CW00956542

Tank
Commanders
KNIGHTS OF THE MODERN AGE

George Forty

Motorbooks International
Publishers & Wholesalers ®

This edition published in 1993 by Motorbooks International Publishers & Wholesalers, PO Box 2, 729 Prospect Avenue, Osceola, WI 54020 USA

First published in the U.K. in 1993 by Firebird Books, Poole, Dorset BH15 2RG

Library of Congress Cataloging-in-Publication Data
ISBN 0-87938-720-3

Designed by Kathryn S.A. Booth
Line illustrations and maps by Mike Haine
Typeset by Inforum, Rowlands Castle, Hants
Monochrome origination by Castle Graphics, Frome
Printed and bound in Great Britain by Biddles of Guildford

CONTENTS

Introduction   4
Acknowledgements   6
1   The Beginnings   7
2   On to Victory   24
3   Between the Wars   39
4   Blitzkrieg   54
5   Tanks across the Desert   70
6   The Russian Front   93
7   The Underbelly of Europe   114
8   D Day   123
9   Normandy to Berlin   134
10 The Far East 1942–1973   154
11 Israelis versus Arabs   168
12 The Gulf Wars   183
    Bibliography   189
    Index   190

INTRODUCTION

When the publisher first approached me on the subject of great tank commanders, we were contemplating a book about a limited number of linked personalities, each of whom would be the subject of his own separate study, the principle adopted with their highly successful 'Heroes and Warriors' series.

However, the more we discussed the subject of tank commanders, the more difficult it became to choose, say, the four greatest tank commanders ever, and at the same time harder to do justice to the history of that remarkable piece of military hardware, the armoured fighting vehicle (AFV). Eventually, we decided that the book should cover not just four great tank commanders, but would endeavour to take in the entire gamut, including some of the bravest in the field as well as the greatest tacticians and leaders.

Such a treatment has enabled me to give the book more depth. However, at the same time it presented me with a well-nigh impossible task. How can anyone cover the entire history of the development of the AFV and of armoured warfare, making sure to mention all those who deserve to be mentioned? What I have done therefore, is to try to give the best examples. The more obvious ones, like Swinton and Estienne, Guderian and Patton, Zhukov and Tal, are easy to choose, but what about all the others who deserve to be included? For better or worse, I have made my own selection and in doing so have been mindful of the need to cover the subject as interestingly as possible and to include, for example, the pioneers and trainers, who, although they did not necessarily command in battle, exerted such an influence on the tactics of armoured warfare as to make their omission unthinkable.

I have also included some of the 'aces' whose prowess as individual tank commanders deserves recognition. But it must always be remembered that a tank commander is only as good as the rest of his crew. A tank crew is a team and all members play their vital part. For example, in a four-man tank crew, the driver, the gunner and the loader/radio operator work with the commander to get the tank and its weapon system at the right time to the right place, where it can inflict the maximum damage upon the enemy. Commanders like the legendary Tiger tank company commander, Oberstürm führer Michael Wittmann, notched up a phenomenal number of 'kills', but would have been the first to admit that they would have got nowhere at all without the rest of their crews.

The same applies to the other tanks in the troop or platoon, the squadron or company, the regiment or battalion. They are all part of a fighting machine that itself is part of the all-arms team. What also makes tank commanders, at any level, different to many other commanders over the years, is the fact that, whatever their rank, they have had to command from the front if they were to be successful. Men like Rommel, Guderian and Patton did not lead from some cosy bunker well to the rear of the front line. They were up at the sharp end, sharing all the dangers and difficulties of their tank crews and urging their tanks forward as much by their own personality and sheer presence as by anything else. It is for this reason that I have called them 'Knights of the Modern Age' – like the knights of old, they have had to fight to survive as well as to command.

The tank ended WW2 in a pre-eminent place upon the land battlefield and has lost none of its usefulness during the turbulent days of 'peace' that have followed. In the last two chapters of the book I have discussed some of the later wars in which tanks have featured. I am conscious that I have almost completely ignored Europe and the Cold War. Clearly, there are great tank commanders on both sides of the Iron Curtain who would have leapt to prominence if the Cold War had turned 'hot'. Fortunately, their skills were never tested.

With the end of the Cold War, it looked very much as though the tank would become just another obsolete weapon system; but aggression can and does occur all over the world. Will the 1990s herald in yet more dynamic tank commanders to join the list? I certainly think so, although I am sure that no sane person wants it to happen. The Gulf War has already shown how effective armour can be – the tank is still a potent force on the battlefield. Operation 'Desert Storm' has also shown clearly that a tank is only as good as its crew and, in particular, its commander. The fourth largest army in the world has been decisively beaten and almost completely destroyed by a much smaller force of highly professional and well-trained soldiers, who have used the capabilities of their weapon systems to the full. In the hands of a great tank commander, the tank still lives!

GEORGE FORTY
Bryantspuddle
Dorset, 1992

ACKNOWLEDGEMENTS

As always, I have many individuals and establishments to thank for their generous assistance with the preparation of this book. First and foremost I must thank all those authors and publishers who have allowed me to quote from their books, together with all those who have equally generously allowed me to use their photographs and those who have sent me valuable background information. They include: Maj Derek Allhusen; Col Michel Aubry, Directeur du CDEB et du Musée des Blindés, France; FM Sir Nigel Bagnall; Jacques Banin, Curator du Musée du Souvenir 'Général Estienne' de Berry au Bac; Brig Madan Bakshi; Brig Gen John Bahnsen USA (Ret); the Canadian Forces Photographic Unit; Maj Patrick Cooney, Editor in Chief *Armor* magazine; Col Owsley Costlow USA (Ret); Lt Col Haynes Dugan USA (Ret); Col David Eshel, late IDF; Brig Gen Thomas Greiss USA (Ret); Col Robert Grow; HA Halliday, Senior Curator of Collections, Canadian War Museum; the High Commission of India and the Director General of Mechanised Forces of the Indian Army; the Embassy of Israel; Military (IDF) and Defence Establishment Archives of Israel; Kari Kuusela of Finland; Samuel Katz; Dr William McAndrew, Director of History, National Defence HQ of Canada; John Purdy, Director of the Patton Museum; Public Relations HQ UKLF; the Embassy of Pakistan; Col Sacha Schevechkov, CAFM; Brig Gen (aD) Horst Scheibert; Maj Gen Lawrence Schlanser USA (Ret); Lt Robert Sutton USA; Shabtai Teveth; and Mike Willis.

GF

Photographs
The following are gratefully acknowledged as sources of the photographs used in the book; each photograph is individually credited as follows: (AWM) Australian War Memorial; (B) Brasseys; (CAFM) Central Armed Services Museum, former USSR; (CDEB) French Tank Museum, Saumur; (CFPU) Canadian Forces Photographic Unit; (CM) Charles Messenger; (DE) Col David Eshel; (GF) author's collection; (HS) Brig Gen (aD) Horst Scheibert; (IA) Indian Army; (IDF) Israeli Defence Forces; (IWM) Imperial War Museum; (KK) Kari Kuuisela; (MGE) La Musée Gen Estienne, Berry au Duc; (PM) Patton Museum; (SD) Simon Dunstan; (SI) Sikorski Institute; (TM) Tank Museum, Bovington (*supplied to the Tank Museum by CDEB Saumur and Musée Gen Estienne); (UKLF) Public Relations Dept, United Kingdom Land Forces; (US) United States Army.

1 THE BEGINNINGS

To open this survey of great tank commanders through the ages, we must go back to the very beginnings and to the invention of the first real armoured fighting vehicle (AFV) early in WW1. At that time there emerged a select band of men who had within them the ability and imagination to appreciate the potential of the tank and to push ahead with the formation of tank units, despite the scepticism and prejudice that surrounded the introduction of this revolutionary new weapon system – men like Ernest Swinton in Great Britain and Jean Baptiste Estienne in France, who became known as the 'fathers' of their respective tank corps. Although these men did not necessarily command the first tanks in battle, their contribution was such as to merit their inclusion.

Ancestry and Evolution

From the very earliest times man has searched for bigger and better weapons with which to defend himself and to destroy his enemies. Each new weapon – the club, the spear, the bow and arrow, the first firearm – must have appeared invincible at first to those engaged in the fighting. Each weapon has in some way been more fearsome than its predecessor. Only today have we perhaps reached the ultimate horror, with the invention of the weapons of mass destruction – nuclear, bacteriological and chemical – each capable of wiping out the entire human race if anyone is ever foolish enough to use them.

All these new weapons have had their impact on the battlefield, but perhaps none has been more effective than the tank. Initially a revolutionary weapon system, it has been developed and refined over the seventy-five years since its spectacular appearance. However, its three basic and essential characteristics – firepower, protection and mobility – have remained constant. Reduced to the simplest terms a tank is a means of carrying protected firepower about on the battlefield, to wherever it is needed.

War chariots are normally considered to have been the original ancestors of the tank – chariots like those of the ancient city of Ur of the Chaldees, which date from about the year 3500 BC, and those 'iron chariots' mentioned in Judges (1.19–20): 'And the Lord was with Judah, and he took possession of the hill country, but he could not drive out the inhabitants of the plain, because they had chariots of iron.' Other possible ancestors are the armoured elephant, as used by Hannibal, the early-fifteenth-century battlewagons used by the Hussites in Bohemia, and also Leonardo da Vinci's war machine.

However, not until the twentieth century did it become possible to propel a vehicle with suitable armoured protection for its crew and weapons across all types of terrain. The internal combustion engine, modern methods of fabricating armour-plate and the caterpillar track all made the tank possible.

Nevertheless, these new developments would not have been combined for military use had there not been a reason to stimulate fertile imaginations to design the strange new vehicle that would become called a 'tank'. This reason came early in WW1 and was brought about by the stalemate that existed on the Western Front after the First Battle of Ypres in 1914. Neither side could advance, because the defences of the other were too strong. The artillery shell, the machine-gun bullet, the barbed-wire entanglement and the mile upon mile of opposing trench systems and defence works, which stretched from the Belgian coast to Switzerland, had brought the war to a grinding halt. Until some way could be found of providing attackers with fire support and protection against enemy fire while they negotiated the barbed-wire and other obstacles, any attack was bound to fail, with horrendous casualties.

FIRST DESIGNERS Before WW1 plans for various strange mechanical devices had been proposed to the war departments of Britain and France, but all had been summarily discounted or, at best, pigeon-holed. In Austria, the design for a *Motorgeschütz* (motor gun) was rejected because it was felt to infringe the patents for agricultural tractors! One of the most interesting of these bizarre early designs was submitted to the British authorities in 1912 by an Australian engineer, Lancelot de Mole. It bears a striking similarity to the actual design of the first real tank, although Mole received no credit for the tank's final invention.

Ad-hoc armoured vehicles, motor cars with sheets of armour-plate bolted on their sides, had already been used by both Britain and Belgium, by the Royal Naval Air Service (RNAS) to rescue downed pilots and protect airfields and by the Belgians as a light-cavalry raiding force. These vehicles had convinced the commander of the RNAS, Capt Murray Sueter, of the value of armour and prompted him to suggest to Winston Churchill, then First Lord of the Admiralty the development of a tracked armoured vehicle using Diplock caterpillar tracks. Another RNAS officer, Flt Comdr Hetherington, suggested a similar vehicle, but his was to be propelled on three enormous wheels, each 40ft in diameter, rather than on tracks. The *Pedrail* and *Big Wheel* land battleships were thus naval proposals. The Army had its own ideas. Foremost among these was a proposal made by a Royal Engineer officer, Lt Col Ernest D. Swinton, for an armoured vehicle employing American Holt farm-tractor caterpillar tracks as the means of getting across rough terrain.

Ernest Swinton was born at Bangalore in Mysore on 21st October (Trafalgar Day) 1868. He was the fourth son of a large family (six boys and three girls); his father was a judge in the Madras Civil Service. He passed out fourth from the Royal Military Academy, Woolwich, on 17th February 1888 and was gazetted to the Royal Engineers, with orders to report to Chatham. After two years at the School of Military Engineering, learning his profession, he was posted to India and served there until returning as assistant instructor to Chatham, where he was responsible for teaching pioneer duties (bridging, demolitions etc.) to young cavalry officers. At the start of the Boer War, Swinton was posted to South Africa. In 1900 he was awarded a DSO while commanding an irregular unit, the 1st Railway Pioneer Regiment. Swinton was an able, observant and literate soldier. His splendid little tactical manual, *The Defence of Duffer's Drift*, which he wrote under the pseudonym of 'Backsight-Forethought', was considered a classic in its day and became required reading for all newly commissioned subalterns. It was followed by a series of stories about future warfare, collected in 1909 under the title *The Green Curve*. This time he chose as his pseudonym 'Ole-Luk-Oie', which he went on using for the rest of his life. He became chief instructor of the Royal Military Academy in 1906, then three years later joined the historical section of the Committee of Imperial Defence and was employed writing the official history of the Russo-Japanese war. He was awarded the Chesney Gold Medal of the Royal United Service Institution for this work and became assistant secretary of the Committee of Imperial Defence in October 1913. At the outbreak of war he was appointed Deputy Director of Railway Transport.

In his capacity as a member of the Committee of Imperial Defence, he was sent to France as a war correspondent in September 1914. In his autobiography he wrote about this period:

Since I had been at the front all the information I had gathered – whether from official reports, from the hospitals or from any other source – had seemed to me consistently to bear out the fact that apart from his artillery, the main strength of the enemy resistance – still only of an improvised nature – lay in his skilful combination of machine guns and wire. Throughout this time I had been wracking my brains to discover an antidote; and within the last two weeks my vague idea of an armoured vehicle had definitely crystallised in the form of a power-driven, bullet-proof, armed engine, capable of destroying machine guns, of crossing country and trenches, of breaking through entanglements and of climbing earthworks.

But the difficulty was to find or evolve something which would fulfil these conditions – especially the last three.

Swinton goes on to explain how, while he was concentrating on this problem early one morning near the lighthouse at Calais, the solution came to him:

Like a beam from the same lighthouse the idea flashed across my brain – the American Caterpillar Tractor at Antwerp! I recalled its reputed performance. If this agricultural machine could really do all that report credited it with, why should it not be modified and adapted to suit our present requirements for war? The key to the problem lay in the caterpillar track!

However, it was all very well for Swinton and his contemporaries to have the ideas. They would have remained unknown and untried had it not been for the vision and determination of one man, the then First Lord of the Admiralty, Winston Churchill. He quickly saw the merit of their proposals and diverted £70,000 of Admiralty money to fund the trials and development of what was very much a land-based weapon system. A Landships Committee was formed, under the chairmanship of Tennyson d'Eyncourt, Director of Naval Construction, which contained such remarkable men as William Tritton, managing director of William Foster & Sons of Lincoln, the firm that would eventually build the first tanks, and Lts Walter Gordon Wilson and Albert Stern of the RNAS. The basis of their work was a memorandum, 'The Necessity for Machine-Gun Destroyers', which Swinton had submitted to the General Staff in France. It gave the following description of the proposed new weapon system:

These machines would be petrol tractors on the caterpillar principle, of a type which can travel at 4 miles an hour on the flat, can cross a ditch up to 4ft width without climbing, can climb in and out of a broader cavity and can scramble over a breastwork. It is possible to build such tractors. They should be armoured with hardened steel plate, proof against the German steel-cored, armour-piercing and reversed bullets and armed with – say – two Maxims and a Maxim 2-pdr gun.

LITTLE WILLIE Designed by William Tritton and Walter Gordon Wilson, 'Little Willie', or 'Tritton Machine', as it is sometimes called, was designed and constructed between 2nd August and 8th September 1915. It weighed about 18 tons and was to have had a centrally mounted turret with a 2-pdr gun. However, this was not fitted – a dummy turret of the correct weight was used when the machine was tested. 'Little Willie' had been designed before the Landships Committee had received Swinton's specifications and, when it was trialled, it showed that it suffered from certain technical shortcomings, chiefly concerned with the tracks. 'Ole-Luk-Oie' had not been impressed by the trial, nor by the apparent lack of security, so he was vastly relieved when he was taken to a nearby building where, behind tightly closed doors, he saw a nearly completed, full-sized wooden mock-up of a much larger tracked vehicle, expressly designed to meet his specifications. He wrote later:

Although an engineer, it took me some minutes to size the thing up at close range. Its most striking features were its curious rhomboidal, or lozenge, shape, its upturned nose, and the fact that its caterpillar tracks were led right round the hull, instead of being entirely below it . . ... Unwieldy as this contrivance appeared in the confined space in which it was housed, it promised to solve the most difficult problems involved – the power to climb and the ability to span broad trenches; and I felt I saw in front of me – though only in wood – the actual embodiment of my ideas and the fulfilment of my specification . . ... Dinner on the train on the return journey to London was a joyous occasion.

Big Willie The wooden mock-up seen by Swinton that day was that of 'Big Willie', known originally as 'HMLS Centipede' or, more affectionately, 'Mother' – even though 'she' was strictly a 'male' tank, being armed with two long-barrelled 6-pounder guns in her side sponsons, while 'female' tanks were designed to carry only machine-guns. As Swinton explains: 'The "Centipede" which became "Mother" was the prototype of all Mark I tanks, or "Big Willies", which took the field in 1916'.[1]

'Mother' was completed in January 1916 and moved secretly by rail to a trials area on the Marquess of Salisbury's estate, near Hatfield. Here Swinton and Flt Cmdr T.G. Hetherington RNAS, another member of the Landships Committee, had been laying out a 'steeplechase course', to enable 'Mother' to prove that she could pass all the official and active service tests.[2] On 2ND FEBRUARY 1916, the trial took place, watched by representatives of the Cabinet, the Army Council, the Admiralty and GHQ France. Swinton wrote later:

Wednesday, 2 February, was the great day of the official trial. So far as was humanly possible everything had been done to ensure that there should be no breakdown. On this point I was particularly nervous, for so much hung in the balance. . . . The demonstration was attended by Lord Kitchener, Mr Balfour, Mr Lloyd George, Mr McKenna, members of the Admiralty staff, General Robertson, several senior officers from the War Office, those connected with the creation of 'Mother', and last but not least, representatives of GHQ.'

The trial was a great success and 'Mother' performed magnificently. Most observers were impressed, especially the GHQ representatives whom Swinton described as being the 'potential buyers'. They agreed to recommend the CinC (FM Earl Haig) to ask for some machines to be built. King George V was the next VIP to watch 'Mother' perform, being given a private trial on

8th February. The King was most impressed and even congratulated the driver personally. He was to take a great interest in the new machines and their crews from then on.

Swinton was overjoyed at the success of 'Mother', especially when the initial order for 40 machines was increased to 100 on his insistence. Later, at a meeting of the Landships Committee, he and Lt Col Dally-Jones, who were acting as assistant secretaries to the committee, coined the name 'Tank'. 'The structure of the machine in its early stages being boxlike, some term conveying the idea of a box or container seemed appropriate. We rejected in turn – container – receptacle – reservoir – cistern. The monosyllable Tank appealed to us as being likely to catch on and be remembered. That night in a draft report of the conference the word "Tank" was employed in its new sense for the first time.'[3]

THE FIRST TANK CREWS   A few days after the first order for 100 tanks had been placed, Swinton was told by Gen Sir W.D. Bird, then Director of Staff Duties at the War Office, that he had been selected by the Army Council to raise and command the 'Tank Detachment', as the new unit to man the machines was first called. Swinton later wrote that: '. . . the ensuing eight months proved to be the most strenuous, stimulating, and trying period I have ever experienced.' Nevertheless, he set to with a will and Siberia Farm, near Bisley Camp in Surrey, was chosen as the birthplace of the Tank Detachment on 16th February 1916. This choice was not a haphazard one, but was made because it was close to the depot and training school of the Motor Machine-Gun Service, which had been formed in late 1914 to increase the machine-gun strength in infantry divisions by the addition of specially trained batteries of motorcycle and sidecar combinations, carrying Vickers medium machine-guns. Trench warfare had rendered this highly trained unit virtually useless, so there were numbers of excellent, mechanically minded soldiers immediately available for transfer to the 'Armoured Car Section of the Motor Machine-Gun Service', which was the cover name given to the Tank Detachment for security. The CO of the Motor Machine-Gun Service, Lt Col R.W. Bradley, DSO, South Wales Borderers, and about seven hundred other ranks were transferred to the Detachment at the beginning of March 1916.

Swinton had earlier written a memorandum, which he entitled 'Notes of the Employment of Tanks', spelling out his basic rules for their tactical employment. He sent copies to GHQ in France, but they were studiously ignored, which needlessly wasted a lot of tanks and their crews when the time came for them to be used in action. His 'tank tips' are as relevant today to any tankman as they were when he wrote them, in down-to-earth, easily understandable language.

The first one hundred drivers, and the first mechanics for the repair workshops, came from 711 Company, Army Service Corps, who mostly had been serving with the Caterpillar Companies in France and the Siege Batteries of the Royal Garrison Artillery. The editor of *Motor Cycle* magazine, Geoffrey

TANK TIPS

Remember your orders

Shoot quick

Shoot low. A miss which throws dust in the enemy's eyes is better than one which whistles in his ear

Shoot cunning

Shoot the enemy while they are rubbing their eyes. Economise ammunition and don't kill a man three times

Remember that trenches are curly and dugouts deep – look round corners

Watch the progress of the fight and your neighbouring tanks

Watch your infantry whom you are helping

Remember the position of your own line

Shell out the enemy's machine guns and other small guns and kill them first with your 6pdrs

You will not see them for they will be cunningly hidden

You must ferret out where they are, judging by the following signs: Sound, Dust, Smoke

A shadow in a parapet

A hole in a wall, haystack, rubbish heap, woodstack, pile of bricks

They will be usually placed to fire slantways across the front and to shoot along the wire

One 6pdr shell that hits the loophole of a MG emplacement will do it in

Use the 6pdr with care; shoot to hit not to make a noise

Never have any gun, even when unloaded, pointing at your own infantry, or a 6pdr gun pointed at another tank

It is the unloaded gun that kills the fool's friends

Never mind the heat

Never mind the noise

Never mind the dust

Think of your pals in the infantry

Thank God you are bullet proof and can help the infantry, who are not

Have your mask always handy

Smith, was also very helpful in recruiting men from the motor-engineering industry. However, still more volunteers were needed, especially officers, so Swinton and Bradley toured the country visiting officer cadet units and similar establishments, looking for likely men. Others were tempted by an order from the War Office, marked 'Strictly Secret and Confidential', inviting volunteers for 'an exceedingly dangerous and hazardous duty of a secret nature'.

During April and May 1916, after a number of differing organizations had been tried out, it was eventually decided to form six companies (lettered A to F), each of 25 tanks, thus making a total of 150 machines, of which half would be male and half female. The company establishment was 28 officers and 255 ORs, while the total strength of the 'Heavy Section, Machine Gun Corps (HSMGC)', as it was now called, was 184 officers and 1,610 ORs.

The six companies moved during June 1916 from Bisley to Lord Iveagh's estate at Elveden, near Thetford, where training on the few available Heavy Mark I tanks took place.

FRANCE Meanwhile, Great Britain's main ally, France, was also experimenting with a form of armoured tracked vehicle. The French too had made use of armoured and semi-armoured cars, such as those built by the Société Charron-Giradot et Voight in 1902. They had also done some work on evolving unarmed tractors to crush barbed-wire entanglements. However, French tank development did not start until Col Jean Baptiste Estienne,[4] having witnessed trials of the Holt caterpillar tractor as used by the British to tow artillery guns, put forward plans for developing a land battleship – a *cuirasse terrestre* – a tracked, armoured vehicle armed with both cannon and machine-guns. Despite the indifference which appears to have greeted all early tank enthusiasts, Estienne persevered and eventually managed to get support from the C in C of the French Army, Gen Joffre. In December 1915 he was given permission to take his ideas to the Schneider works at Le Creusot and there the tank that eventually bore the Schneider name was developed. Thanks to Estienne's drive and enthusiasm, an initial order for 400 Schneider tanks was placed in February 1916. It was followed in April by another order, again for 400 tanks, which this time went to the Compagnie des Forges d'Homecourt (FMAH), who were ordered to produce an entirely different type of tank, the 'Saint Chamond', designed by Col Rimailho. This was nowhere near as good a tank as the Schneider. Like the Schneider it was turretless and had a 75mm gun as its main armament. It was driven by a petrol-electric motor and weighed 23 tons against the Schneider's 13½ tons. The initial delivery was made to the French Army in September 1916, just after the British had first used their tanks on the Somme.

In the meantime, of course, like their British counterparts, the French had been organizing a unit to man the new weapon systems. Col Estienne was promoted to Brigadier and appointed commander of the *Artillerie d'Assaut* (assault artillery) as the new arm was to be called. The name gives a clue as to how the French initially envisaged the main use of the tank, namely as a source of mobile fire support. The tanks were organized into *groupes* of four batteries, each of four tanks. Three or four *groupes* made up a *groupement*. There was no higher organization and hardly any tactical control within the *groupement*, which was merely administrative. Sadly, also, the tanks themselves were of poor design and suffered from many mechanical faults. Nevertheless, training centres were established, at Marly, Cercottes and Champlieu, so that by April 1917 ten *groupes* – nine of Schneider and one of St Chamond tanks – were in training.

Estienne had also pressed for the building of a simple, light, inconspicuous, easily manufactured small tank that could advance in front of the infantry, like the skirmishers of old. They would be available to give immediate fire support to the infantry and would also be able to exploit success by independent armoured action. His proposals met with considerable opposition, but 'Père' Estienne again persevered and an order was eventually placed for 1,000 Renault two-man tanks, weighing about six tons. They featured the first fully rotating cast turret to be mounted on any tank. Although the turret had no gearing, it could be moved around by hand on a ball race and locked into any desired position. The FT 17, as it was called, was a highly successful light tank and was subsequently produced in different forms (as a wireless tank, for example, and as SP artillery with a 75mm gun). Renault produced it in vast numbers. After the successful counterstroke against the Chateau-Thierry salient, in which these little tanks were used to great effect, they were built at the rate of one battalion's worth a week. After the war it was copied by the Americans, Italians and Russians.

THE UNITED STATES OF AMERICA The Americans, who entered the war later than the other Allied nations, used British heavy tanks and French light tanks in battle, although there were a few 'home-grown' designs which never got very far, such as the CL Best Tractor Co 75 tank of 1916, the weird 'Skeleton tank' of 1918 and the 'Steam tank' produced by the US Engineer Corps of 1918 and based upon the British Heavy Mark IV. At this stage the real 'Father of the American Armored Force', Adna R. Chaffee, had not appeared on the scene.

RUSSIA The Russians produced some remarkable proposals early in the twentieth century. One was the armoured track-laying vehicle designed by Vasiliy Dmitriev Mendeleyev between 1911 and 1915, which sadly came to naught, never even getting off the drawing board. Another was the *Vezdekhod*, designed by an engineer called Porokovskikov, which got only as

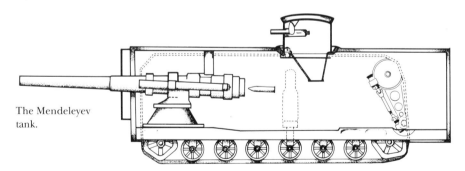

The Mendeleyev tank.

far as a wooden mock-up. The Russians took some interest in armoured cars, but their real emergence as a tank nation would not come until the post-Bolshevik revolutionary period in the 1920s and 1930s.

ITALY The Italians too, while producing armoured cars as early as 1907, took little interest in tanks in WW1, although, to be fair, their area of the battlefields did not lend itself to AFV movement, being far too mountainous. Their first tank design, the Fiat 2000, originated in about 1916–17 and was built in prototype form in the following year. Instead of producing their own tanks immediately, however, the Italians decided to buy French FT 17s and Schneiders, but only a few were delivered before the Armistice and the Italians then decided to build their own version of the ubiquitous FT 17.

GERMANY   Like the Italians, the Germans initially took little or no interest in tanks, but did produce some good armoured cars. Their one and only successful foray into tank construction in WW1 came with the building of the A7V Stürmpanzer, designed by Joseph Vollmer in 1917. Only some twenty of these box-like, unwieldy machines were completed, but they did see action, as will be recounted later. However, for the most part the Germans used captured British tanks (*Beutepanzerwagen*) – mostly Mark IVs but also some Mark Vs – which had been overhauled and rearmed (males with ex-Russian 57mm Sokol guns as used on the A7V; females with MG08 Maxim machine-guns).

CANADA   Although Canada would not form its small Tank Corps until 1918, it is worth mentioning here Brig Gen Raymond Brutinel, in view of his pioneering work on armoured tactics. Brutinel, who had been born in France in 1872, emigrated to Canada before WW1 and was active in Edmonton, mainly in coal and streetcars. On the outbreak of war, he organized the 1st Canadian Motor Machine Gun Brigade, equipped it with Autocars – open-topped vehicles mounted on truck chassis, crewed by six men and carrying two Vickers .303 water-cooled machine-guns in an armour-plated body. Brutinel took his unit to England in October 1914 and then on to France in 1915. He there evolved a tactical grouping of troops travelling by armoured car and bicycle, and supported by light artillery, which in some ways foreshadowed the armoured division of WW2. Its mobility was demonstrated when No 1 CMMG Brigade moved a hundred miles in one day and then went into action on the next, blocking the German advance in support of the British 5th Army. They took 75% casualties and there now remains just one single Autocar in existence. Brutinel was decorated with the CB, CMG and DSO, was mentioned in despatches seven times and awarded the Légion d'honneur and the Croix de Guerre by France. He died in 1964.

Into Battle

On 13th August 1916, the first detachment of British tanks left for France, the crews from Southampton, but the tanks from Avonmouth because no crane at Southampton was capable of loading them. They were then moved by rail to the forward battle area. The great Somme offensive had opened on 1st July, with horrendous casualties – the British alone had over 60,000 on the first day, of whom over 20,000 were killed. Haig, conscious of mounting criticism, was desperately seeking a solution and seized upon the tanks as the means of providing a way out of his difficulties. Despite the fact that there were so few of them available and that they had no battle experience, he would brook no

16

argument from Swinton, who recalled: 'On 19 August I paid a hurried visit to Advanced GHQ at Beauquesne. Sir Douglas saw me and pointed out on the map the sector where he proposed to throw in the tanks. He did not enter into any discussion of his reasons for using them at that time.'5 Swinton's visits to France were never very happy occasions. He was met everywhere with a strange mixture of amused tolerance and contemptuous scepticism by many senior officers. Others were so convinced that the tank was the panacea for all their ills, that they proposed impossible tasks for them to perform. Everywhere there was a feeling that the tank was some new kind of toy and the poor Heavy Section was forced to put on an endless series of demonstrations, which completely ruined any possible period of preparation for battle, as the crews had barely time to eat and sleep, let alone do any work on their tanks.

Haig had decided to spread all the available tanks (49 in total) in twos and threes across the entire front of the intended attacking force, so XIV and XV Corps on the right and centre-right were allocated 17 tanks each; III Corps in the centre had eight; while the remaining seven were kept in Army Reserve. The main task for the tanks would be to deal with the enemy strongpoints and to provide fire support for the infantry.

THE FIRST ACTION   The morning of 15th September 1916 was fine, although there was a thin ground mist. Zero Hour was set for 0620 hours, but the tanks had to be on the move well before then in order to reach the start line on time. It had been planned to precede the main attack with a small operation to clear a pocket of enemy between Ginchy and Delville Wood, where the Germans were occupying a trench called 'Hop Alley'. Three tanks were allocated to this task, but unfortunately one broke down and one was ditched while moving forward, so tank D1, commanded by Capt H.W. Mortimore, advanced on its own at about 0515 hours, followed some fifteen minutes later by two companies of the 6th King's Own Yorkshire Light Infantry, who thus became the first infantry to go into action with tanks. Mortimore and the KOYLIs cleared out the pocket successfully, but D1 was disabled by a shell which hit its steering gear. The location of D1's gallant action was later appropriately chosen as the site of the Tank Corps Memorial.

Because the tanks were so spread out across the battlefield, the actions during the advance were in the main fought by single tanks. These, however, had an effect on the battle out of all proportion to their small numbers. Perhaps the most famous exploits were those of D17 (Dinnaken), of 3 Section, D Company, commanded by Lt Hastie, which was enthusiastically reported in the British press as being seen 'Walking up the High Street of Flers with the British Army cheering behind!' German war correspondents were even more dramatic in their reporting, one writing:

When the German outposts crept out of their dugouts in the mist of the morning of 15 September and stretched their necks to look for the English, their blood was chilled to their veins. Two mysterious monsters were crawling towards them over the craters. Stunned as if an earthquake had burst around them, they all rubbed their eyes, which were fascinated by the fabulous creatures. . . . One stared and stared as if one had lost the power of one's limbs. The monsters approached slowly, hobbling, rolling and rocking, but they approached. Nothing impeded them; a supernatural force seemed to impel them on. Someone in the trenches said: 'The devil is coming' and the word passed along the line like wildfire.

The British press was ecstatic, giving the tanks names like 'Motor Monsters' and 'Jabberwocks with Eyes of Flame', but of course the military view was the one that really mattered and this was somewhat mixed. Some senior officers, who should have known better, poured scorn upon the tanks' performance and talked only of their faults. Fortunately, Haig was highly pleased with all that they had done and thanked Swinton and Stern most warmly when they next visited his Advanced HQ on the 17th. According to Stern's account of the meeting, Haig said that 'wherever the tanks advanced we took our objectives and where they did not advance we did not take our objectives'. He now wanted as many tanks to be built as possible and so a firm order was placed for 1,000 bigger and better tanks and another 100 Heavy Mark Is were ordered, to keep the factories going until the new designs could be settled.

ELLES TAKES COMMAND   There now followed a period of expansion, which culminated in the Heavy Section being expanded to nine battalions – four formed in France from the twelve tank companies now in existence[6] and five, based on the two existing companies, in the UK. And there were changes at the top. It was considered by GHQ that the commander of the Heavy Section in France should be someone with active service experience on the Western Front who was also persona grata with GHQ. Neither Lt Col Brough, who had brought the Heavy Section to France, nor his replacement, Lt Col Bradley, were considered suitable by GHQ (probably because they argued too much about what their tanks should or should not do!), so Swinton chose another Sapper, Lt Col Hugh Jamieson Elles, who had some knowledge of the new weapon system, having been selected by Haig some time before to enquire into the subject of tanks on his behalf. In Swinton's words, Elles was 'a first class officer . . . persona gratissima at GHQ who knows everyone and all the "ropes" . . . in spite of the fact that he knew as little about tanks as his two predecessors did about the niceties of the tactics current in France . . . I could think of no one more suitable.'

Elles was born on 27th April 1880 and commissioned into the Royal Engineers on 25th June 1899. He saw service in the Boer War and, at the outbreak of WW1, was serving as a captain with his Corps. He went to France on the staff in 1914 and had held various staff appointments before Swinton chose him to command the Heavy Section in France.

Thus, on 25th September 1916, the next great tank commander came on the scene, when Elles was appointed to command the Heavy Section in France, in the rank of colonel. His HQ consisted of just one small hut in the village of Beauquesnes, and his staff of just four other officers beside himself: Brigade Major, Capt G. Le Q. Martel; DAA and QMG, Capt T.J. Uzielli; Staff Captain, Capt J.H. Tapper; and Intelligence Officer, Capt F.E. Hotblack. One of Elles's first actions was to move the HQ to Bermicourt, a small village near St Pol, where it would stay for the rest of the war. The staff would grow in size, being joined by such 'greats' as 'Boney' Fuller (GS02), undoubtedly another great tank commander in his own right, who was considered by many to be the real brains behind the new corps. Stephen Foot in his book *Three Lives* described Fuller thus:

For success tanks require tactics no less than petrol: Fuller devised them. Before an attack can be launched there must be a plan: Fuller made it. After an attack lessons must be learnt both from success and failure: Fuller absorbed them. And sad to relate, in the case of the Tanks, a constant war had to be waged against apathy, incredulity and short-sightedness of GHQ. Fuller fought that war and won.

Notwithstanding the fact that the Heavy Section was now a self-contained organization, with its own brigades and battalions, the War Office appeared deliberately to denigrate the new arm. Elles was not even promoted to brig-adier until May 1917, even though at that time he was commanding two full tank brigades in the field and had formed the HQ of a third ready to receive fresh battalions from England. Elles had ten battalions under him before he became a major general. For a long time his brigade commanders held only the rank of colonel and were thus junior to every infantry brigadier with whom they had to work. 'Apart from the slur on the Corps and its officers, this deliberate omission caused serious inconvenience. In its early days the Tank Corps needed every ounce of authority it could get to help it through inevit-able difficulties.' The author of that last quotation, Capt D.G. Browne MC, in his book *The Tank in Action*, makes another telling observation about the attitude of the War Office towards the expansion of the new corps:

Unhappily, the official attitude toward this expansion was marked by a grudging spirit which the pedants in every Government Department manifest when they have to adopt an innovation against their will. There seemed to be a tacit understanding in Whitehall that the budding enterprise must be kept in its place and reminded continually of its youth and status.

SWINTON REPLACED   Meanwhile, at home in England, a dramatic change was taking place. The War Office decided that, while Elles should continue to command in France, Swinton was to be replaced at home by Brig Gen Gore-Anley and return to his old duties with the War Cabinet Secretariat. Swinton was understandably bewildered by this decision. He wrote in his autobiography:

I thought it best to go direct to the Chief of the Imperial General Staff, to whom I reported what I had heard, asked if it was correct and if so, the reason. General Robertson's reply was to the effect that France wanted a big expansion of the Heavy Section and that I was not considered the man to carry it out. . . . As I walked down the passage of the War Office, bereft of my child, consolation came with the thought that the child was waxing strong.

Swinton was too much of a gentleman to express even in his autobiography his true feelings at the scandalous way in which he was treated. It was left to Capt D.G. Browne MC, himself a Tank Corps officer, to express the opinion of those in the Corps:

Somebody said (or so it will be most charitable to suppose), 'Hullo, here's another of these infernal sappers! This won't do! The whole war is being run by RE's and gunners, as it is. We must get rid of him!' And he was got rid of. . . . An infantry brigadier, who had performed a very notable feat of arms in the first few months of the war, but knew nothing about tanks, came down to Thetford to take over command, and gave an encouraging tone to the proceedings by declaring quite openly, the moment he arrived, that he was come to put some discipline into the corps, that he took no interest whatever in the tanks and that he did not want to see them.

'From then on I faded out of the picture', wrote Swinton in his autobiography *Over My Shoulder*, 'until in the autumn of 1934, just twenty years after I had initiated them, I renewed my official connection with the Tanks when I was appointed one of three Colonels Commandant of the Royal Tank Corps'. Maj Gen Sir Ernest D. Swinton KBE, CB, DSO, 'Ole-Luk-Oie', was back with his 'ewe lamb' and was, he wrote, '. . . much touched by the welcome I received from many I had known in the early days of the new Arm'. Swinton died in 1951, after teaching military history at Oxford University for a number of years, '. . . content in the knowledge that the credit, at least for being father of the tank was recognisably his'.7

BRITISH OPERATIONS Elles and the Heavy Section did not have much time to contemplate the changes taking place at home, which had included a move from Thetford to Bovington Camp in Dorset, the 'home of tanks' from November 1916 onwards. In France operations on the Somme continued, with the tanks playing as full a part as they were permitted but still being used only in small groups. On many occasions the tanks proved to be battle-winners, for example on 1st October 1916, just west of Flers, when two tanks assisted 141 Brigade when it was held up short of the German trenches. The tanks drove along the trench line with their guns blazing and the enemy were so frightened that they surrendered en masse and 141 Brigade was able to capture their objective and push forward to Eaucourt L'Abbaye. Cross-country going in the morass of mud which the battlefield had become in the early winter rains was so terrible that officers used long ash sticks to test the depth of the mud in front of the tanks. It is now the custom for Royal Tank Regiment officers to carry ashplants instead of the normal swagger cane.

January 1917 saw the formation of the first Tank Brigade (comprising C and D Battalions), and a month later 2 Brigade was formed from A and B Battalions. Then, in late April, a third Tank Brigade came into existence, with the arrival in France of F Battalion. Elles was everywhere at this important, formative time, exerting his influence on his brigades, and, as Fuller records, '. . . endowing the Corps with a high morale, that fine "esprit de corps" and jaunty "esprit de cocarde" which impelled it from one success to another.'

NEW TANKS March/April 1917 also saw the Heavy Mark IV go into production. This had many improvements over the previous models and it would be produced in greater numbers than any other British tank, a total of 1,220 being built. It had smaller sponsons which, being hinged, could be swung inboard for rail movement, rather than having to be taken off and carried separately; it had a 60-gallon armoured petrol tank mounted outside the tank between the rear horns; it was built of thicker steel, making it proof against the German anti-tank rifle bullet; the long (40 calibres) 6-pdr guns had been replaced by shorter ones (23 calibres) so they were less liable to damage from hitting trees and buildings; it carried a special, metal-bound unditching beam which, when fixed by chains to the tracks, would be taken underneath the tank as the tracks revolved, thus giving more purchase on the mud to assist in unbogging the tank.

THE FIRST FRENCH TANK ACTION   The tank arm that Estienne had formed fought its first battle at Berry-au-Bac on the River Aisne, on 16th April 1917, some eight months after Flers. One hundred and thirty-two Schneiders, in eight companies, were organized into two columns: in the west Groupement Chaubes and in the east Groupement Bossut (both named after their respective commanders). Their objective was to take Chemin des Dames in an attack by the French 5th Army. The tanks had to make a long approach march, in column, part of which was in broad daylight. German aircraft discovered them soon after they started and directed artillery fire on to them. Part of the approach route was also in full view of the German artillery. These factors led to heavy tank casualties as they moved up.

Of the eight companies, five were assigned to 32nd Corps, who were to make the main attack between the Aisne and the Miette, while the remaining three companies were with 5th Corps, west of the Miette. Those with 32nd Corps encountered many obstacles – blocked roads and poorly made trench crossings over the German trenches (the Germans had widened their trenches after Flers, so that the Schneiders could not cross without assistance). Enemy artillery caused even more casualties, as the Schneiders caught fire far too easily when struck by artillery.

The attacking force of 32nd Corps reached its objectives, but was then subjected to intense enemy fire which forced it to withdraw. Of the 82 tanks in support, 31 were knocked out by artillery and 13 by other causes, making a total of 44 tanks lost, with 26 officers and 103 men killed and wounded.

Those in support of 5th Corps lost eight tanks immediately when they got stuck in marshy ground on the approach march. Artillery fire, directed from the air, caused more problems, so the tanks had to increase their speed, leaving the infantry behind. Clearly the lack of training and poor co-operation with the supporting infantry caused many problems, and of the 50 tanks with 5th Corps 32 were lost, 26 being knocked out by artillery. Losses in personnel were seven officers and 44 men.

Thus, 76 Schneiders were lost in total, 57 being completely destroyed by artillery. This undoubtedly made the Germans conclude that tanks were not really very effective weapons, so they would not build them. They would certainly live to regret this decision. In fact, one of the main reasons for such heavy losses was the vulnerability of the Schneider's fuel tanks and the fact that they were vulnerable to the new German 'K' anti-tank bullet. The same applied of course to the British Heavy Mark Is, in which, however, thicker armour would rectify these problems.

Chef d'Escadrons Louis-Marie-Ildefonse Bossut, Commandant of the 1er Groupement d'Artillerie d'Assaut, was killed in the attack. He was one of France's first tank heroes, being awarded the Légion d'honneur, the Croix de Guerre (with seven citations) and the Croix de Sainte-Anne.

The British Tank Corps

While the new tank crews trained, GHQ was busy planning a new offensive. Sadly, they had learned nothing over the intervening months and still chose to use the tanks in 'penny packets', spread out across the battlefield, thus frittering away the true potential of the new weapon. Elles and his staff did their best to make higher authority see reason, but without much success. However, they must have been heartened by the news that the King had approved the Heavy Section becoming a new Corps in its own right. On 28th July 1917 the Tank Corps came into existence, with the issue of a new metal cap badge to go with the tank arm badge which Swinton had designed and which had been worn for some time as a unifying symbol.

Fate played its part in the choice of colours for the new corps. Elles and Hardress-Lloyd (commanding 3 Tank Brigade) could find only a very limited selection of coloured materials when they visited the local dressmaker's shop. They chose brown, red and green, a combination which Fuller later proposed should be interpreted: 'From mud, through blood, to the green fields beyond'. The Corps motto, 'Fear Naught', was also chosen at that time, in preference to the earlier 'Dread Naught', suggested by Swinton, because of the latter's use by the Royal Navy to describe one of its classes of warships.

The morale of the new corps received a staggering blow when Elles was told by Maj Gen Sir John Capper, who had been appointed as Director General of the Tank Corps in May 1917, that the expansion of the Tank Corps was to be postponed, the excuse being the heavy casualties sustained on the Somme. Fortunately, Haig saw the danger this presented to the new corps and agreed to give the tanks a final chance to prove themselves, by planning and executing a tank battle on a suitable area of ground of their own choosing. It was to be the acid test of the Tank Corps and Elles was determined that they would succeed. THE FIRST VICTORIA CROSS Meanwhile, the Tank Corps had been awarded its first VC. As Capt Clement Robertson of 'A' Battalion was the first tank commander to be awarded his country's highest decoration, he should have his citation included in full. It reads:

From 30 September to 4 October this officer worked without a break under heavy fire preparing a route for his tanks to go into action against Reutel. He finished late on the night of 3 October 1917, and at once led his tanks up to the point for the attack. He brought them safely up by 3am on 4 October, and at 6am led them into action. The ground was very bad and heavily broken up by shell fire and the road demolished for about 500 yds. Capt Robertson, knowing the risk of the tanks missing their way, continued to lead them on foot. In addition to the heavy shell fire, intense machine-gun and rifle fire was directed at the tanks. Although knowing that his action would inevitably cost him his life, Capt Robertson deliberately continued to lead his tanks when well ahead of our own infantry, guiding them carefully and patiently towards their objective. Just as they reached the road he was killed by a bullet through the head, but his objective had been reached, and the tanks in consequence were enabled to fight a very successful action. By his very gallant devotion, Capt Robertson deliberately sacrificed his life to make certain the success of his tanks.

A further three VCs would be awarded to members of the Tank Corps before the Armistice.

NOTES TO CHAPTER 1

1   Maj Gen Sir Ernest D. Swinton, *Eyewitness.*
2   The official test included climbing a 4ft 6in high parapet and crossing a 5ft wide ditch. The active-service test course that 'Mother' had to negotiate contained a series of obstacles – it had to crawl into a dug-out shelter, climb out and cross a British-style trench and two 12ft-wide by 6ft-deep shell craters, ford a stream with marshy edges, climb a slope through a German wire entanglement, cross the trench beyond, then turn round and go back to the stream, down its marshy bed and finally over a double breastwork of 5ft 6in. 'Mother' did all this with ease and then achieved a final feat (as demanded by Kitchener) of crossing a 9ft-wide trench.
3   *Eyewitness.*
4   Jean Baptiste Eugene Estienne was a remarkable man who had been born in a small village on the Meuse on 7th November 1860. He entered the Artillery School at Fontainebleau in 1883 and was commissioned as a lieutenant of artillery the following year. His career in the artillery took a spectacular change in 1909, when he was appointed to command the newly-formed military aviation establishment at Vincennes, so he played an important part in the early development of French military aviation. In 1914, on mobilization, he was appointed to command the 22nd Artillery Regiment and took part in the battle of the Marne and the retreat from Belgium. He became what Swinton was to Britain, the 'father of the tank' (*père des chars*), although he was treated very differently. As Browne comments bitterly, in *The Tank in Action*: 'In England, it seems we do not know how to do these things – or at least to whom to do them'. Estienne would go on to become Inspector General of the Artillerie d'Assaut, retiring from the Army in 1923. However, his enthusiasm for new developments continued and he became actively involved with the production of the revolutionary Citroen Kegresse half-track. He was awarded the Grand Cross of the Légion d'honneur in 1934 and died in Paris on 2nd April 1936.
5   *Eyewitness*
6   The original four tank companies had grown into twelve in order to man all the new tanks.
7   Kenneth Macksey, *The Tank Pioneers.*

2 ON TO VICTORY

Despite Haig's agreement that the Tank Corps could plan its own battle on ground of its own choosing, Elles and his staff had to work very hard to find an ally from among the Army commanders. Eventually, though, they found that Gen Sir Julian Byng, whose Third Army was occupying an ideal area of ground, liked the idea of the proposed 'tank raid'. However, he was anxious to make it a far grander affair, involving larger resources – so much larger that GHQ promptly vetoed the plan! It was clear that Haig still considered the tank to be only a minor weapon, 'an adjunct to infantry and guns', rather than a battle-winner in its own right. Fortunately Byng was not prepared to let the matter drop. Eventually GHQ grudgingly agreed, but the plan was now so changed that the simple raid had become a large-scale offensive.

Vindication at Cambrai

The area of operations chosen was a stretch of firm, rolling countryside, relatively undamaged by shellfire and lying just south of the town of Cambrai, between the Canal du Nord and the Canal St Quentin. The soil was hard, chalky and well drained, so the cross-country going for the tanks would be good. The objective contained a number of villages and was defended by the hitherto impregnable Hindenburg Line, a tough nut to crack. The aim of the offensive was to capture and hold the objective, so that another offensive could then be launched.

The Tank Corps had much to do to prepare for the battle. It had to learn new basic tactics to enable the tanks to cross the strong German defences of the Hindenburg Line. It had been decided that surprise was essential, so there would be no long preliminary bombardment, which would in any case only churn up the ground, making tank movement even more difficult. Every tank would carry a 'fascine', a special obstacle-crossing device of some seventy-five large bundles of brushwood bound together with chains to form one large bundle 10ft long and 4ft 6in in diameter mounted on the nose.

Tank sections had been reorganized, reducing them from four to three tanks, so that every company now had a fourth (reserve) section. The new drill was that each section would advance in arrow-head formation. The leading tank (advanced guard tank) would go through the wire, up to the enemy line and then turn left, still on the friendly side of the first trench, and open fire with its starboard guns. The left-hand tank of the following pair (infantry

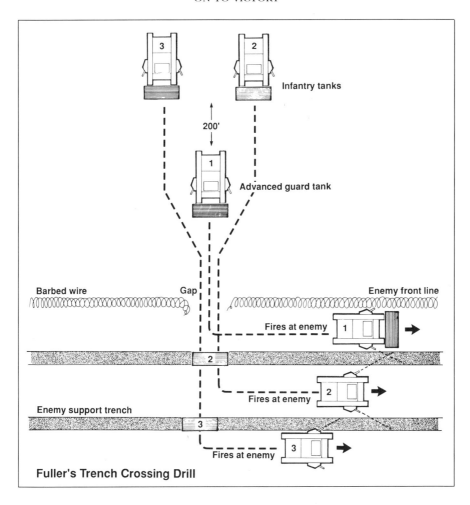

Infantry tanks

200'

Advanced guard tank

Barbed wire   Gap   Enemy front line

Fires at enemy   1   →

2

Fires at enemy   2   →

Enemy support trench

3

Fires at enemy   3   →

Fuller's Trench Crossing Drill

tanks), which were initially some 200 yards behind, would then move up to the first trench, drop its fascine into the trench, cross it and then also turn left, this time along the rear of the enemy trench, firing its guns in both directions. The third tank would cross that trench by the same fascine, advance to the support-line trench, cross it using its own fascine and then also turn left, this time along the rear of the second trench. Next, the advanced guard tank would cross the first trench via the fascine and meet up with the left-hand infantry tank. Both would then cross the support trench, where they would join the third tank. All three tanks in the section were now beyond the enemy support line, with one fascine still in hand. It was Fuller who had evolved this attack drill, which was to work very well in the battle. It was not used, though, in the area of 51st Highland Division, whose commander rejected the scheme as being 'too fantastic and unmilitary' and instituted his own. The later failure at Flesquieres was directly caused by his stupidity.

Against the advice of Elles, it was decided to attack with all the tanks spread out along the entire frontage, rather than concentrating them at one selected point, or retaining any in reserve. This foolhardy plan was supported by all the infantry divisional commanders, who naturally wanted the fullest tank support possible to be available. Fuller likened this lack of a reserve to '. . . playing cards without capital – it is sheer gambling. To trust to the cast of the dice is not generalship. . . . To leave the present plan as it is and the distribution as it is, is to court failure.'[1]

The entire Tank Corps, three brigades of three battalions each, was used:

III Corps sector: three divisions forward and one in support, 2nd and 3rd Tank Brigades split from left to right
> 12th Division – 'C' and 'F' Battalions
> 20th Division – 'A' Bn (minus one company) and 'I' Bn
> 6th Division – 'B' and 'H' Bns
> 29th Division – one company of 'A' Bn

IV Corps sector: only two divisions initially, but with the important objective of taking Bourlon Ridge in the second phase, with 1st Tank Brigade allocated and split
> 51st Division – 'D' and 'E' (minus one company) Bns
> 62nd Division – 'G' Bn plus one company of 'E' Bn

Each Tank Battalion had a full complement of 36 fighting tanks, plus six in immediate reserve. In addition, each brigade had 18 supply tanks[2] and three signal tanks equipped with wireless, while there were 32 tanks fitted with special grapnels to pull away any wire on the cavalry attack routes, and a further two loaded with bridging material, again for the cavalry advance. Finally, one tank was used to carry a telephone cable for Army HQ, making a grand total of 476 tanks in all.

On the morning of the attack, Elles drafted and issued his Special Order No 6, probably the most famous order ever to be written in the entire history of the Tank Corps. He explained how, at long last, the Corps would get the opportunity to operate on good going, in the van of the attack. He ended the order with the words: 'I propose leading the attack of the centre division.' It was unheard of in modern war for a general to lead his troops into battle. Even such great commanders as Wellington and Napoleon had not done so, although they had at least occupied vulnerable positions of observation on the battlefield in sight of their soldiers. Haig and his Army commanders were so far behind the line as to be totally invulnerable to shot and shell, seeing nothing of the battle and relying on line communication or liaison officers for information. As Fuller commented later on Elles's decision: 'To lead his command was to give life and soul to all our preparations – it was spiritually the making of the Tank Corps, and in value it transcended all our work.' It was this act, above everything else,

Special Order No 6.

1. Tomorrow the Tank Corps will have the chance for which it has been waiting for many months, – to operate on good going in the van of the battle.

2. All that hard work & ingenuity can achieve has been done in the way of preparation

3. It remains for unit commanders and for tank crews to complete the work by judgment & pluck in the battle itself.

4. In the light of past experience I leave the good name of the Corps with great confidence in their hands

5. I propose leading the attack of the centre division

Hugh Elles.
B.G.

19th Nov. 1917.   Commanding Tank Corps.

Distribution to Tank Commanders .   .

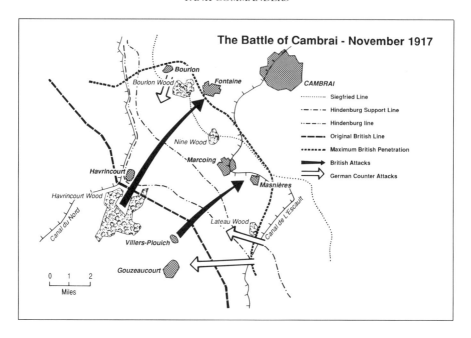

The Battle of Cambrai - November 1917

CAMBRAI

.... Siegfried Line

.—.—.— Hindenburg Support Line

..—..—.. Hindenburg line

▬▬▬ Original British Line

■■■■■■ Maximum British Penetration

➤ British Attacks

⇨ German Counter Attacks

Bourlon

Bourlon Wood

Fontaine

Nine Wood

Marcoing

Havrincourt

Masnières

Havrincourt Wood

Canal du Nord

Lateau Wood

Canal de L'Escault

Villers-Plouich

Gouzeaucourt

0   1   2

Miles

which made Elles one of the great tank commanders, setting the seal of success upon all his Corps' endeavours on that memorable day.

By 0500 hours on 20th November 1917, the tanks were drawn up in one long line, stretching for six miles in front of the British trenches. Zero hour had been set for 0620 hours, but the tanks were on the move 10 minutes earlier, so that they would be in their correct positions to lead the infantry forward. At zero hour an artillery barrage from 1,000 guns started and the tanks were on the move again, with Elles in 'Hilda', flying the Tank Corps colours. Major Gerald Huntbach of 'H' Battalion recalled:

I visited my tanks while they were warming up before zero, and as time got close we – Parsons, McCormick and myself – stood by Lt Leach's 'Hilda'. A lithe figure strode past the infantry and the rear rank tanks, pipe aglow, and an ash stick with mysterious cloth wrapping tucked under his arm: unheralded, unexpected then and there, and unattended, Brigadier-General Elles had arrived. 'Five minutes to go,' he said, 'This is the centre of our line and I'm going over in this tank'. He tapped 'Hilda's' off-side sponson, I swung the door open and informed Leach of his distinguished passenger. . . . The General glanced at his wrist. Shaking out his stick, he disclosed the brown, red and green flag soon to be historical, and then he squeezed through the doorway. As I shut the door, simultaneously with its clang came the sudden boom of a naval long-range gun somewhere behind Beauchamp. At this knock on the Kaiser's door, the flame and blast of our massed artillery crashed out, and the tanks moved as one to this mighty overture.[3]

Huntbach tells how later he met Gen Elles again, after they had crossed the first enemy trenchline: 'we met General Elles walking briskly towards Beauchamp, still pulling at his pipe, and with his fondest theories vindicated, exultant. He gave us a cheery wave with the now shot-riddled, victorious

28

banner. Behind him, at a respectful interval, came several crowds of German prisoners.' Elles was walking because 'Hilda' had been ditched in a trench near Ribecourt. (It was later towed out.)

In another account of the battle, Capt D.E. Hickey, who was then a section commander in 23 Company, 'H' Battalion, in the third wave, describes how he saw: 'Ahead of us, the General himself . . . with head and shoulders sticking out of the top manhole of his flag-tank, 'Hilda', leading the attack.'

The attack went well. The enemy was thrown into confusion by the ease with which the tanks had been able to break through their 'impregnable' Hindenburg Line. Hundreds of enemy surrendered, throwing away their weapons and equipment as they ran. Almost all first objectives were taken by 0800 hours, but there was still hard fighting in the Ribecourt area, where the enemy were strongly ensconced in the cellars and in deep dugouts. The second phase of the attack took the Hindenburg Support Line everywhere except near Flesquieres, where the 51st Highland Division was held up for the reasons already explained. Artillery in this area also succeeded in knocking out a number of tanks too far in front of their supporting infantry.

By 1600 hours the battle was won as far as the Tank Corps was concerned. The most rapid advance of the entire war had been achieved. From a start line 13,000 yards long, a penetration of some 10,000 yards in depth had been achieved in under twelve hours. To put the achievement into proper perspective, this was the equivalent of a previous penetration that had been achieved only at a cost of over 250,000 casualties, while in the first two days at Cambrai, the total casualties were under 6,000 (over 600 being Tank Corps men). This success had been achieved by using a tank force of just 690 officers and 3,500 men, without the usual weeks of preparatory bombardment or expensive artillery wire-cutting operations. However, a number of tanks had been lost. With none in reserve, it was necessary for further operations to rally those few remaining, select the fittest and form composite companies.

This should have been the moment when the cavalry poured through the gap and took up the advance, thus setting the seal upon the tanks' spectacular victory. Unfortunately, this was not to be. For a variety of reasons the cavalry arrived late and were then cut to pieces by enemy fire as they tried to advance, their horses killed or wounded so that they were reduced to fighting as infantrymen. They gained nothing and next day the battle reverted to the normal static dogfight. Over the next few days the situation went from bad to worse until, on 30th November, the Germans launched a major counter-attack. The tanks had all been withdrawn by then, back to the railheads, but some were quickly rounded up – in some cases being taken off the railway flat cars, patched up and sent off into battle in small groups. Eventually the position was stabilized and the tanks were able to withdraw completely, to prepare for the 1918 campaign. As a German officer wrote later: 'If the English Army leader had taken full advantage of his opportunity, it would not have been possible to limit his breakthrough in that region. The attack was a complete surprise. . . . Without tanks it would have been impossible to over-run the excellently built and invulnerable positions. . .'.4

Gen Elles and his Tank Corps had proved themselves beyond all expectations. Haig wrote in his despatches that 'the great value of the tanks in the offensive has been conclusively proved.' Gen Byng made his feelings clear in a letter to Elles:

> To say that the operation without tanks was an impossibility is merely a truism, but to say that the far-reaching success was due to the co-operation of your Corps with the infantry and artillery is the point of view I wish you to realise.
>
> No one could have been so well supported, so greatly helped and so consistently strengthened in the plan, as I have been by you and your staff. And no Army has ever been so splendidly led and so fully assisted as mine by your Corps.
>
> The many calls on you and your men's endurance have been answered with the greatest alacrity – their losses have been heavy and their work prodigious, but they have established a record now which none can dispute.5

The anniversary of the Battle of Cambrai, 20th November 1917, is now always celebrated as Regimental Day throughout the Royal Tank Regiment.

The Yanks are Coming!

It was misty and drizzling on 12th September 1918, when the 304th US Tank Brigade, under the command of Lt Col George Smith Patton Jr, supported an attack by the 1st and 42nd Divisions of the US IV Corps in operations against the St Mihiel Salient. The Brigade consisted of the 344th and 345th Tank Battalions, both of which were equipped with French Renault light tanks. These were the first American tanks ever to go into action.

ORIGINS When the United States of America entered the war in April 1917, the tank was still virtually unknown in that country. The tank's performance on the Somme, where, as we have seen, it had only been used in small numbers on impossible terrain, had not impressed the American Military Mission in Paris, which had concluded that tanks were useless. An American Expeditionary Force (AEF) tank arm had not even been considered. All this changed with the arrival in France of Gen John J. ('Black Jack') Pershing as CinC AEF. On 19th July 1917 Pershing ordered a special board to be formed to look more closely into the employment of tanks. This far-sighted board concluded that: '. . . the tank is considered a factor which is destined to become an important element in this war.' It also recommended that the tanks be organized into a separate corps and be equipped with a mixture of French light tanks and British heavy tanks. The initial size of the American Tank Corps was to be 20 combat divisions and the board recommended that 2,000 light and 200 heavy tanks be procured, with further production geared at a 15% a month replacement rate.

Pershing ordered a member of his staff, Lt Col LeRoy Eltinge, to take charge of all tank matters, and, after examining the situation, Eltinge sent the following cable back to the War Department's chief of ordnance:

Careful study of French and British experience with tanks completed and will be forwarded by early mail. Project includes 350 heavy tanks of British Mark VI pattern; 20 similar tanks equipped for signal purposes; 40 similar tanks for supply of gasoline and oil; 140 tanks arranged to carry 25 soldiers or five tons of supplies; 50 similar tanks with upper platform for field gun; total 600 heavy tanks. Also following Renault tanks: 1,030 for fighting purposes; 130 for supply; 40 for signal purposes; total 1,200 Renault tanks. Replacement of tanks requires 15% per month after arrival here.[6]

Eltinge further reported that the French were prepared to allow the manufacture of the FT 17 in the USA and would supply a model to assist production. The British also promised to produce complete plans of their projected Mark VI tank but when this project was abandoned agreed to substitute Mark V and Mark V* heavy tanks.

GEORGE S. PATTON   One of Pershing's staff who showed immediate interest in tanks was a young cavalry captain, George S. Patton Jr, who was unhappy with his mundane job as post adjutant and commander of the AEF HQ Company at Chaumont. Patton had graduated in 1909 from West Point, where he excelled at Drill Regulations. He was top of his class in conduct at the end of his second year, appointed second-ranking corporal at summer camp, and was adjutant in his final year. He also had a fine record in sporting activities, being awarded his 'A' for athletics and playing football for the last four of his five years there, breaking both arms, his nose (three times) and dislocating his shoulder. He represented the USA in the 1912 Olympic Games in Stockholm, taking part in a new event, the modern pentathlon. This comprised the five skills of riding, running, swimming, shooting and fencing – the perfect military combination, especially for a cavalryman. Patton was placed a creditable fifth overall, although he always felt that he should have done better. After the Games, he stayed on in Europe to take his wife on a second honeymoon. They managed to include a visit to the French Cavalry School at Saumur in the Loire valley, where Patton took fencing lessons from the school adjutant, who was a renowned fencing master. He returned there in 1913 to take sabre lessons and again took his wife touring Normandy and Brittany, which he later said helped him greatly during the 1944 Normandy campaign.

Returning to the USA, Patton was posted to the Cavalry School as a weapons instructor, teaching sabre (he had already written a new manual entitled *Saber Methods* and designed a new pattern of the weapon, based on his Saumur experience). His tour at the school ended in 1916, when he was posted to the 8th Cavalry, just in time for the outbreak of the Mexican War. He was a member of Gen Pershing's expedition to capture Pancho Villa and his gang. Patton was Pershing's aide, but also often acted as leading scout for the force. On one occasion he caught up with Villa's personal bodyguard, Julio Cardenas, who was holed up in a hacienda with some of the gang. Patton, getting inside the house, shot it out with the bandits, killing Cardenas and one other. He brought the bodies back to Pershing's HQ, strapped on the front mudguards of his open touring car. Pershing was delighted, remarking: 'We have a bandit in our ranks, this Patton boy,! He's a real fighter!' This incident was to serve Patton well – when he arrived in France in June 1917 he was immediately appointed as Pershing's ADC and later became post adjutant. However, the job quickly became too boring for the young fire-eater. When towards the end of September, Eltinge asked him if he wanted to become a tank officer Patton immediately said 'yes' and was told to write a letter to Gen Pershing, requesting his name be considered if a tank arm was organized.

In the letter, which is quoted by Martin Blumenson in *The Patton Papers*, Patton highlighted his cavalry experience, which he felt would be similar to working with light tanks, wrote about the knowledge he had gained as a machine-gun troop commander, which would also be most important, because, as he put it, 'accurate fire is very necessary to good use of tanks'. He also mentioned his excellent knowledge of French, his mechanical ability and his aggressive spirit, claiming to be 'the only American who has ever made an attack in a motor vehicle' – a reference to his days in Mexico. Patton's application was supported by Maj Robert Bacon, the HQ commandant, who considered Patton to be 'unusually well equipped and fitted in every way for the command'. Patton had to wait for a while, but in early November Pershing told him that he could either have command of an infantry battalion or go into the newly forming Tank Corps. Patton chose the tanks, was promoted to major, and sent as CO to the new US Army Tank Training School, which was being set up at Langres, some twenty miles from HQ AEF. This school would teach tank tactics and tank command, while a second school, at the nearby village of Bourg, would teach tank driving, maintenance and the other necessary crew skills. Patton was in charge of both schools and rapidly became the AEF's leading tank expert. He was supported by First Lt Elgin Braine, a reserve artillery officer, who became his assistant. Braine was a mechanical engineer with a thorough knowledge of engines, which made him the ideal choice for the job. However, neither he nor Patton knew much about tanks, so they were ordered to report for a two-week course at the French Light Tank Training School. As Dale E Wilson explains in *Treat 'em Rough!*, his history of the formation of the US Tank Corps: 'During the first week at Chamlieu, Patton had time to become thoroughly acquainted with the Renault tank. He drove the vehicle, noting its ease of handling and surprising comfort in contrast to the heavier British tank. . . . In addition to driving tanks, Patton fired their guns, observed a manoeuvre, worked on tactical problems, toured the repair shops and tank parking area, and spent long hours discussing how best to employ tanks in combat.' On several occasions he was able to meet and talk to Estienne, and he was at Chamlieu during Elles' attack at Cambrai. Following their course Patton and Braine returned to GHQ AEF, where they reported verbally and then in writing to Eltinge, who was still nominally in charge of the tank project. Patton was delighted to be '. . . in on the ground floor. If they [the tanks] are a success I may have the chance I have always been looking for', he wrote in his diary.

True to his West Point upbringing, Patton was a strict disciplinarian, so the two schools soon earned a reputation throughout the AEF for discipline, dress and military behaviour. However, at the same time, the instruction was sound and Patton ensured that members of his staff also received battle experience with frequent attachments to operational French tank units. In less than five months Patton had trained a complete brigade of tank crewmen, so he was not particularly pleased to hear a rumour, which circulated in early December 1917, that another cavalryman, Col Samuel Dickerson Rockenbach, who was then serving with the Quartermaster Corps, was to be appointed to command both the light and heavy tanks of the AEF. The rumour turned out to be fact and Patton had to swallow his pride, commenting in a letter to his wife, '. . . I guess he [Rockenbach] does not care a whole lot for me, but my theory that if you do your best no one can hurt you will be put to the proof'.[7] Rockenbach was officially appointed as Chief of the Tank Service, AEF, on 23rd December 1917, the Tank Corps of the US Army being officially created a few days later, on 26th January 1918. That same month he and Patton visited Elles and Fuller at the British Tank Corps HQ at Bernicourt.

Patton did not find it easy working with Rockenbach – 'the most contrary old cuss I ever worked with. As soon as you suggest any thing he opposes it, but after about an hour's argument comes round and proposes the same thing himself. So in the long run I get my way, but at a great waste of breath.'[8] Patton may be guilty of exaggeration, but he, not Rockenbach, was the real driving force in the US Tank Corps. More officers began to arrive, who would form the nucleus of Patton's first tank brigade and the two schools increased in size and tempo under Patton's strict regime. 'Our chief fault as an army', he wrote to his wife, 'has been that of taking things too easily. When the days get longer I can work them more, which will be a help to them.'[9]

By the middle of April the level of training was such that Patton decided he could start some practical manoeuvres, including a demonstration to the members of the General Staff College on 22nd April. It featured 10 of Patton's light tanks, plus a battalion of infantry, and went very well indeed. On 28th April the 1st Light Tank Battalion was formed, with Patton as CO.

About this time Patton set the officers of the tank centre the task of designing for the embryo Tank Corps a shoulder patch, specifying that, because tanks had the firepower of artillery, the mobility of cavalry and the ability of the infantry to hold ground, red, yellow and blue had to be featured. The resulting three-coloured 'pyramid of power' was accepted by Patton, who immediately paid out of his own pocket to have a suitable number of sets made up locally. Later, the triangular patch was embellished with an endless track, a cannon and a lightning bolt superimposed upon the three colours. It is still used to denote the various armoured divisions in the US Army. The chosen collar insignia and button design featured the silhouette of a British Heavy Mark IV tank. Patton did much to heighten the *esprit de corps* of the new unit, his obsession with proper saluting being so well known that a really smart salute was known throughout the AEF as a 'George Patton'.

While Patton was busy at his Light Tank School in France in early 1918, the

2nd American Tank Center was established under Lt Col Conrad S. Babcock at the UK Tank Training Centre at Bovington Camp in Dorset. Patton and Rockenbach visited Bovington in March 1918, during the preparations for the arrival of the first heavy tank battalion from the USA. Meanwhile, back in the United States, another young officer was busy creating the first Tank Corps training centre in the USA at Camp Colt, near Gettysburg in Pennsylvania. The officer was Capt Dwight D. Eisenhower, who was to become the most famous American officer of WW2. He later recalled that at the time his 'mood was black', as he believed he was missing possible battlefield glory. However, as Dale E. Wilson comments, 'He would not have been quite so despondent, had he known what the future held in store for him. . . . within just seven months he would be a lieutenant colonel commanding a training post with more than 10,000 enlisted men and 600 officers. The experience he gained in this assignment would prove far more valuable to him in his later career than any battlefield exploits he might have accomplished as an infantry company or battalion commander in France.'

INTO BATTLE   The US Tank Corps was thus undergoing a hectic expansion, which would eventually produce six battalions in Europe and eleven more in the USA. However, the immediate aim was to produce two fully trained battalions by the spring of 1918, so that they could be used in the new offensive being planned for the American First Army, namely to reduce the St Mihiel salient by two simultaneous attacks – one from the south and one from the west. The 505th French Tank Regiment would support the southern attack, together with the 304th American Tank Brigade, which contained the two battalions armed with Renault FT 17s. Patton was the brigade commander and he later recalled how, while he was waiting for the attack to start, his position was sprayed with German machine-gun fire, the bullets cutting the grass along the ridge where he was lying:

Occasionally a man would be hit and he said he could tell by the grunt or the scream and the way the body fell whether the hit was high or low. He said he was getting more and more scared, his mouth dry and his hands were sweating, and he felt like turning and running like hell toward the rear. He happened to look up, and there, on a low bank of cloud he saw the faces of his ancestors watching him; he recognized his grandfather, George Patton and his great Uncle Tazewell, and General Mercer, from their pictures, but he said there were scores of others, in different dress, some almost fading into the cloud, but they all had a family look and he said to himself, 'Here is where another Patton gets his'. The command came to move forward, and he suddenly was not scared at all.[10]

Patton had, like Elles at Cambrai, issued his final instructions before the battle. He ordered that no tank was to be surrendered or abandoned to the enemy. 'You must establish the fact,' he told his men, 'that American tanks do not surrender. . . . As long as one tank is able to move it must go forward. Its presence will save the lives of hundreds of infantry and kill many Germans. Finally, this is our BIG CHANCE; WHAT WE HAVE WORKED FOR . . . MAKE IT WORTHWHILE.'[11]

With Patton at its head, the attack went in at 0500 hours on 12th September 1918. The 345th followed the 42nd Division until it had passed the Tranches d'Houblons and then the tanks took over the lead. Despite thick mud and heavy shellfire, the tanks overran several machine-gun posts, destroyed a complete battalion of artillery and took some thirty prisoners. The 344th were operating with the 1st Division and they succeeded in cutting through the enemy wire and taking on a number of machine gun posts around the Bois de Rate. On the second day there was a shortage of fuel for the tanks, which curtailed operations, but on the 14th an eight tank patrol from the 344th attacked and dispersed an enemy battalion near Woel.

After the operation, and despite the tanks' considerable success, Patton received a dressing-down from a furious Gen Rockenbach, who had been trying to find out what was happening since the start of the operation! He told Patton that he did not consider it was a commander's place to lead his troops from the front. Patton managed to smooth things over and, although he promised to conform in future, clearly appreciated better than Rockenbach, that an armoured leader must be up at the front at all times, where he can rapidly influence events in a fluid tank battle. Patton later wrote to his wife, 'Gen R. gave me hell for going up (with the forward elements) but it had to be done. At least I will not sit in a dug-out and have my men out in the fighting.'[12] During the two-day action the brigade, which had comprised 144 tanks, lost only two tanks from enemy action, but a further 22 were ditched and 14 broke down. Fourteen men were hit, but only two while inside their tanks.

Commanding the 344th was another remarkable officer, Maj Sereno Brett, who had served as chief instructor at Patton's Tank School. Later, when Patton was wounded in the Argonne, Brett took over the brigade, supporting nine different divisions and being constantly in action, both then and throughout the rest of the campaign. He was awarded the DSC, DSM and the Silver Star with Oak Leaf Cluster. Two of his soldiers, Cpls Harold W. Roberts and Donald M. Call, were awarded their country's highest decoration, the Congressional Medal of Honor. Roberts' citation tells how, when he was driving his tank into a clump of bushes to protect a disabled tank, it slid into a shell-hole 10-feet deep and full of water. Knowing that there would be time for only one of the two-man crew to escape, he pushed the gunner out of the back door and was himself drowned. Cpl Call was in a tank conducting operations against some enemy machine-gun nests, when half of the tank's armour-plate was knocked off by a direct hit from an artillery shell. Choked by fumes from the exploding shell, he got out and took cover in a shell-hole some 30 yards away. When the officer who had been in the tank with him did not follow, he returned under heavy machine-gun fire and shell fire, rescued the officer and carried him over a mile to safety, under intensive machine-gun and sniper fire.

After their first triumphant engagement, the Americans went on to take part in the bloody Meuse-Argonne battles at the end of September, Patton being wounded early on in the offensive. However, he had by then already proved himself an outstanding combat commander and had imbued his brigade with such a sense of duty and aggressive spirit that it continued to fight with great courage and skill. As Dale Wilson says: 'This first generation of American tank crewmen truly earned the nickname "Treat-'em-Rough Boys" with which they had been tagged.'[13]

The heavy tanks of 301st Heavy Tank Battalion, under Maj Ralph I. Sasse, also proved themselves, while supporting an attack by the British Fourth Army's Australian Corps. The attack began on 29th September. The 301st, who were equipped with British Mark V and V* heavy tanks, had a difficult and bloody baptism and by the end of the first day had only 17 tanks operational. Nevertheless, after a period for rest and reorganization, they went into action again on 23rd October, which proved to be their last action of the war. Sasse was awarded a British DSO and many of his men won other British gallantry awards.

French Tanks in Action

Following Berry-au-Bac, the French fought an increasingly large number of tank battles, involving varying numbers of tanks. Soissons, on 18th July 1918, in which three *groupements* of Schneiders (approx 123 tanks) and three *groupements* of St Chamonds (about 100 tanks) were involved, together with six battalions of Renaults (255 tanks), must count as the largest concentration of French tanks employed in any one battle of the war, although in the Forêt d'Argonne, which followed on from St Mihiel, no fewer than 544 Renaults were engaged – seven and one-third battalions of which were French-manned, while the remaining four battalions (214 tanks) had American crews.

SOISSONS   The allocation of tanks for the battle was as follows:

Tenth French Army	Sixth French Army
3 *groupements* Schneider (123 tanks)	1 *groupe* St Chamond (10 tanks)
3 *groupements* St Chamond (90 tanks)	3 battalions Renault (125 tanks)
3 battalions Renault (130 tanks)	

Operating as part of the Tenth French Army were two American divisions (1st and 2nd), both of which had French tanks allocated in support.

As at Cambrai, no preliminary bombardment was allowed and the final moves of the tanks to their jumping-off positions took place at night, so as to retain the element of surprise. However, unlike Cambrai, the allocation of tanks was such as to allow for reserves at every level. Where brigades were attacking in line, tanks were allocated to the assault, support and reserve battalions; where they were attacking in column, each brigade received its own allocation of tanks, irrespective of its position in the column. Thus every division had its own tank reserve. In addition, three of the Renault battalions in the Third French Army were held in Army reserve.

Zero hour was timed for 0435 hours, the tanks and infantry moving forward under covering artillery fire. The Germans, taken by surprise, offered little resistance initially, but from about 1100 hours resistance stiffened. From then on the battle was by no means easy. Nevertheless, the attacks, which went on for the next seven days, were generally successful, although the infantry tired quickly and could not always complete all the phases. The tanks in support of both Armies were very effective, and gave great acceleration to the initial advance. This enabled both Armies to move as far and as fast as their infantry would allow. It soon became obvious that a continuous supply of fresh infantry was needed, in order to take full advantage of the continued successes of the tanks and to hold the ground they had captured. If the tanks moved too slowly then they were found to be vulnerable to enemy artillery fire, while tanks on their own had difficulty in dealing with large numbers of artillery and machine-guns. Even in these early days the importance of the all-arms team was becoming clear. Between the 18th and 23rd, the tanks in support of the Tenth Army lost 102 of their original 223, while 25% of the personnel were killed or wounded. The tanks with the Sixth Army went on operating for a further three days, by which time they had lost 58 tanks, 25% of their officers and many of their men.

Tanks against Tanks

As we have seen, the Germans took little interest in tanks and built only a handful of A7Vs. However, tank-*versus*-tank combat was bound to occur sooner or later and the first recorded engagement took place on 24th April 1918. The Germans had assigned 14 of their heavy A7V tanks to support operations in the area around Villers-Bretonneux. They were deployed in three groups. The first, of three tanks, was with 228th Infantry Division and the second, of six tanks, with Fourth Guards Infantry Division, both with the task of attacking Villers-Bretonneux. The third group, of five tanks, was assigned to 77th Reserve Infantry Division, to attack Cachy. Group 1 was involved in heavy fighting in Villers-Bretonneux, capturing many prisoners in the village and destroying the airfield. Group 2 had similar success, until its tanks either broke down or were knocked out by enemy fire. Group 3 lost a tank soon after the action started, when it got stuck in a deep hole. The second tank advanced to a point some 700 yards from Cachy, where it came upon a forward section of 1st Battalion, Tank Corps, equipped with one male and two female tanks. The females were the first into action, but could make no impression on the enemy tank with their machine-guns and were both knocked out. Then the male tank, commanded by Lt F. Mitchell MC, arrived and engaged the enemy, scoring five direct hits with its 6-pdrs. Trying to avoid this fire the A7V ran onto a steep bank and overturned. The remaining three A7Vs then arrived, but were engaged and routed, one crew abandoning their tank during the fight. As the Tank Corps regimental history recalls: 'It was most appropriate that the victor in this first tank versus tank fight was No 1 Tank of No 1 Section, A Company, 1st Battalion, Tank Corps.'[14]

37

Victory

August 1918 saw the start of the last phase of WW1, with the Battle of Amiens, which began on 8th August and ended 100 days later with the Armistice on 11th November 1918. British, French and American tanks all played a major role in the battles. The numbers employed were considerable. To support the British offensive at Amiens over 600 tanks assembled, providing a massed tank assault even larger than at Cambrai. By 6am on 9th August these tanks had penetrated seven-and-a-half miles, taken 16,000 prisoners and captured over two hundred guns. During the non-stop fighting up to the end of the war, nearly two thousand tanks and armoured cars of the British Tank Corps alone were in continuous action, 3,000 officers and men being killed or wounded out of a total Corps strength of only 10,500. Tank Corps losses between 1916 and 1918 were a staggering 7,116.

Between September 1916 and November 1918, French tanks took part in no less than 4,356 separate engagements,[15] British in 3,060 and American in 250, a grand total of 7,666. It is certainly no wonder that the Germans would claim that they had been defeated, as one historian put it, 'not by the genius of Marshal Foch, but by "General Tank"'.[16]

Although the tank had done so well in the war and its future looked secure as the war ended, the coming days of peace would quickly sound the death knell of a large portion of the tank forces in the three Allied armies, shattering the dreams of many of the young, enthusiastic, highly trained members of these élite forces, to the great delight of their opponents. There were unfortunately, all too many senior officers in the British, French and American armies who despised the new tank arm and who longed for a return to more sedate methods of making war – 'a return to real soldiering' was the way one such critic put it. To anyone who cared to look closely, the days of the horse on the battlefield were clearly numbered, but the tank would, once again, have to struggle long and hard before proving itself a major battle-winner.

NOTES TO CHAPTER 2

1 Basil Liddell Hart. *The Tanks,* Vol. 1.
2 This was before the invention of the Mark IX Supply tank, so these were merely elderly fighting tanks, 'de-gutted' so that they could take stores.
3 *The Tanks* Vol. 1
4 *The Fighting Tanks 1916–1933*
5 *Tank Corps Book of Honour* (edited by Maj Maurice)
6 Cable No 159-S as quoted in Dale E. Wilson, *Treat 'em Rough!*
7 Martin Blumenson, *The Patton Papers*
8 *ibid*
9 *ibid*
10 From a letter to the author by Mrs Ruth Ellen Patton Totten, Gen Patton's daughter.
11 *Treat 'em Rough!*
12 *The Patton Papers*
13 *Treat 'em Rough!*
14 *Short History of the RTR*
15 Col Ramspacher, *Le Général Estienne*
16 Attributed to General der Infanterie AWH von Zwehl.

3 BETWEEN THE WARS

The early days of peace were unhappy ones for the British Tank Corps, which found itself swiftly reduced from the 25 battalions that were in existence when the Armistice was signed – 18 in France, all of which had seen action except for the 18th Tank Battalion, and seven in the UK, four of which were trained and ready for battle. In addition, there was the training and reinforcement centre at Swanage, which comprised two more battalions plus a complete battalion of officers. This entire reserve disappeared soon after the Armistice and in just over a year there were only five battalions left.

British Tanks – the Lean Years
Sir Hugh Elles, now reduced to the rank of brigadier general,[1] took over command of the Tank Corps Centre, which included the Central Schools, the Tank Corps Depot and the Workshops Training Battalion at Bovington and the Gunnery School at Lulworth. He and his erstwhile staff, in particular 'Boney' Fuller, had to fight long and hard to keep the Corps alive, because of the strong element in the Army at the time that wanted to see the new Corps abolished, or amalgamated with some other arm. The Army Council changed its mind endlessly, vacillating between forming a *corps d'élite*, instituting a twin-corps system (one to provide tanks for infantry support and one for independent action), and making tanks part of the Royal Engineers. It was not until 1922 that a firm decision to retain a permanent Tank Corps of four battalions was made. The Corps became the Royal Tank Corps on 18th October 1923.

The sniping, however, continued, with much bad feeling against any kind of mechanization in general and tanks in particular – such dirty, noisy machines should be abolished so that the horse could return in all its glory! However, it was soon discovered that the Army could not do without AFVs, because the armoured car provided a cheap and effective way of policing the British Empire, in particular India and the Middle East. Thus, between January 1920 and July 1921, twelve Armoured Car Companies were raised and manned by Tank Corps personnel. Lt Col (later Maj Gen) George Lindsay was an early exponent of armoured car/aircraft co-operation in the Middle East, which proved to be a highly effective and cheap way of exercising control. Thus, Tank Corps soldiers served, first in armoured cars and later in light tanks, all over the world, gaining valuable experience in such faraway places as the North-West Frontier of India, Shanghai, Palestine and Egypt.

'THE RUSSIAN STUNT' Apart from the tank element of the British Army of Occupation in Germany and such brief but exciting episodes as 'the Russian Stunt', when British tanks and crews were sent to southern Russia to help fight against the Bolsheviks, most tank activity took place at home. However, one incident from the operations in Russia is well worth including here, as it shows, once again, both the tremendous latent power of this new weapon system and the bravery of the tank commanders. A single British tank crew was responsible for the capture of an entire city, namely the important centre of Tsaritsin – renamed Stalingrad after the Revolution and now called Volgagrad – together with the surrender of 40,000 Bolshevik troops. Initially some tanks (three Heavy Mark Vs and three Whippets) had been among reinforcements to be called up, after numerous attacks on Tsaritsin had been repulsed. One of the Mark Vs had a British crew under Capt Walsh and this tank in company with one other (Russian-manned) broke through the enemy wire and crossed the first trench line. In true Cambrai style, Walsh then turned and drove parallel with the trench, clearing it of enemy, so that the Cossack cavalry could advance and consolidate. After an enforced wait for petrol, which took two days to arrive and then was only sufficient to refuel one tank, Walsh's Mark V continued its advance, under the personal command of Maj E.M. Bruce, who was the commander of the entire South Russian Tank Detachment (then comprising 57 Mark Vs and 17 Whippets). He drove straight into Tsaritsin and succeeded in capturing the entire city, which was something a complete German Tank Army could not achieve during WW2!

THE BLACK BERET In March 1924 the black beret was officially adopted by the Royal Tank Corps (RTC) in place of the peaked field-service cap, which had been found totally unsuitable for wearing inside tanks. Elles was responsible, having been impressed during the war by the berets worn by the French Chasseurs Alpins, although he considered their pattern to be too large and floppy, while the Basque beret was too skimpy. A compromise was achieved and worn, despite much initial mirth and ridicule from outside the Corps, by all ranks of the RTC from then on. In time, the black beret would become the symbol of armoured troops throughout the world.

MECHANIZATION Despite all the prejudice against mechanization that pervaded the Army, it was very clear to anyone who looked at the situation objectively that, unless the British Army mechanized soon, it would be left far behind every other army in the world. When Gen Sir George Milne became Chief of the Imperial General Staff in March 1926, he declared that it was his intention to mechanize the Army, with the tank in a principal role. As if to emphasise his resolve, he chose Fuller as his Military Assistant. There was, however, much opposition and it was to take far too long to achieve full mechanization. A measure of the hostility against all things mechanical can perhaps be gauged by the fact that as late as 1936 the Secretary of State for War (Duff Cooper) was apologizing to the cavalry for having to mechanize them with the words, 'It is like asking a great musical performer to throw away his violin and devote himself in future to the gramophone'. Such stupidity at such a high level would leave the British Army woefully short of tanks when war came.

Despite these idiocies, the tank pioneers persevered. This was an exciting period when revolutionary new ideas were expounded and occasionally put into practice, such as the formation of an experimental, entirely mechanized brigade, and when men like Fuller, Lindsay, Broad, Martel and Liddell Hart, all exerted their influence on the evolution of the tank and on the tank tactics of the future. They did not always speak with one voice, except to aver that mechanization was essential, all having their own ideas on what types of tanks were needed and how they should be handled. Sadly, despite the fact that a well-balanced Experimental Mechanised Force came into being in May 1927, and that this force proved itself superior to more conventional military forces time and time again on exercises, no proper notice was ever taken of its achievements by the higher echelons of command in the UK.

Theorists and Practical Men

Fuller and Liddell Hart are prime examples of the thinkers who produced a continual stream of books and articles on the theory and practice of armoured warfare. Both looked into the future and postulated all-conquering, fully armoured forces, containing a mix of all arms (tanks, artillery, engineers and infantry) and working in close co-operation with aircraft. Fuller's *Lectures on FSR III*, published in 1932, for example, put forward this concept and, while his words fell upon deaf ears in Britain, both Germany and Russia took heed. Fuller was later swayed towards advocating that tanks should operate on their own, uncluttered by the other arms, who inevitably slowed up their cross-country movement. Liddell Hart became the acknowledged armoured expert of the 1920s and 1930s, his teachings being studied all over the world. However, towards the late 1930s even he, strangely enough, began to have doubts about the promise he had once imagined the tank to hold and recanted some of his own teachings. Nevertheless, his earlier writings were avidly read, in particular, once again, by the Germans.

If Fuller and Liddell Hart were the thinkers, then Martel in the UK and J. Walter Christie in the USA were the engineers who put theory into practice by designing and building tanks. Martel's tiny tankettes were cheap and thus popular with those in authority, but they did not provide adequate protection for their one- or two-man crews and were too small to be effective apart from in a reconnaissance role. Christie was an exceptionally difficult man to deal with and, like so many inventors, was virtually ignored by his own country. However, his revolutionary type of suspension, which allowed for high-speed cross-country movement, was adopted by the Russians for what was to become arguably the best tank of WW2 (the T34) and the start of a line of highly successful AFVs capable of great things even on modern battlefields.

Then there were the soldiers – men like Lindsay, Broad and later Hobart, Pope and Crocker in the UK; Chaffee and Voorhis in the USA; Lutz and

Guderian in Germany; and de Gaulle in France. All had to fight against the prejudice which pervaded their respective armies, while they tried to get on with the job of forming tank units and training armoured soldiers in the new doctrines. Their task was in some ways the hardest of all, as they constantly had to deal not only with the inevitable shortages of both men and material, but also with the putting into practice of the theories of the 'thinkers' in the vehicles provided by the 'engineers'. These difficulties varied considerably between countries, and even the Germans had problems.

Neither of Britain's two great tankmen of WW1, Swinton and Elles, featured to any major degree in this pioneering work. Swinton, who had retired in 1919, continued to show interest in the importance of cross-country movement and was actively associated with the makers of the first half-tracked vehicles (made by the French company Citroen-Kegresse). He also became the Representative Colonel Commandant of the RTC in 1934, holding that post until 1938. Elles was of course indissolubly tied up with the Corps as its head and had to bear the great strain of fighting for its very existence, while at the same time endeavouring to protect the interests of those who had served under him in the war. In an appreciation of Elles which appeared in *The Tank* magazine soon after his death, Maj Gen Lindsay said of the 1920s: 'These were very difficult times for the young Corps in its fight for existence against old-established institutions and vested interests, and I was helped enormously by his ever ready advice and assistance. . . . I think that few of the present day members of the Corps realise the great work that Hugh Elles did to establish the Corps on a sound foundation.' Elles became MGO in May 1934 and a Colonel Commandant of the RTC in the same year, an appointment he held until 1945, being Representative Colonel Commandant after Swinton for just one year (1939).

The Royal Armoured Corps

On the 4th April 1939, the British Secretary of State for War, Leslie Hore-Belisha, announced in Parliament that the newly mechanized cavalry regiments would combine with the battalions of the RTC in order to create the Royal Armoured Corps (RAC). Sadly there would be no time for the newly formed Corps to settle down before war came. Even after the obvious lessons which came from the German Blitzkrieg in Poland, the War Office was still determined to keep tank formations subordinated and would not allow the creation of the required number of senior RAC positions. All that they would permit was the creation of an Inspector RAC and an Advisor RAC for the BEF. Vyvyan Pope would be appointed as the first Inspector and later become the first armoured advisor to the BEF.

Commonwealth Armour

Although the first mechanized unit in the Australian Military Forces (AMF) had been formed in 1908 (the Australian Volunteer Automobile Corps) and the 1st Australian Light Car Patrol (six Model 'T' Fords equipped with Lewis guns) had been very successful in the Middle East during WW1, the AMF showed little interest in tanks until 1926. They then decided to send an officer (Lt E.W. Lampered) to the UK to train as a tank instructor. They also decided to buy four Vickers medium tanks and the following year, on 15th December 1927, the Australian Tank Corps was gazetted, although the 1st Tank Section, commanded by Capt E.T. Penfold, did not hold its first parade until 22nd March 1930. Their history reports that he 'brought great enthusiasm and a strong sense of duty to his new unit'. Lampered, now a captain, was appointed as tank instructor and adjutant. Another important member of the small unit was an ordnance artificer named George Davidson, who kept the tanks in running order for many years, all through the Depression years 1930 to 1937. Further tanks were ordered in 1935 (35 Vickers Light Mark VIAs) and a second tank section was formed two years later.

The unit colour patch was a rectangle of three equal bars in the RTC colours (brown, red and green), the badge a tank backed by the AMF 'rising sun', with the motto 'Paratus' on a scroll at its base. After trying various types of headgear the OC eventually appealed to the Colonel Commandant, RTC, who sent them 60 black berets.

Meanwhile, between 1933 and 1939 three armoured car units were formed, which together with the Tank Sections, became the basis of all the Australian Armoured Corps units raised after the outbreak of WW2.

On the other side of the world, the Canadians had made their start during WW1, when two tank battalions were mobilized. Both saw service in England but never went to France. As soon as war ended they were disbanded. The man who was to become the 'father' of the Royal Canadian Armoured Corps began his service as an infantryman, was wounded and decorated in France, then commissioned into the 1st Canadian Motor Machine Gun Brigade. Two MCs and two MMs were evidence of the bravery of 'Worthy' Worthington, who in 1936 was given the job of organizing and commanding the Canadian Tank School at London, Ontario. The school moved to Camp Borden two years later, when the first tanks arrived from the UK, but it was not until 12th August 1940 that the Canadian Armoured Corps was authorized. It would eventually reach a strength of over 20,000 men. Worthington organized and commanded the 1st Armoured Brigade, which he was to take overseas in 1941, his name becoming synonymous with tanks in the Canadian Army.

Hard Times in the USA

At the end of WW1, the US Tank Corps consisted of just over 20,000 officers and enlisted men – some 12,000 in France, the rest divided equally between Camps Colt and Polk. Although the Tank Corps had an authorized complement of 1,803 officers and 25,535 enlisted men on 11th November 1918, by May 1919 most of these had been demobilized, all that remained being 300 officers and 5,000 enlisted men, in three tank brigades, the Tank Centre (with repair and depot companies) and the Tank Corps GHQ. A few months later Congress fixed the size of the corps at just 154 officers and 2,508 men. An extraordinary collection of AFVs was assembled for them to operate – some 218 Renault FT 17s, 450 American-built Renaults, 28 British Heavy Mark Vs and 100 Mark VIIIs.[2] Rockenbach was appointed as Commandant of the Tank Corps, but as Dale E. Wilson explains in *Treat 'em rough!*, 'Unfortunately for the Tank Corps, the methodical, hidebound general was not the right man for the job. He was more interested in maintaining the status quo than in promoting research, development and training – three essentials for the creation of a vigorous, improving force.'

The Tank Corps was never really given a chance to flex its muscles in peacetime, because in 1919 a War Department board, which had been set up to study tank tactics, came to the conclusion that the 'Tank Service should be under the general supervision of the Chief of Infantry and should not constitute an independent service.' Tankers like Patton, Eisenhower and Sereno Brett did their best to put forward opposite views, but their arguments were in vain and, on 2nd June 1920, Congress passed the National Defense Act, which abolished the Corps, assigned all existing tank units to the Chief of Infantry and directed that all tankers should be designated as serving with Infantry (Tanks). Pershing had been the main instigator of this plan, so there was no recourse. Battalions were broken up, companies being assigned on a basis of one per infantry division. War Department policy stated that the primary role of the tank was to 'facilitate the uninterrupted advance of the riflemen in the attack.' It also stated that there should be only two types of tanks, light (under 5 tons) and medium (under 15 tons), so that all could be carried by rail and all would be able to use existing road bridges and pontoons.

Rockenbach protested at the butchering of his infant Corps, but to no avail. He was demoted to the rank of colonel, while Patton had to revert to captain. With the Tank Corps' loss of status, Patton quickly saw that he would stand a much better chance of promotion if he returned to the cavalry. He submitted a formal application during August 1920. His application was approved and in the following month his three years with tanks ended. However, he maintained a strong interest in tanks, keeping himself well informed of all progress being made abroad. He did not take much part in the subsequent mechanization of the cavalry – perhaps because of personality clashes – and did not come back into the picture until the Armored Force had been formed. Rockenbach also faded from the scene, spending his last few years as commander of the handful of tanks that remained at Camp Meade, right up to his retirement in 1933.

Fortunately, however, some people were taking an interest in tanks, and the Secretary of War, Dwight F. Davis, visited England in 1927, to watch the manoeuvres of the British Experimental Armoured Force. He was very impressed and determined that the US Army should follow the British example. On his return to America he immediately ordered Gen Charles P.

Summerall, then Chief of Staff, to organize a similar force. In the following year the Experimental Mechanized Force was assembled at Fort Meade. Although it was initially heralded by the press as being 'the pride of the Army', it was in fact little more than a collection of worn-out equipment, and its performance quickly earned it the new and less polite nickname of 'the Gasoline Brigade'. The state officials in Maryland didn't help either, by banning the tanks from their roads in case they tore up the surfaces!

Despite this abortive start, nothing could prevent the coming of mechanization and, in November 1930, the Mechanized Force returned once again, thanks to the recommendations of an 11-man Mechanization Board, of whom Adna R. Chaffee was the main driving force. This remarkable officer, who became known as the 'father' of the US Armored Force, fought hard in the cause of mechanization, especially for his own arm, the cavalry. Adna Romanza Chaffee was born in Junction City, Kansas on 23rd September 1884 and entered the US Military Academy in 1906. He was a brilliant horseman and followed his father into the cavalry, but did not get the opportunity to shine in WW1, serving mainly on the staff during the St Mihiel and Meuse-Argonne offensives. It was not until after the war that he really came to prominence as the main advocate of mechanization. Despite his love of the horse, or perhaps because of it, he became convinced of the need for armour on the battlefield, to replace animals and to provide firepower, protection and mobility for the erstwhile horsed cavalry. It was on his desk in the G3 Section of the War Department General Staff that Gen Summerall's now famous 'pink slip of paper' bearing the words 'Organize a Mechanized Force' landed. Chaffee eventually rose to become the Commanding General of 7th Cavalry Brigade (mechanized) in 1938, this being the brigade that grew out of the Mechanized Force.

In 1930, the Board had recommended that the force should comprise an HQ, a light tank battalion, two mechanized infantry battalions, a field artillery battalion, an engineer company and a medical detachment, in all just over 2,000 all ranks. The Force was to be commanded by Col Van Voorhis, then commanding 12th Cavalry. Bob Grow, his S3 (which equates to adjutant in the British Army), accompanied him to the new appointment and later wrote:

The Mechanised Force at Eustice was not Cavalry. Although the commander and S3 were cavalrymen and the Armoured Car troop was a cavalry unit, the force was a composite group of all Arms and Services. . . . In the first demonstration given to orient Van Voorhis and me, Brett (the Executive Officer) led the attack on foot, with colored signal flags. From this we made our first basic decisions: that all equipment must be capable of high battlefield, as well as road, mobility and, most important, leaders must learn to think and to command mounted.[3]

Van Voorhis, who later rose to the rank of lieutenant general, laid down the basic principles of the new Mechanized Force and has become known as the 'grandfather of armor'.

As in the UK, there was a lack of funds (a rhyme of the time read: 'Tanks is tanks and tanks is dear: There shall be no tanks this year'), and considerable professional jealousy within the rest of the US Army, which hindered mechanization. The Mechanized Force took part in 10 field exercises and 10 marches during early 1931 and did a good job. However, it was then felt that its mission – to introduce mechanization to the rest of the Army – was completed, so it was disbanded. The then Army Chief of Staff, Gen Douglas MacArthur (who was later to become famous in the Pacific fighting against the Japanese) directed all arms and services to '. . . adopt mechanization and motorisation as far as is practicable and desirable.' All were allowed to carry out experiments, the infantry, for example, being told to develop combat vehicles which would enhance their power in the roles of reconnaissance, counter-recce, flank action, pursuit and similar types of operation, normally undertaken by the light cavalry.

Unfortunately for the cavalry, the 1920 National Defense Act had laid down that only the infantry were allowed to have tanks, so, in order to get around this legal obstacle the cavalry decided to call their tanks 'combat cars'. This led to such anomalies as the T2 light tank being also the T1 combat car. Thus, while mechanization slowly took effect, the Armored Force was no more, a sad blow for people like Van Voorhis and Grow who had worked so hard for an independent mechanized force. Nevertheless, the disbanded force became the nucleus of a mechanized cavalry unit at Camp Knox, Kentucky, and, in 1933, this nucleus was combined with the 1st Cavalry Regiment, which added the word Mechanized to its title. Gradually the 7th Cavalry Brigade grew from this small beginning, so that by the time WW2 began the brigade consisted of two mechanized cavalry regiments, with a total of 112 combat cars, one mechanized artillery regiment (16 75mm howitzers), plus ordnance, quartermaster and medical detachments.4 On 16th January 1933, Congress changed the name of Camp Knox to Fort Knox and it became the permanent home of mechanized forces in the US Army. As the leaflet advertising the 50th anniversary celebrations of the Armored Force (held at Fort Knox 'The Home of Armor and Cavalry' on 10th July 1990) explained: 'These pioneers had a new idea. They visualized the first Mechanized Force in the US Army as having the capability of performing missions based on speed, firepower, shock effect and a wide operating radius. They conceived of Armor as a strategic threat – a weapon that commanders could use to decisively affect the outcome of any war. They conceived of Armor as a weapon of shock, a weapon to paralyze the minds of the enemy with fear.'

US Armor was to show dramatic growth once WW2 started and the success of the new Blitzkrieg tactics became apparent. But, like the British Army, the US Army between the wars suffered from a lack of funds and an almost total lack of interest in tanks by those in authority. Elsewhere in the world, though, it was a very different story.

Rise of the Panzers

The foundations of the *Panzerwaffe*, the 'armoured weapons' that would sweep so swiftly across Europe in 1939–40 were laid some ten years before, by Gen

46

Hans von Seeckt, first CinC of the Reichswehr (1920–26). Under the terms of the Versailles Treaty the German Army was limited to not more than 100,000 men. The relevant clause of the treaty reads:

Article 160. By a date which must not be later than March 31, 1920, the German Army must not comprise more than seven divisions of infantry and three divisions of cavalry. After that date the total number of effectives in the Army of the States constituting Germany must not exceed 100,000 men, including officers and establishments of depots. The Army shall be devoted exclusively to the maintenance of order within the territory and to the control of the frontiers. The total effective strength of officers, including the personnel of staffs, whatever their composition, must not exceed 4,000.[5]

This was humiliating to the once-proud German Army, but von Seeckt was determined to make the best of the situation. He ensured that every member of this small force was a highly trained leader and instructor, well capable of training others. Thus the 'Versailles Army' became merely a cadre for the much greater army of the Third Reich that would follow once Germany had recovered from its defeat. Gen von Seeckt was convinced that any future war would be a much more mobile affair, with ground and air forces working closely together. 'In brief,' he wrote, 'the whole future of warfare appears to me to lie in the employment of mobile armies, relatively small but of high quality and rendered distinctly more effective by the addition of aircraft.'[6]

HEINZ GUDERIAN   Seeckt also made certain that his tiny officer force (just 4,000 strong) took every opportunity to travel abroad, to visit other armies and to glean new ideas. Nowhere were these more readily available than in Great Britain, and no-one took more heed of these new philosophies than Heinz Guderian. Born on 17th June 1888, son of a Prussian officer, Guderian had been educated at cadet school and commissioned into the 10th Hano-verian 'Jaeger' Battalion in February 1907, at which time the battalion was commanded by his father. In January 1908 he became a lieutenant and lived the life of a normal young officer, riding well and enjoying hunting and shooting. He was a natural linguist and later in his career qualified as an interpreter in French, also becoming fluent in English. He attended the *Kriegsakademie* (war academy) in 1913 and later took part in one of the earliest military trials, using wireless, working with cavalry. Unfortunately, thanks more to the incompetence of the divisional commander and his staff than to any faults of Guderian's wireless section, the trials were deemed a failure. Thus, wireless was not used to its full potential by the German Army at the start of WW1. Guderian initially served with 5th Cavalry Division, then was sent as IO at HQ Fourth Army.

At the end of the war he was sent to help organize volunteer forces in the Baltic states, which Germany was trying to retain, having taken them from Russia at the treaty of Brest-Litovsk. After the collapse of this enterprise, he was chosen to become one of von Seeckt's 4,000 officers and began to special-ize in the military use of mechanical vehicles. The prejudice and lack of interest in things mechanical also pervaded the German Army at that time, so

Guderian did not have things all his own way. But Hitler, when he came to power, quickly realized the potential of the tank. He watched one of Guderian's demonstrations of an armoured force consisting of light tanks, armoured cars, motorcycles and anti-tank guns and is said to have exclaimed excitedly, 'That's what I need! That's what I'm going to have!' From then on Guderian received his unreserved support.

THE PANZER DIVISIONS It was Guderian who first visualized the panzer division as the weapon of decision for the new German Army, and it was he who guided the development of this new weapon. He saw armoured forces as comprising not only tanks, but as a mix with all other fighting arms and services, so he differed from both the 'all-tank' theories of Fuller and from the policy of tying tanks to infantry that both the Americans and French had adopted. His new panzer divisions would be the primary striking arm in the coming war and not just supporting players.

The years 1934–5 were the most important in the early formation and building of the *Panzerwaffe*. With Hitler's full support, and despite considerable opposition from within the Army, the *Panzertruppe* was created, with Gen Oswald Lutz at its head and Guderian as his Chief of Staff. The first tank unit – Panzer Regiment 1 – was formed in October 1934 and earlier that year the basic specifications of the *Panzerkampfwagen* (Pzkpfw) II (light) and IV (medium) were approved. These two tanks, together with the tiny Pzkpfw I and the later light-medium Pzkpfw III, formed the basis of the early highly successful Nazi tank formations.

The first three panzer divisions were formed on 15th October 1935, their initial organization bearing a close resemblance to that of the British experimental armoured force of 1927. Officers and men of these early divisions would gain much useful combat experience as 'volunteers' in the German Condor Legion, fighting for Franco during the Spanish Civil War (July 1936–March 1939), four tank battalions and 30 anti-tank companies forming the ground element. They were able to perfect the new tactics that would form such a vital part of the *Blitzkrieg* (lightning war) to come, such as air-ground support, the Stuka dive-bomber and tank formation working closely together.

The French Approach

The French Army had enthusiastically adopted the light tank during WW1 and probably produced more tanks than any other nation. After the war there was not the same wholesale disbandment of tank units as in the UK and the USA, but in some ways the course chosen was even worse. Despite the fact that Gen Estienne, who was Director of Tank Studies from 1921 to 1926, went on propounding the idea of mechanized forces with tanks as their most important ingredient, and another tank enthusiast, Gen Doumenc, proposed the formation of complete armoured divisions, the French High Command thought otherwise. Marshal Pétain had not been particularly impressed by the work of tanks in the war and saw them only as a useful adjunct to infantry action. In 1925, for example, he imported tanks into Morocco to help crush the Riffs, but never once did he develop new tactics within the French Army to make the most of their potential. In 1920, tanks had become an integral part of the infantry and the Artillerie d'Assaut was disbanded.

Estienne continued to declare publicly, in lectures and pamphlets, his conviction that new tactics had to be developed for armoured warfare, that what was needed was a force that could cover great distances by night or day, with all its vehicles and equipment, and then strike an overwhelming blow at the enemy. He also pressed for the construction of a new medium tank. These were eventually produced in fair numbers in 1926, but were then grouped into *Chars d'ensemble* and held in reserve under divisional or corps control, for use in support of infantry formations. Sadly, French thinking remained very inflexible. The French saw the tank merely as a supporting weapon to the all-powerful infantry. This approach was, they considered, vindicated by the success of the anti-tank gun in the Spanish Civil War, from which they wrongly concluded that independent armoured formations were of little value. Speaking to the British CIGS in 1936, Gen Gamelin, the French Chief of Staff, described the German tanks operating in Spain as being badly protected and fit only for the scrapheap! On another occasion he is quoted as saying, 'You cannot hope to achieve real breakthroughs with tanks. The tank is not independent enough. It has to go ahead, but then must return for fuel and supplies'.7 France never got the armoured message until it was too late for them to do anything about it, despite the fact that Charles de Gaulle, another great tank commander, had appeared on the scene.

CHARLES DE GAULLE   Born in Lille on 22nd November 1890, son of a professor, Charles de Gaulle graduated with distinction from St Cyr in 1913, and was commissioned into the 33rd Infantry Regiment, which was then under the command of Col Philippe Pétain (later to become a marshal of France and subsequently head of the Vichy government). De Gaulle fought bravely during WW1, until he was wounded and taken prisoner during the Battle of Verdun in 1916. He remained in captivity until the Armistice was signed. After the war he instructed at St Cyr and then went to the École Superieure de Guerre, the French staff college, in 1924, joining Pétain's staff the following year. Gradually his ideas on future warfare crystallized along the lines of the mechanized concept which Fuller, Liddell Hart and Guderian were advocating, namely, the need for highly mobile, mechanized forces. Unfortunately for him, this was entirely in opposition to the stated French military policy of the day, which was based upon positional defence, enshrined in the building of the Maginot Line. In 1933, de Gaulle first put his views into print in an article which promoted the case for a properly established armoured division in the French Army. Then, one year later, he expressed his ideas more fully, in a short pamphlet, *Vers l'armée de métier* (Towards a professional army). In this he set out the views of Liddell Hart, Estienne and Doumenc, then made the logical conclusion that the French Army needed a special tank corps, composed of regular soldiers, rather than of one-year conscripts, whom it was impossible to train properly in the time available. He advocated a separate tank arm comprising 3,000 tanks in special mechanized divisions and laid down the way in which they should be used. While this may have found favour among some of the more radical thinkers abroad, it certainly did nothing for de Gaulle at home. Pétain was so furious that he struck him off the promotion list in 1936, ensuring that de Gaulle remained in relative obscurity until WW2 had started. He was then given a chance to prove his theories, too late to have any effect upon the well-organized Panzers of Guderian and the other German tank commanders.

MECHANIZING THE CAVALRY   In his book, *To Lose a Battle*, Alistair Horne quotes a splendid French Army saying of the mid-1930s, 'Oil is dirty, dung is not', which probably encapsulates the feelings of all French cavalry officers towards mechanization. One cavalry general (Brecart) went so far as to advocate, as late as 1933, that the cavalry should be maintained just the way it was and that the tanks should never be used again! Nevertheless, as in every other European army, the conservatives eventually had to accept the inevitable. And they did so with far more flexibility and open-mindedness than their British opposite numbers. There had always been a small number of armoured cars in cavalry regiments since 1917, and, in 1930, one of the three horsed brigades in each cavalry division was mechanized (i.e. converted to motorized infantry), while a complete regiment of armoured cars replaced the small number previously allowed. Like the US Cavalry they adopted a similar subterfuge, calling the AFVs *automitrailleuses* (machine-gun cars), because only the infantry could have tanks. In 1934, the first light division, the Division Légère Mécanique (DLM) was formed, containing a tank brigade, a motorized rifle brigade, a recce regiment, a towed artillery regiment, an engineer battalion and normal supporting arms. Thus it was very similar to the experimental armoured forces of other nations, but the tanks were far too light, and so, although the DLM was ideal for its main role of strategic reconnaissance, which it inherited directly from the cavalry, it was no match for the panzer divisions and would be badly mauled by the better-trained, better-handled and much more cohesive German tank forces.

During the mid-1930s the *chars de manoeuvre d'ensemble* of Estienne's days did re-emerge in the formation of embryo armoured divisions, in which heavy tanks were to be organized into battalions. The process was painfully slow and it was not until September 1939 that four battalions of the heavy Char B tanks then in service were grouped into two demi-brigades, each with a newly formed motorized infantry battalion. They were then grouped together to form the very first Division Cuirassée Rapide (DCR). More would follow, but they were never an effective fighting force, as we shall see.

Like Elles, Swinton and Rockenbach, Estienne had less and less influence on the way tanks were employed and faded from the scene, those in authority being unable or unwilling to see how much the tank had changed the way that future wars would be fought.

Soviet Expansion

The Soviet Union did not really begin to take a great interest in tank development until the start of the first Five Year Plan in 1929. Before that, the basic Soviet tank had been the 'Russkiy Renault', which was simply a copy of the French FT 17. John Milsom in his book *Russian Tanks 1900–1970* quotes from D. Bibergan's history of the Soviet tank industry from 1914 to 1925: 'Only in 1929, when we began to carry out the first Five Year Plan and our industry matured – not by days but by hours – did we have a basic home tank industry. The leader of the nation, Comrade Stalin, became personally involved in the problems of tank design and put us on the right road.'

Whether that is entirely true, or whether it was merely Bibergan's way of ensuring that he was not sent to the salt mines, is a matter of conjecture. It is clear, however, that the Soviet Union would not have devoted so much of its resources to building tanks had not the Supreme Soviet given their full approval. At Army level it was Voroshilov, the People's Commissar for Military Affairs, who in 1926 pressed for a large tank force that would equal or surpass those of all other nations. He wanted quality as well as quantity, so new plant had to be built, engineers and technicians found who could design and develop the necessary machinery to build the tanks, while soldiers had to be trained to use the new weapons. This all led to the establishment of a secret tank school at Kazan on the Volga. It was a combined Russo-German project, the former hoping to gain technical knowledge and experience from the Germans, while the latter had to keep the whole thing secret because of the Versailles Treaty which prohibited them from having tanks. The project began in 1927, but took some years to get under way and there was always a considerable amount of distrust between both sides, Voroshilov, for example, realizing that war between the two countries was inevitable. In view of his effect upon the tank building industry, Kliment Yefremovich Voroshilov fully merits a place in this book. He eventually became a marshal of the Soviet Union, although he was more a politician than a soldier. In 1934, he became Commissar for Defence (merely a change of title) and remained the effective political head of the Soviet services until May 1940. He was in charge of the Red Army during the period when Gen Pavlov had such a disastrous effect upon Russian tank units' organization and must take some of the blame for their poor showing in Finland and at the start of the German invasion.

The first Five Year Plan was launched on 3rd April 1929 and many new tanks – none very successful – began to be built. In addition, German prototypes of their new tanks were secretly shipped to Kazan and tested, while the Russians also purchased various types of tanks from abroad for evaluation. The first mechanized brigade came into existence in May 1930, comprising two tank battalions, two motorized infantry batalions (known in Russian parlance as 'motor-rifle'), a recce battalion, artillery battalion and supporting services. However, in general terms, the first Five Year Plan did not produce tanks in any significant numbers and this did not happen until the second Five Year plan got under way. From 1933 to 1934, the military budget was almost quadrupled (from 1.5 to 5 thousand million roubles), the output of motor vehicles and tanks increased and building programmes were established for light, medium and heavy tanks. By 1935, the Russian tank strength was estimated by the Germans as being a staggering 10,000 tanks.[8] Other sources put the figure even higher, while the numbers of lorries and tractors were equally enormous.

By 1937, Soviet armoured forces were divided into various tank-heavy organizations. There were the motor mechanized corps, each containing some 500 tanks, which were in battle intended to be divided among the infantry battalions, purely as tank support; motor mechanized brigades, containing light tanks and motorized infantry; mechanized brigades containing a similar mix, but with a larger number of tanks; and tank brigades consisting primarily of three battalions of medium tanks. Mobile warfare had been studied in great detail by men like Marshal Mikhail Tukhachevsky and Col Kalinovsky, whose theories of deep penetration and the use of armour were enshrined in Red Army Field Regulations of 1936. However, their theories, which were based to some degree on the teachings of Liddell Hart and other foreigners, would find little favour with Stalin in the Great Purge of 1937.

Misha Tukhachevsky was born in Byelorussia, some 150 miles from Moscow, in February 1893. He passed out of the Alexandrovskii Military College in 1914, with one of the highest sets of marks in its history, and was commissioned into the Tsar's Imperial Bodyguard. He served in WW1, was captured and spent several years as a POW. After the war he became a Communist and rejoined the army, doing extremely well. He was highly respected – Lenin, for example, spoke of his 'inquiring mind, ebullient energy and broad initiative'. He was one of the main architects in the formation of a regular Red Army, creating with Mikhail Frunze the foundations for armoured, mechanized and airborne forces, and eventually succeeded Frunze as Chief of General Staff. None of this saved him from Stalin's firing squad. His writings were destroyed (except for one set in the restricted-access section of the Lenin Library in Moscow), together with everything else about him. As Richard Simpkin said in his book *Deep Battle*, 'those who Stalin purged were not just liquidated, they were eradicated.' Nevertheless, it was Tukhachevsky's thinking and concepts that provided the basis for both the Russians' eventual success against the Germans in WW2 and their post-war strength.

By the start of WW2, or the Great Patriotic War, as the Russians call it, the USSR had undoubtedly caught up, and in some cases passed, the other European tank producers in sheer numbers of tanks. Over the period 1935 to 1938, the Red Army had doubled its offensive capability. *Pravda* in 1939 included statements to the effect that the previous five years had seen an increase in tank numbers from 6,000 to 10,000. These tanks included both amphibians and well-armed heavy tanks, although the majority were still light tanks and tankettes. Some, although not all, were well-made, robust machines, capable of giving an excellent account of themselves on the battlefield. The Soviets had, for example, taken great note of the designs of J. Walter Christie, thinking, though, that, 'it is unfortunate that he was born in the imperialist camp and hence not given the chance to exploit his ideas to the full!'[9]

During the Spanish Civil War, the Republicans employed a number of Russian tanks, mainly T26 light tanks. It was found that their armour-plate was easily penetrated and tanks were lost both to the mine and the anti-tank gun, giving rise to the opinion that they should not be used independently, but always had to be in support of infantry. Gen Pavlov, the supposed Russian tank expert, returned from Spain and reported to Voroshilov and Stalin that 'the tank can play no independent role on the battlefield.'[10] He recommended that the existing tank units should be broken up and the tanks distributed throughout the army in an infantry support role. His new 'practical' experience was rated higher than Tukhachevsky's theories, and Tukhachevsky's 'deep penetration' idea went out of the window. Thus Russia, like most other nations with the major exception of Germany who had now fully espoused the new doctrine, was convinced that the tank would fail in any future war.

It did not help the cause of Russian tank development that Stalin carried out his savage purge of the Soviet Army, removing many of those who had been advocating the theories of Fuller and Liddell-Hart – now considered to be 'reactionary, bourgeois and unworthy of Marxist society'[11]. Pavlov became indisputably the leading tank-warfare specialist and the armoured divisions were frittered away in penny packets. The Soviets would pay dearly for this folly when the Germans launched 'Barbarossa'.

NOTES, CHAPTER 3

1 This rank was abolished in 1921, being replaced by 'colonel commandant' until 1928, when the simpler term 'brigadier' was revived.

2 The Mark VIII, also known as the 'International' was much larger than the Mk V, weighing 37 tons and powered by a 300hp engine. It was going to be built in France in large numbers by Britain and the USA, to win the war in 1919, but did not see action. In 1939 a few American-built models were refurbished and given to the Canadians for training at the start of WW2!

3 Maj Gen Robert W Grow, *The Ten Lean Years* (privately published).

4 Figures from Richard M Ogorkiewicz, *Armour*.

5 Bart Whalley, *Covert German Re-armament 1919–1939*.

6 *Thoughts of a Soldier* published in 1928 and quoted in Brig H.B.C. Watkins, *Panzer Divisions of WW2*.

7 Quoted by Alistair Horne in *To Lose a Battle*.

8 *Russian Tanks 1900–1970*, p. 42.

9 *ibid.*, p. 41

10 *ibid.*, p. 50

11 *ibid.*, p. 51

4 BLITZKRIEG

In Germany in 1938, Gen Oswald Lutz was dismissed because of his involvement with Gen Werner von Fritsch, who had been falsely accused by the Nazis of homosexual behaviour. Guderian took his place as head of the panzer arm, with the rank of lieutenant general. He was thus in charge of all the panzer units that entered Austria at the Anschluss of March 1938. No doubt he was disappointed with the number of breakdowns that occurred at that time, but at least he had the opportunity to rectify such problems before war began. Popular with his panzer troops, Guderian was a tough, demanding commander, probably the most expert panzer leader in the German Army, so it is not surprising to find that his corps was handled with both brilliance and confidence when battle was joined.

Into Poland

At dawn on 1st September 1939, two German Army Groups swept across the Polish frontier – Fedor von Bock's in the north and Karl von Rundstedt's in the south. Spearheading both Army Groups were two Panzer Corps – XIX (Guderian) in the north and XVI (Kleist) in the south, their aim being to encircle the Polish Army in a gigantic pincer movement and then to destroy it completely. The Germans had appreciated that the Poles would fight stubbornly, buoyed up by the promises of support given them by their British and French allies. But, unbeknown to the Allies, Hitler held a trump card – the secret clauses of the Nazi-Soviet Pact, signed on 23rd August 1939, in which he and Stalin had agreed to divide Poland between them after the Russians had attacked the beleaguered Poles from the rear.

It was a bitter and hard-fought campaign, lasting for only 35 days – still considerably longer than the Germans had expected, although most of their aims were achieved within 18 days. Warsaw held out until the 27th and some other isolated places for even longer, but the Germans had destroyed most of the Polish forces by the 18th. Despite the speed of the German advance, the Poles fought with great courage and used what armour they had to advantage, but they were not equipped to fight a modern war against well-trained and mechanized troops.

Britain and France both declared war upon Germany on 3rd September, two days after the invasion, but they were unable to give the Poles any practical assistance. When the Russians invaded on the 17th, they met with little oppo-

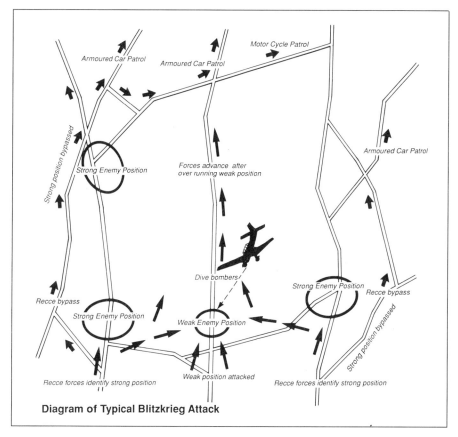

Diagram of Typical Blitzkrieg Attack

sition and quickly occupied the east of the country as already agreed with Germany, thus dividing Poland roughly in half.

BLITZKRIEG IN ACTION   The blitzkrieg that broke upon the Poles in September 1939 was simply a tactical system that Guderian had perfected to pierce the enemy's front, and then to encircle and destroy all or part of his forces. Its major elements were surprise, speed of manoeuvre, shock action from both ground and air and the retention of the initiative by the attacking force. It required that all commanders used their initiative to the full.

Imagine that a panzer division is advancing towards the enemy. Out in front are reconnaissance elements, whose task is to look for the enemy positions. These recce elements consist of armoured cars on the main routes and motor-cycle patrols on the side-roads and tracks. They would be accompanied by Artillery Forward Observation Officers and Luftwaffe Forward Air Controllers, who could quickly call for fire support from ground and air. Having located the enemy and reported back, the recce forces would then try to bypass the main positions, pressing on as quickly as possible so as to maintain the momentum of the advance. They would be in constant radio communication with the force commander, who controls the speed of their advance, deciding whether the whole force should bypass or engage any enemy positions they discover. The commander is well forward, travelling just behind the vanguard. If he decides to attack then he will give out orders over the air, the striking force will concentrate as quickly as possible, immediately off the line of march (*Aufmarsch*), to attack on a narrow front with as much power as possible.

The centre of gravity (*Schwerpunkt*) of the assault will clearly be where the commander thinks is the best place to attack and he will endeavour to concentrate overwhelming forces at that point – as Guderian advised, *Klotzen nicht Kleckern!*' ('Thump them hard, don't pat them!'). The aim of this initial attack is to punch a hole through the enemy line. It will be immediately followed up by another element of the force, who will pass through and then press on, avoiding the main enemy positions. These were the tactics of space and gap (*Flachen und Lückentakit*), the aim being to get armoured forces behind the enemy positions so that they could take control of his lines of communication.

Meanwhile, just behind the leading troops who have made the breakthrough are additional forces, probably based upon motorized infantry. Their task is to mop up any remaining pockets of enemy and generally to tidy up and make safe the hole in the enemy line where the break has been made. This rolling up (*Aufrollen*) is to ensure that the gap is permanent. The spearhead will be constantly pressing forward, with the aim of encircling as many of the enemy forces as possible. The faster and deeper it can penetrate into the rear areas, then the larger will be these envelopments and the more chaos and fear they will cause. Guderian's dictum was to reinforce success and abandon failure, switching forces from any unsuccessful attacks to other parts of the battlefield where they could be of more use. Such operations required teamwork, good command and control, careful timing, continuous radio communications and, where possible, surprise. Instead of a massive build-up, a long artillery barrage before the attack and a long-drawn-out period of manoeuvring, giving the enemy time to prepare his defences, the overwhelmingly powerful attacking force would suddenly hit the enemy without warning, smashing through his positions on a narrow front. No wonder that Guderian earned the nickname *Schnelle Heinz* ('Hurrying Heinz') and *Heinz Brauseweter* ('Heinz Hothead')!

THE STUKA DIVE-BOMBER The other essential ingredient of the blitzkrieg was the dive-bomber. The most famous was the Junkers Ju 87, whose thick angled wings and fixed undercarriage make it instantly recognizable. To support a major attack, an entire *Gruppe* of 30 aircraft would be used. Aircraft would have to climb to about 15,000 feet to begin their attack, as they needed some 8,000 feet of dive to reach the limiting speed of 350mph, after which the Stuka's velocity remained constant. It took about half a minute to dive from 15,000 feet to the release altitude of 3,000 feet, when the bomb was released automatically. After pull-out the pilot regained control of his aircraft, opened the throttle and got away as quickly as possible. The Stuka struck terror in the early days of the war, with a siren adding to the aircraft noise as it dived towards the enemy positions at a frighteningly steep angle.

GUDERIAN IN ACTION   Guderian's XIX Corps, operating in the north, provided an excellent example of the new blitzkrieg tactics in action. Racing ahead of the main advancing troops it pierced the Polish defensive line, then swept around to bottle up a much larger infantry force. Leaving this to be dealt with by the follow-up forces, it pressed on eastwards, carrying out a similar operation against another Polish army. Guderian's corps covered some 400 miles in 28 days during the Polish campaign, the longest mechanized advance in wartime ever recorded up to that time. Guderian was awarded the Knight's Cross of the Iron Cross for his achievements, which were probably the most daring of all the panzer forces employed in Poland. Elsewhere, the other tanks, for example XVI Corps under von Kleist, spearheading the Tenth Army in the south, were handled far more cautiously. Paul Ludwig Ewald von Kleist was a cavalryman of the old school and not a Nazi. He had commanded the 2nd Cavalry Division in 1934, then VIII Army Corps until 1938, when he was retired, but brought back again in 1939. Initially he had not been an advocate of tanks, so Guderian did not think much of him and they would have some differences of opinion in France, when von Kleist again acted more cautiously than Guderian would have liked – and, to make matters worse, on that occasion Guderian was his subordinate!

Guderian, like Elles and Patton in WW1, was right at the sharp end with his leading troops, the very first corps commander ever to use an armoured command vehicle (ACV) to accompany tanks into battle. He had a fortunate escape during the very first minutes of the campaign. He was with the leading elements of 3rd Panzer Brigade when they crossed over the frontier, in the area north of Zempelburg, where the first fighting took place. There was a thick ground mist which prevented the Luftwaffe from giving any air support, so, despite the fact that he had given them clear orders not to fire, the heavy artillery of 3rd Panzer Division began firing into the mist. In his autobiography Guderian records:

The first shell landed 50 yards ahead of my command vehicle, the second 50 yards behind it. I reckoned that the next one was bound to be a direct hit and ordered my driver to turn about and drive off. The unaccustomed noise had made him nervous, however, and he drove straight into a ditch at full speed.

The steering of the ACV was so badly damaged that Guderian had to get out and walk back to his corps command post to get himself another vehicle. On the way, as he drily points out, he: '. . . had a word with the over-eager artilleryman'.

POLISH ARMOUR   The Poles fought with great bravery and stubbornness. Most of their armour, such as it was, had been split up in 'penny packets' among the infantry formations. Only one all-arms mechanized brigade (10th Cavalry Brigade), established in 1937, remained as a cohesive force. The peace-time brigade had included both the 24th Lancers Regiment and the 10th Mounted

Rifle Regiment, while the tank content, added in 1939, included a company of Vickers 6-tonners and a recce company of the tiny TK tankettes. Known as the 'Black Brigade', because of their unique black leather coats, they fought a remarkable delaying action near Cracow, holding up XXII Panzer Corps who were spearheading the Fourteenth Army in the far south. The 10th Polish Cavalry Brigade was under the command of Col Stanislaw Maczek, who later went on to command the Polish 1st Armoured Division. Maczek was a tough, uncompromising leader, much in the same mould as Guderian, and, as part of Army 'Krakow', his Black Brigade fought a series of delaying battles, never allowing the numerically superior panzer forces to gain the upper hand. As their history records:

The soldiers proved splendid fighters, without a trace of any 'armour panic', especially the anti-tank units [whose] 37mm anti-tank guns confirmed the hopes we had placed in them. In the course of the day the enemy lost about 30 tanks. The 2nd of September had an excellent influence on the morale of the Brigade.

Eventually, on 19th September, the Black Brigade was ordered to cross into Hungary, complete with their remaining arms and equipment, so they lived to fight another day when the Polish Army was reformed in France. I have talked with surviving members of the Polish 1st Armoured Division and they are unanimous in choosing Gen Stanislaw Wladyslaw Maczek as the great Polish tank commander of WW2. Maczek was born near Lwow in 1892, saw service on the Italian front during WW1 and after the war was commander of a storm company in 4th Infantry Division. Steady promotion followed, and in 1938 he was appointed commander of 10th Motorized Cavalry Brigade. After crossing into Hungary, Maczek took his brigade to France, where he was promoted to major general and appointed commander of all Polish units at Coetquidan. He then took part with his brigade in the operations covering Paris. With the fall of France he made his way to England and in 1942 when the 1st Polish Armoured Division was formed he was the obvious choice as its commander. He would take his division to Normandy in 1944 and continue to command it until final victory in 1945, his last operation being the capture and occupation of Wilhelmshaven. Promoted lieutenant general in June 1945, he was GOC 1st Polish Corps until 1947 and at the same time GOC Polish Forces in Great Britain. Demobilized, he settled in Edinburgh, where he still lives.

THE LESSONS OF POLAND   Poland proved a most useful training ground for Guderian's Panzerwaffe. They realized, for example, that their Pzkpfw Is and IIs were of little use as fighting vehicles because they were under-gunned and under-armoured. In future they would be used only for recce or other purposes – such as gun platforms for self-propelled anti-tank guns. The heavier Pzkpfw IV was singled out by Guderian as being a most effective weapon which could be continually up-armoured and up-gunned. Consequently, it remained in full-time production from 1934, throughout the war, until 1944. Guderian also recommended basic tactical and organizational changes to panzer units. Battalion and regimental HQs were to be located further forward, from where they might direct the battle more successfully; all HQs had to be smaller, more mobile and composed of ACVs equipped with radio.

The campaign in Poland spread alarm and despondency throughout the West and led to much panic and rumour-mongering, which was not entirely disadvantageous as it stopped any lingering doubts about the need for mechanization. Undoubtedly, however, it gave the Panzerwaffe an aura of invincibility which it did not really possess. Nevertheless, the German achievement was considerable, bearing in mind that most of the German Army was still unmechanized, with most infantry marching, while artillery and supply trains were still pulled by horses. Battle losses and the bad roads of Poland, together with poor production figures at home, had so reduced the number of trucks in combat units that Gen Franz Halder, then Army Chief of Staff, went so far as to propose a major de-motorization programme and the replacing of motor vehicles with horses!

The tankmen, though, were in the ascendancy, their prowess eulogized in German propaganda, in the propaganda magazine *Signal*, for example: 'Tank units mobile, fast and hard-hitting, and directed by wireless from headquarters, attack the enemy. This armoured machine paves the way to victory, flattening and crushing all obstacles and spitting out destruction.' In his black uniform and his *Schutzmütze* (the large black tank beret with its inner padded head protector and flamboyant outer), the tank soldier was the new élite of the German ground forces.

THE ARMORED FORCE During the lull that followed the Polish campaign, Germany feverishly prepared for *Fall Gelb*, as the plan of attack upon the West was called, and the Allies vacillated and waited behind the Maginot Line for something to happen. Far away, on the other side of the Atlantic, the Armored Force was born. Undoubtedly, the shock of the blitzkrieg in Poland added impetus to the start of the transformation of the entire US Army into the most mechanized force the world had ever seen. Sir Winston Churchill once described this transformation as a 'prodigy of organisation'. And this was perfectly true. Of tanks alone, the USA built a staggering 88,410 – having started just before the war with under 400! They reached a production peak in 1943, when 29,497 tanks were built in that one year. A total of 16 armoured divisions and more than 100 separate tank battalions would be raised and trained.

On 25th May 1940, a recommendation was made after a meeting in the basement of a high school in Alexandria, Louisiana, between Gen Chaffee, Col (later Maj Gen) Alvan C. Gillem Jr, Col (later Gen) George Patton and Gen Frank Andrews (a member of the War Department General Staff). The Alexandria Recommendation was to authorize and create an Armored Force. Soon after the meeting, 'a War Department Order of 10th July 1940 created the US Armored Force. The Armored Force School and Replacement Training Centre, now the Armor School, was established on 25th October. This ended once and for all the infantry's stranglehold on armour. Commanding this force was Brig Gen Adna R. Chaffee. A week later 1 Armored Corps, comprising 1st and 2nd Armored Divisions, was activated, with the first 'marrying-up' of tank and mechanized cavalry elements of the Army. 1st Armored Division was organized from the Provisional Tank Brigade, which had been made up from elements of infantry tank battalions. Back into the armoured fold came WW1 tank commanders like Col George S. Patton, who had been serving with the cavalry since 1920. In 1940 he was transferred to 2nd Armored Division at Fort Benning, as commander of an armoured brigade, by Gen George C. Marshall, who, as Chief of Staff, was trying to modernize the US Army. A few months later, on 19 April 1941, he was appointed Commanding General 2nd Armored Division. He earned the nickname 'Old Blood and Guts' about this time, thanks to a newspaper reporter misquoting his words (something that was going to happen quite often in the future!). Patton had said not that an armoured division needed 'blood and guts', but that it needed 'blood and brains'. Patton was well and truly back in the fold, revelling in his new command, even designing his own uniform, which included a golden helmet, green trousers with a black stripe and a green leather jacket which earned him the nickname 'the Green Hornet'.

The Winter War

On 30th November 1939 Russia invaded Finland with five massive armies (800,000 men, 1,500 tanks and 1,000 aircraft). The Russians found themselves opposed by the tiny (150,000 total) Finnish armed forces, who were aided by deep snow and the forested terrain. The Finns fought bravely, inflicting heavy casualties and knocking out many enemy tanks. When the war began Col Ernst Ruben Lagus was on the staff of the Army of Karelia, which took the main weight of the Russian attacks, as it was responsible for the front at the vital Karelian Isthmus. Despite their bravery, the Finns were eventually forced to sue for peace in March 1940, and to cede various areas of the country to Russia, although Finland as a whole retained its independence. After the war Lagus was appointed as commander of the *Jaakariprikaati*, a light infantry brigade which was partly motorized. It was later expanded to form Group Lagus, which contained the only Finnish tank battalion. Not unnaturally, the desire to get back their territory later drove the Finns into limited collaboration with Germany and they declared war on Russia again on 26th June 1941. In the limited actions that took place thereafter, Lagus gained prominence, first as commander of Group Lagus, then as GOC of the only armoured division (*Panssaridivisioona*) to be formed, which took part in heavy fighting against the Soviets in the Karelian Isthmus during the summer of 1944. Lagus was undoubtedly Finland's greatest tank commander, being the very first soldier to be awarded the Mannerheim Cross (on 22nd July 1941). He retired in 1947, died in 1959 aged 63, and is buried in Helsinki.

Russia too had its tank heroes in the Winter War. Gen Dmitry Danilovich Lelyushenko, who commanded 39th Armoured Brigade, was made a Hero of the Soviet Union on 7th April 1940, after displaying great personal bravery and leading his brigade with great success. A Ukrainian, Lelyushenko had joined the Soviet Army in 1919 and the Communist Party in 1924. He went on to command 4th Tank Army in the Great Patriotic War and was responsible for the destruction of enemy dispositions in the Kielce-Radom area and the forcing of the River Oder, being awarded the Gold Star Medal for a second time in April 1945. Lelyushenko continued a distinguished military career after the war and died on 20th July 1987. A bronze bust has been raised to him in Rostov-on-Don.

The Phoney War

During the period October 1939 to May 1940, there existed an uneasy 'truce' between the combatants in western Europe. This period, known as the 'Phoney War', should have given both Britain and France time to better organize their armoured forces, so as to be ready to combat the inevitable blitzkrieg attack which had shown itself so effective in Poland. Instead, neither Britain nor France did anything to change their agreed defensive strategy. They were of course hampered by the fact that the Belgians and the Dutch were both determined to remain neutral, so Allied forces could not occupy their Dyle Line positions in Belgium, or prepare them in any way. Along the Franco-German frontier, it was assumed that the Maginot Line would provide all the protection necessary. Tanks would, in general, remain split into small groups, with their main role being infantry support. French armoured forces were at the time both larger and better equipped than those of their enemy, but they lacked training, their organizations were wrong for modern war, and, on the whole, their generals totally unprepared for command in what was going to be a fluid, fast-moving campaign. Instead of being up with their leading forces, they preferred to remain well behind the front line, cut off from reality apart from telephonic communications and liaison officers – the use of wireless for the passage of orders was almost unheard of in the French Army.

The winter was spent digging in (in many cases the trenches and fortifications were dug in entirely the wrong places and would be of no use whatsoever when battle was joined), doing some training and, especially among the French conscripts, getting thoroughly bored and dispirited. Over the border, the Germans worked their forces up to a peak of training, their successes in Poland lifting morale to an unbelievably high level.

BRITISH ARMOUR The British Expeditionary Force (BEF), which had been so expertly and safely delivered across the Channel by the Royal Navy in September 1939, was the most mechanized army the British had ever assembled. However, it contained very few tanks. Compared with the 10 panzer divisions now in existence – the Germans had converted their four light mechanized divisions to panzer soon after the Polish campaign ended – the BEF initially had just two Light Armoured Reconnaissance Brigades, armed with scout carriers and light tanks whose main armament was a machine-gun, and the 1st Army Tank Brigade (4th and 7th RTR) with the heavier Matilda Mk Is and IIs, the only tanks in the British Army capable of surviving in a tank *v* tank engagement. 1st Armoured Division, the only British armoured division ready for despatch to France by May 1940, arrived just in time to see some action, but, as we shall see, lost most of its tanks needlessly, because the higher command of the BEF was totally unused to handling armour, so, as always, spread them out in the inevitable 'penny packets'. 'For myself', wrote the most famous of all British WW2 generals on his autobiography, 'I never saw any tanks during the winter or active operations in May. And we were the nation which had invented the tank and were the first to use it in battle, in 1916. It must be said to our shame that we sent our Army into that most modern war with weapons and equipment which were quite inadequate.' Those are the words of FM Montgomery, who was then commanding 3rd Infantry Division in the BEF, and they reflect the years of neglect of tanks and tank warfare which would now have to be paid for in blood.

The BEF were as short of experienced armoured commanders as they were of tanks, Brig (later Gen Sir) John Crocker being the only one of the tank soldiers of the inter-war years who was still in an armoured appointment. Lindsay, who had been sent to India pre-war, had retired. Broad, who had also been sent to India, as GOC-in-C Eastern Command, stayed there until his retirement. Hobart had been sacked and was retired, but would fortunately 'live to fight another day'! Crocker, who was destined to reach the highest levels of the Army, was at least commanding an armoured brigade in 1st Armoured Division, and would later become GOC of 6th Armoured Division and then, in 1943, Commander 9th Corps. Other highly competent and experienced RTC officers were side-tracked into other jobs, the most glaring example being the fate of Gen Sir Frederick Pile, who

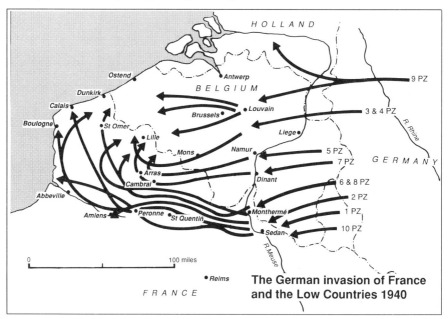

The German invasion of France and the Low Countries 1940

had commanded the Fast Group in the Experimental Mechanized Force. He was made GOC-in-C of Anti-Aircraft Command in July 1939, a post which he performed brilliantly and held throughout the war. However, as Liddell-Hart rightly comments in his history of the RTR, 'It was a cruel stroke that, just when an expansion of the tank arm was in prospect, its leaders were pushed aside. That was sad for the Corps, and bad for the Army – while worse still for the nation.'

War in Western Europe

At 0535 hours on 10th May 1940, Germany launched *Fall Gelb*, with Armies invading Holland, Belgium and Luxembourg. First into action were two different types of special forces – the 'Brandenburgers', an élite and highly trained force of commandos whose targets were various bridges over the River Meuse and the Juliana Canal, and an equally highly trained force of Luftwaffe paratroops, whose targets included other vital bridges, the key Belgian fortress of Eban Emael and The Hague – to eliminate the Dutch government and capture the Dutch Royal Family. All these operations, which were in the main, highly successful (apart from the capture of the Royal Family), relied upon a swift link-up by ground forces, with the panzers playing a major role.

Allied reaction was to rush to man their Dyle Line positions, with full support from the Belgians now that they had been attacked. Unfortunately, this was exactly what the Germans wanted, because their plan called for a feint through Belgium, in accordance with the Allies' expectations, while the main weight of the attack would be through the Ardennes (considered impassable by French tactical experts) with a large panzer force to cross the Meuse around Sedan.

The assault went better than Hitler could even have hoped. Even the feint through Belgium was more than a match for the Allied opposition – Hoepner's XVI Panzer Corps soundly defeated the French cavalry corps of 2nd and 3rd DLM[1], who were acting as a screen for the French 1st Army. 1 DCR suffered just as badly as the DLMs. The armoured division had been kept in reserve for use in Belgium, with the mission of reinforcing the Dyle Line forces. They were sent forward on the 11th, got snarled up in the traffic chaos, were separated from their fuel and ammunition supplies and did not reach the Dinant area until the 15th, where 5th and 7th Panzer divisions made short work of them.

ACROSS THE MEUSE Meanwhile, south of Aachen and Liège, the panzers of the main assault force (Army Group A) had moved up to the Meuse. XV Pz Corps of Kluge's Fourth Army had reached the river between Namur and Dinant on the evening of the 12th – right at the junction point between the French 9th and 2nd Armies. In the centre Panzer Group Kleist had reached the Meuse in the area of Sedan and Montherme, the 'impassable' Ardennes having proved to be no problem for the tanks. There was a mass of armour – over 2,400 tanks – in three Panzer corps: Hoth's XV (5th and 7th Pz Divs), Reinhardt's XLI (6th and 9th Pz Divs) and Guderian's XIX (1st, 2nd and 10th Pz Divs), which, it was said stretched back for over a hundred miles over the frontier and on into Germany. This was to provide the *Schwerpunkt* – it would cross the river and then drive for the Channel coast, spreading chaos in its path.

Although Guderian's XIX Corps was to be the *Schwerpunkt* around Sedan, he was in fact not the first to cross the river. This honour was taken from him by 7th (Ghost) Division, whose commander, Maj Gen Erwin Rommel, would swiftly gain a reputation which equalled if not excelled Guderian's. Erwin Johannes Eugen Rommel was born at Heidenheim near Ulm on 15th November 1891. He joined the German Army in July 1910 and served with great distinction in WW1. As a young infantry officer, he was awarded the Pour le Mérite, or 'Blue Max' as it was popularly called, the German equivalent of the VC. Rommel had been in charge of a small force of some six companies in the Battle of Caporetto, and had succeeded in capturing key Italian positions, taking nearly 10,000 prisoners and 81 guns. After the war, he served with 13 Infantry Regiment, then became an instructor at the infantry school in Dresden. In 1933, he was promoted to lieutenant colonel and given command of a mountain battalion. While commanding the Jaeger Goslar he first met Hitler and clearly made a good impression on his Führer. In 1938, he was appointed commandant of the war academy at Wiener Neustadt, where his textbook on infantry tactics attracted the interest and approval of Hitler, who made him commander of his personal headquarters bodyguard (*Fuehrergleitbataillon*), and later promised him command of a division. Although he was an infantryman, Rommel specifically asked for a panzer division, having been very impressed by the way the panzers had fought in Poland. He took over 7th Panzer Division in February 1940 and it was immediately apparent that he had found his true vocation as an armoured commander. The Rommel legend began on the Meuse, when the men of his division saw their commander up to his waist in the water, helping his engineers move heavy baulks of timber to construct a ferry. 'I'll give you a hand,' he had said and then stayed around under heavy fire until the job was finished. The Belgians had tried to counter-attack but were beaten off, and by last light on the 13th the panzers had started to cross, with Rommel's ACV on the first pontoon. He was wounded shortly afterwards by a shell splinter on his right cheek, which bled a great deal, but was not serious.

XIX Corps had crossed the frontier on 10th May and by the 12th had reached the Meuse. Guderian was as usual right up with the leading troops. Von Kleist issued his orders, namely that XIX Corps should attack on the 13th, after a mass bombing attack. This was not what Guderian wanted, as he had already arranged with the supporting Luftwaffe commander, Gen Lorzer, that the Luftwaffe would supply continuous support throughout the operation rather than one initial massive strike. However, it proved 'too difficult' to issue von Kleist's new orders and so Guderian let the original orders stand, which cannot have endeared him to von Kleist! Fortunately all went well, with Guderian going over in the first assault boat of 1st Panzer Division, the CO of 1st Motor Rifle Regiment admonishing him for 'joy-riding in a canoe over the Meuse' – something which he, Guderian, had said was forbidden in his

64

'Father of the Tanks' Colonel Ernest D. Swinton, whose memorandum entitled *The Necessity for Machine-Gun Destroyers* was the basis of the work of the Landships Committee. (TM)

An artist's impression of the design for a tank by the Australian engineer Lancelot de Mole, which he submitted to the War Office in 1912. Mole received no acknowledgement for his work. (TM)

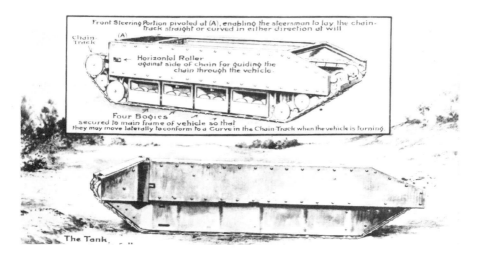

Front Steering Portion pivoted at (A), enabling the steersman to lay the chain-track straight or curved in either direction at will

Chain-Track (A)

Horizontal Roller against side of chain for guiding the chain through the vehicle

Four Bogies secured to main frame of vehicle so that they may move laterally to conform to a Curve in the Chain-Track when the vehicle is turning.

The Tank.

The very first tank to be built in the world was the No. 1 Lincoln Machine, fitted with American Bullock tracks, which proved unsatisfactory. The modified version, seen here at William Foster's Lincoln factory, was known as 'Little Willie'. (TM)

'HMLS Centipede', which became affectionately known by the Tank Corps as 'Mother' (despite being a male tank), is seen here on trial at Burton Park in 1916, easily crossing a gap 5 feet wide – the average German trench width at that time. (TM)

Colonel Jean Bapitiste Estienne, 'Pere des Chars', who put forward plans for a French land battleship after witnessing trials of the Holt caterpillar tractor as used by the British to tow artillery guns. (TM*)

Loading a train with Schneider Ca 1s, the first French tank to be built, at Contay in the Somme. They were first used at Berry au Bac on 16th April 1917. The Schneider mounted a 75-mm gun on the right-hand side, but not in a sponson. (TM)

French light tanks advancing. The FT 17 was the first tank to have a fully traversing turret. The FT 17s of the Tank Force (*Artillerie Speciale*) were organised into squadrons each of four platoons which were identified by playing card symbols, such as the diamond seen here. The French light tanks were far better and more numerous than their heavier models. (TM)

The amazing looking American Skeleton Tank, was built by the Pioneer Tractor Company of Winona, Minnesota. It weighed only 9 tons despite the fact that its dimensions were as for the British 28 ton heavy tank. Needless to say, it didn't get any further than prototype stage! (TM)

Two of the handful of German A7Vs to be built. With an enormous crew of 18 men, it weighed 30 tons and was armed with a 57-mm gun and six machine guns. Its cross country performance was poor. The Germans took little interest in tank design during WW1. (TM)

These Canadian-manned Auto-cars were built in the USA and employed successfully in France from 1915 onwards, but notably during the German offensive on the Somme in March 1918. (TM)

'D' Company's part at Flers, on 15th September 1916, scene of the very first use of tanks, is commemorated by this drawing by Sam Goddard Crowder. (TM)

Hastie's tank 'Dinna ken' (D17 of No 3 Section, D Company), 'walking up the High Street of Flers with the British Army cheering behind!' (TM)

(*left*) Maj Gen Sir Hugh Elles, KCMG, CB, DSO, who was appointed to command the Heavy Section in France on 29th September 1916. At that time he was a Colonel in the Royal Engineers. (TM)

(*right*) 'Bony' Fuller, Elles's GSO 2 and the real brains behind the new Corps. It was he who designed the tactics and fought a constant war against the '. . . apathy, incredulity and short-sightedness of GHQ'. (TM)

Swinton, wearing the tank armbadge which he designed, seen here shortly before his totally unwarranted replacement by Brig Gen Gore-Anley, who had little interest in the new weapon system. Swinton's part in the formation of the Tank Corps was fundamental. (TM)

Gen Estienne and his staff are pictured here at their HQ in the Chateau d'Orrouy, September 1917. (TM*)

Elles and some of his headquarters staff at Bermicourt, 1917. From left to right: Fuller (GSO 2), Uzielli (DAA & QMG), Elles, Atkin-Berry (Staff Capt A), Dundas (Staff Capt Q) and Butler. (TM)

The Tank Corps' first Victoria Cross was awarded posthumously to Captain Clement Robertson of 'A' Battalion for conspicuous gallantry and devotion to duty over the period 30th September to 4th October 1917, preparing the route for his tanks and then guiding them forward under heavy fire until he was killed. (TM)

Unloading for Cambrai. Mark IVs, equipped with fascines (for trench crossing) being unloaded at the railhead at Plateau, which was the scene of great activity as the tank trains arrived prior to the battle. (TM)

Commandant Bossut, who commanded the eastern *groupement*, is seen here (back towards the camera) as he guides his tank – appropriately named *Le Trompe la Mort* (The Trumpet of Death) towards the Start Line. Bossut was one of the most highly decorated French tank commanders of WW1. (TM*)

'The sunken road at La Vacquerie, dawn 20th November 1917'. This evocative painting by W. L. Wyllie shows the attack beginning. (TM)

'The Yanks are coming!' US tank units were equipped with either French Renault FT 17s (seen here), or British Heavy tanks. (US)

Brigadier General Samuel Dickerson Rockenbach, first chief of the US Army Tank Corps in World War One. Patton considered him to be: '. . . the most contrary old cuss I ever worked with.' (PM)

'This Patton boy! He's a real fighter!' So said Gen 'Black Jack' Pershing, after Patton had captured and killed some of Pancho Villa's gang in Mexico in 1916. (PM)

This interesting photograph of a very young Captain Dwight D. Eisenhower was taken at Camp Colt, Gettysburg in June, 1919. With him are Col Clopton US Army, plus Lt Col Frank Summers and Major Philip Hamond, Tank Corps. Ike had been responsible for creating the first Tank Corps training centre. (TM)

Col George S. Patton poses in front of his FT 17. He commanded 304th American Tank Brigade in its first action on 12th September 1918. (TM)

Sereno Brett, photographed at Camp Meade, Maryland, shortly after WW1. Brett commanded 344th Tank Battalion and had been chief instructor at Patton's Tank School. (PM)

British tanks of the 12th Tank Battalion drawn up in front of Cologne Cathedral, after a visit in 1919 by French Gen Petain. (TM)

Artist's impression of the very first tank versus tank engagement, which took place on 24th April 1918. Lt Mitchell, MC, who was appropriately commanding No 1 Tank of No 1 Section, A Company, 1st Battalion, Tank Corps, routed four A7Vs. (TM)

Members of the Anglo-American Commission standing in front of the Mark VIII pilot model in USA. The 'International' as it was called was to be built in vast quantities to win the war in 1919. However, the Armistice cut short the building programme. A few were re-activated in 1939 and handed over to the Canadians for training purposes. (TM)

The Armoured Car Companies of the Royal Tank Corps helped police the British Empire between the wars. Here a patrol of India-pattern 1925 Crossley armoured cars leave the magnificent Red Fort at Delhi. (TM)

Gen Sir John Capper, first Colonel Commandant of the RTC, (on left in riding britches) inspects 5th Battalion RTC at Perham Down in the early 1930s. The Vickers Medium was the main British tank of the period. (TM)

The irascible J. Walter Christie, seen here in front of his 'fast medium tank' (this model is the T3) which could reach amazing speeds both on its tracks or roadwheels. He was largely ignored by the US Army. Two of these tanks were purchased by the Russians and became models for the BT series. (TM)

Maj Gen George Lindsay, one of a handful of brilliant RTC officers, who was ignored by the War Office and put into jobs far removed from tanks and tank development. (TM)

'Father of the Royal Canadian Armoured Corps' Maj Gen F.F. 'Worthy' Worthington, who won two Military Crosses and two Military Medals in WW1 and was selected in 1936 to organise and command the Canadian Tank School at London, Ontario. Worthy organised and later commanded the 1st Armd Bde. His name is now synonymous with tanks whenever they are mentioned in the Canadian Army. (CFPU)

'Father of the US Armored Force', Lt Col Adna R. Chaffee (in dark shirt) was executive officer of the 1st Cavalry Regiment in the early 1930s. With him is Col Bruce Palmer, CO of 1st Cav Regt. The two men stand in front of an early T4 6 × 4 armoured car built by James Cunningham Company in 1932. (PM)

'Grandfather of the US Armored Force', Col Daniel Van Voorhis, seen here when he was CO of the 7th Mechanized Cavalry Brigade at Fort Knox, 1936–38. (PM)

'Schnelle Heinz' Guderian was one of the most important figures in the formation of the 'invincible' Panzertruppe. A man of foresight, courage and determination, his dynamic energy and strong personality made him a difficult and dangerous opponent. He was undoubtedly the 'father' of Blitzkrieg. (IWM)

Caricature of Charles de Gaulle, whose formidable nose must have been manna from heaven for the cartoonists. His pamphlet 'Vers l'armee de metier' which advocated a separate tank arm of 3,000 tanks, caused Petain to strike him off the promotion list in 1936. (CDEB)

(opposite) Combat Cars on parade. The Cavalry had to call their tanks 'combat cars', so as not to contravene the 1920 National Defense Act. In the leading Combat Car M1 is Ernie Harmon, who went on to become one of the outstanding divisional commanders of the US Armored Force. (TM)

Panzers on parade. This striking photograph was taken in the marketplace of Kamenz near Bamberg, on 2nd October 1936 and shows the new tanks of Panzer Regiment 3 on parade. (GF)

Inauguration of the memorial at Berry au Bac in July 1922. Gen Estienne gives an address, while Marshal Foch and Gen Mangin look on. (TM*)

Marshal Tukhachevsky was the great Soviet exponent of armoured warfare in the early days, but was liquidated by Stalin in the Great Purge and his writings destroyed. This photograph was taken when he was People's Defence Commissioner for Procurement. (B)

Maj Gen Vyvyan Pope was appointed Director of Armoured Fighting Vehicles in 1940, but was sadly killed in an air crash before his full potential as an armoured leader could be realised. Ronald Lewin argues that if Pope hadn't been killed the disasters which overtook British armour during the 'Crusader' operation and the subsequent battles of 1942, might have been averted. (TM)

Architect of Blitzkrieg, Gen Heinz Guderian and his staff in France 1940, having reached the Channel ports, watch as Allied prisoners are led away. (IWM)

Panzer deine Woffe! German propaganda poster typifing the swashbuckling image of the panzer commander in his black uniform and distinctive beret. (TM)

Adolf Hitler and his staff leave his private train at a German station close to the border with Poland. This was done so as to allow Hitler to study the war at close quarters. Hitler wears his 'war uniform' minus the swastika armband. (TM)

Gen (later FM) Fedor von Bock – facing the camera – commanded the northern Army Group in Poland and Army Group B in France. A tall, ramrod-stiff Prussian, he achieved excellent army-air cooperation with Kesselring. (IWM)

Gen (later FM) Gerd von Rundstedt, who commanded the southern Army Group in the attack on Poland and Army Group A in the *Fall Gelb* attack on France. Although not really an armoured commander he nevertheless had large numbers of panzers under his command on both occasions. He and Rommel later worked harmoniously together in Normandy. (GF)

Gen Stanislaw Maczek, who commanded the 'Black Brigade' in Poland and then went on to become GOC 1st Polish Armoured Division. He was undoubtedly the greatest Polish armoured commander of WW2. (SI)

Gen George Patton commander 2nd Armored Division, receives a briefing during the Louisiana manoeuvres in 1941. (PM)

Gen Dmitry Danilovich Lelyushenko, commanded 39th Armoured Brigade in the Soviet-Finnish War and was awarded the title Hero of the Soviet Union on 7th April 1940. He went on to command 4th Tank Army. (CAFM)

Commander of Osasto Lagus and later, the only Finnish armoured division (Panssaridivisioona), Col (later Gen) Ernst Ruben Lagus, who was undoubtedly Finland's great tank commander of WW2. (KK)

(opposite) 'Knights of our times' is the way the German propaganda machine eulogised the panzer leaders, such as this commander in his Pzkpfw IV whose photograph appeared in Signal magazine in June, 1940. (TM)

Cool, unflappable 'Papa' Hoth stands beside the mercurial and brilliant Erwin Rommel in Eplessier, 7th June 1940. Hoth commanded XVth Corps in France which contained Rommel's 7th (Ghost) Division and 5 Pz Div. (TM)

Gen der Kavallerie Erich Hoepner, whose XVIth Panzer Corps soundly defeated the French Cavalry Corps in 1940. He was one of the finest armoured commanders in the German Army and thought by some to be even better than Guderian or Hoth. (HS)

Gen der Panzertruppen Georg-Hans Reinhardt commanded XLIst Corps in France, which comprised 6 and 9 Panzer Divisions. (HS)

'The Little White-Haired Terrier' (Gen Sir Richard O'Connor) talks with 'The Chief' (Gen Sir Archibald Wavell) before the great battles of Operation Compass in which the Western Desert Force soundly defeated the Italians in Libya, outfighting an army more than ten times their strength. (IWM)

This photograph of Gen Sir John Crocker was taken towards the end of the war. However, in 1940 he was commanding an armoured brigade in 1st Armoured Division and was an inspiration to his men. (IWM)

The trainer from England. Maj Gen Percy Hobart was undoubtedly one of the finest trainers of armoured troops the world has ever seen. However, he did not suffer fools gladly and his abrasive, abrupt manner did not endear him to those who disliked tanks. (TM)

(*left*) Gen der Panzertruppe Hans Cramer was the last commander of the DAK, from 5th March 1943 until 12th May 1943. (HS)

(*right*) Gen der Panzertruppe Ludwig Cruewell, became commander of the DAK in August 1941, but was captured the following year in late May, when his Storch light aircraft was shot down. A brave and skilful commander, his capture was a sad loss to Rommel. (HS)

'The Desert Fox', Gen (later FM) Erwin Rommel, wearing the British issue anti-gas goggles which became his trademark, was undoubtedly the most well known German general in North Africa. His reputation was such that Auchinleck caused a special order of the day to be published about 'our friend Rommel' (see text). (GF)

Rommel, sporting a tartan scarf, discusses tactics with Gen Walther K. Nehring (on his right with hand on map), Oberst Bayerlein and Oberst von Mellenthin. Nehring served with distinction in North Africa and later commanded 1st Panzer Army in March 1945. (IWM)

Captured at Tobruk by New Zealand forces, Maj Gen von Ravenstein had commanded 21st Panzer Division bravely and fought with great chivalry. See text for his letter to Gen 'Jock' Campbell after he was awarded the Victoria Cross. (IWM)

A new face on the desert scene. Montgomery at Alam Halfa, with left to right: John Postern (one of Monty's ADCs), Brig Bobbie Erskine (who later commanded 7th Armd Div), Lt Gen Horrocks and Lt Col Pip Roberts. (IWM)

Monty with two of his corps commanders, Sir Oliver Leese and Herbert Lumsden. The latter was a dashing 12th Lancer whose Corps was the designated 'corps de chasse' to provide the follow-up force after Alamein. (IWM)

Two of the greatest British armoured commanders of the desert: 'Strafer' Gott and Jock Campbell (*left*), both commanded the Desert Rats and died in tragic accidents. (IWM)

Another excellent armoured divisional commander was Maj Gen Raymond Briggs, late RTR, seen here with Montgomery. He commanded 1st Armoured Division at the time of El Alamein. (IWM)

The 10th Armoured Division commander at El Alamein was another ex-Royal Tank Regiment officer, Maj Gen Alec Gatehouse. (IWM)

The tall, ascetic Gen Wilhelm Ritter von Thoma took over from Stumme until Rommel returned a few days later. A few weeks later on 4th November, he decided to surrender and is seen here reporting to Monty. (IWM)

Gen der Kavallerie Georg Stumme, who took over command of the DAK when Rommel went home to convalesce. Kesselring wrote of him: 'Being a man of a more even and genial temperament than Rommel, he did much to relax tension among officers and men'. Unfortunately he was not a fit man and died of a heart attack on 24th October 1942, when his car was fired on at the front. (HS)

Gen der Kavallerie Siegfried Westphal, Rommel's Chief of Operations in North Africa, studies his map, while a worried Rommel waits to move on. (GF)

Maj Gen Ernest N. Harmon, who, in February 1943, took over as CG of 1st Armoured Division, 'The Old Ironsides' as they were called, after their disastrous start in North Africa and quickly stamped his personality on the division. (PM)

Last of the German commanders in North Africa, Generaloberst Jurgen von Arnim marches smartly into captivity after surrendering at noon on 12th May 1943. (IWM)

original orders! All that night the corps engineers built tank ferries and by first light the bridgehead on the western bank measured some three miles in width and six in depth.

The French had been trying unsuccessfully to prevent the crossing at Sedan and Gen Flavigny, the corps commander of XXI Corps, had 3 DCR, 5 DLM and 3rd Motorized Infantry Division allocated to contain the bridgehead. Unfortunately, the same chapter of accidents as with 1 DCR was repeated. Orders took far too long to work out and issue, fuel and ammunition were held up. Flavigny was indecisive and the attack was far too slow in starting. After two days of manoeuvring around the bridgehead, it was called off, the tanks split up and given to the infantry for the usual 'static defence' and the opportunity lost. One can perhaps gauge the mood of France and the French Army that day (15th May) by the words of the French premier, who telephoned Churchill and told him that France was beaten, that they had already lost the battle and that the Germans were 'pouring through in great numbers of tanks and armoured cars'.

ON TO THE COAST   From then on, until the evacuation from Dunkirk, which began 10 days later, the German panzers were virtually unstoppable. By the evening of the 15th the bridgehead was over 60 miles wide and getting deeper and deeper. By midday on the 16th, Guderian's forward troops were 55 miles west of Sedan. Then the doubts began to creep in – not at corps level, but rather with Gen von Rundstedt and Adolf Hitler himself, who could see nothing but increasing danger from the south, as both expected the French to unleash a savage counter-attack. Nothing could have been further from the truth, as those at the sharp end fully appreciated. However, as Guderian admitted in his memoirs, he made a great mistake. XIX and XLI Panzer Corps had made a pact that they would press on regardless, ignoring orders from above (it was quite easy to be suddenly plagued by difficult radio communications at the right moment!) and were doing just that, when, on the morning of the 17th, Guderian received a direct order to report to von Kleist on the XIX Corps airstrip, where he was given a severe wigging by his senior officer for disobeying Hitler's personal orders. Guderian's reaction was typical of 'Heinz Hothead' – he immediately asked to be relieved of his command. Von Kleist agreed – there was by now no love lost between them – and told Guderian to hand over to his senior divisional commander. Having done so, Guderian radioed von Rundstedt, who was appalled and ordered him to stay where he was until Col Gen List could be sent to talk to him. As Richard Brett-Smith says in his book, *Hitler's Generals*, 'He could not have chosen better, for, after listening to the arguments, List gave an order to Guderian to which Hitler could hardly object but which he knew Guderian would interpret in his own way. This was: "Reconnaissance in force to be carried out. Corps headquarters must in all circumstances remain where it is, so that it may be easily reached."' Honour was satisfied and Guderian was off again!

On 11th May, after years of waiting in the wings, another great tank

65

commander was to be given his chance. This was Charles de Gaulle, and to be fair to him, his chance was a slim one. On 11th May Gen Georges had sent for him and told him that he was going to be given command of the embryo 4th DCR, sending him on his way with the words, 'There, de Gaulle! For you who have so long held the ideas which the enemy is putting into practice, here is your chance to act!'[2]

De Gaulle decided that he would try to cut across Guderian's lines of supply so as to isolate the free-wheeling panzers. He aimed his attack at the town of Montcornet, an important road centre some 20 miles to the northeast of 4th DCR. Despite the fact that his division was incomplete and not properly trained, de Gaulle pushed forward, destroying German armoured cars and lorries in his way, reaching the town and pressing home his attack with great *élan.* The French 'charge' was stopped only at the last moment, when, short of ammunition and fuel, they were forced to withdraw. It was a gesture, but it did salvage some French honour and, in later life, de Gaulle was inclined to embroider the tale, talking about the exploits of an 'improvized armoured division', which 'did to the Germans what they had been doing to the Allies'. It was good for after-dinner speeches, but hardly true, although it would be wrong to denigrate either de Gaulle's personal efforts or those of his gallant tank crews. He did try again some days later, but this time was seen off by the Luftwaffe. It was time for the British tanks to have a go.

COUNTER-ATTACK AT ARRAS   Guderian pressed on and, during the 20th May, achieved his longest advance to date, from the Canal du Nord to the sea at Abbeville, over 56 miles in a single day, cutting France in two and isolating the northern Allied armies from their supply bases further south.

Above this penetration, the other panzer divisions were advancing, Rommel's Ghost Division pushing forward in a long, thin penetration 30 miles deep but only two miles wide, taking vast numbers of prisoners and destroying many enemy tanks and guns for the loss of fewer than a hundred men killed and wounded. However, they did not have their own way all the time and, on 21st May, suffered their first major reverse of the campaign near Arras, when they were counter-attacked by a mixed force of British tanks and infantry.

The force consisted of 151 Infantry Brigade (6, 8 & 9 Battalions of the Durham Light Infantry), supported by 1st Army Tank Brigade (4th & 7th Battalions of the Royal Tank Regiment), together with some artillery, anti-tank guns and machine-guns. All were battle-weary, the tanks, for example, having driven some 120 miles on their tracks over the past five days and lost about a quarter of their strength through breakdowns. However, the tanks were Matilda Mark Is and IIs, the heaviest, best-protected and best-armed British tanks in the BEF. Although the Matilda I had only a medium machine-gun as its main armament, the Matilda 2 (later to earn the nickname 'Queen of the Desert') had the admirable 2-pdr quick-firing anti-tank gun which could penetrate most German tanks of the period.

This was no well-planned, well-coordinated affair. The basic counter-attack consisted of the force advancing in two columns, each roughly consisting of a tank battalion and an infantry battalion, plus supporting arms, with the columns some three miles apart. Their mission was to counter-attack from Arras southwards, cutting off Rommel's penetration. However, the infantry had never worked with tanks before, there were no infantry/tank radio communications and the force had to leave its concentration area in such a hurry that proper orders were never passed down to individual tank commanders. Nevertheless the operation was, at least to begin with, a spectacular success. It was a perfect example of tank commanders at a low level seizing the initiative and using the capabilities of their AFVs to the full, and of infantry standing and fighting stubbornly with their anti-tank weapons. Rommel's 25 Panzer Regiment lost about 30 tanks – more than at any other time in the whole campaign – while the higher headquarters got a completely false idea of the size of the opposing force. News of the counter-attack sent shock waves all the way back to Adolf Hitler. In the opinion of many historians, this was the primary reason for the Führer giving his famous order to halt in front of Dunkirk. Von Rundstedt later wrote: 'A critical moment came just as my forces reached the Channel. It was caused by a British counter-stroke southwards from Arras on 21 May. For a short time it was feared that the panzer divisions would be cut off before the infantry divisions could come up to support them. None of the French counter-attacks carried the threat of this one'.[3] Liddell Hart, writing in his history of the RTR was even more emphatic: 'It may well be asked whether two battalions have ever had such a tremendous effect on history as the 4th and 7th RTR achieved by their action at Arras. Their effect in saving the British Army from being cut off from its escape port provides ample justification for the view that if two well-equipped armoured divisions had been available, the Battle of France might have been saved.'[4]

'A TRAVESTY OF AN ARMOURED DIVISION' As already mentioned, the only British armoured division to fight in France was 1st Armoured, which did not arrive until 17th May and was far from properly equipped or complete, its artillery and motor battalions having been taken to fight in Norway and then sent to hold Calais, where they were joined by one of its armoured regiments (3 RTR). The division had been in the process of exchanging its light tanks for cruisers when ordered to France, and nearly half its tank strength (134 out of 284) were still light tanks. Crews had not had much opportunity to get themselves accustomed to the new cruisers, which were minus all their tools and even their Besa machine guns (the latter arrived just before sailing, still packed with grease and in their crates!). Their commander, Maj Gen Roger Evans, later wrote of it as 'this travesty of an armoured division'.[5] Amid this chaos, Brig John Crocker remained an inspiration to his men, as they all learned the hard way how effective blitzkrieg tactics could be. Maj Gen Percy Hobart, who was an excellent judge of men had this to say about Crocker, when he was his Brigade Major in 1934: 'An absolutely reliable officer who has never failed me, in spite of a very great pressure of work and completely novel

Panzer Leaders

Although they did not shine as brightly as Rommel and Guderian, these other panzer leaders nonetheless performed with skill and daring. Their corps, reading from north to south, were:

XXXIX Panzer Corps – Gen Rudolf Schmidt. His Corps led the break-through into Holland to link up with the paratroops and air-landed forces. He played a major part in the surrender of the Netherlands. He also tried to prevent the bombing of Rotterdam, but was too late in warning off the Luftwaffe. He was later dismissed in Russia, in July 1943, on the eve of the great tank battle at Kursk.

XVI Panzer Corps – Gen Erich Hoepner. Many historians rated Hoepner at least on a par with Guderian. A cavalryman of the old school, he was, as Richard Brett-Smith so aptly describes him, 'a real thruster, with drive and talent'.[6] He too was to be dismissed later, while commanding 4th Panzer Army in Russia and later became one of the main plotters against Hitler, playing an active role in the assassination attempt on 20th July 1944. He was arrested and later executed by hanging.

XV Panzer Corps – Gen Hermann Hoth. 'Steady rather than dashing, cool, a good strategist and tactician, unflappable and well liked.'[7] His troops called him 'Papa' and he commanded 3rd Panzer Group in the invasion of Russia, but later he also fell foul of Hitler, being blamed for failures of German armour in late 1943, was sacked and spent the rest of the war in retirement.

XLI Panzer Corps – Gen George-Hans Reinhardt. Like Hoepner, he was under-rated, and had much to do with the development of the Panzer-waffe. He was the commander of 3rd Panzer Army from late 1941 until 1945, when he was relieved of his command, after asking Hitler if he could abandon East Prussia in order to avoid being cut off and isolated.

XIX Panzer Corps – Gen Heinz Guderian. Even 'Schnelle' Heinz would later fall foul of his Führer, being relieved by Hitler for the German failure to capture Moscow. He was given no further field commands, but instead was appointed Inspector General of Panzer Troops (1943–4) and then Chief of the General Staff (1944–5), being once again relieved in March 1945 after yet another blinding row with Hitler!

Above the XLI and XIX Panzer Corps was von Kleist's headquarters. Paul Ludwig Ewald, Baron von Kleist, was the senior cavalry general in the German Army. He and Guderian did not see eye to eye, but von Kleist did well in both Poland and France. In June 1941 his Panzer group led the advance to Kiev and in September 1942 he was given command of Army Group A in the Caucasus. Brett-Smith describes him as 'a solid, unflap-pable commander, rather than a brilliant one'.[8] He died in captivity in Russia in 1954.

problems and conditions. His taciturnity does not cover up a slow mind. Far from it. But he always thinks before he speaks. He is popular with officers and men; is quite unperturbed by responsibility or crisis; has unruffled serenity and a cool judgement under all circumstances.'9 No doubt he needed all these qualities to the full, as he led the remnants of his brigade some 200 miles in two days, back to Cherbourg and then home.

HITLER'S 'HALT' ORDER Soon after the Arras counterattack on 24th May, Hitler ordered the panzers to halt, which effectively stopped them from advancing over the line of the Aa Canal for three whole days, long enough to allow the BEF to escape from Dunkirk. The Luftwaffe was supposed to finish them off on the beaches, but in fact 366,162 men were rescued during Operation 'Dynamo' (the code name for the Dunkirk evacuations) in an epic rescue by the 'little ships' from England. One-third of those saved were French and other Allied troops, who would form the beginnings of exiled armies such as the Free French under de Gaulle, who also escaped – although he managed to get away by air from Paris with the senior British Liaison Officer, Gen Sir Edward Spears, in mid-June, just before Pétain asked the Germans for peace terms.

THE FINAL BATTLES After Dunkirk, France was left to continue the battle for the remainder of her territory with no allied support, well knowing that there was no way in which the demoralized and disintegrating French Army could stop the now triumphant panzers. The blitzkrieg tactics continued, Paris surrendered on the 14th and a week later Hitler met the French delegation at Compiègne for the surrender. French armour rallied in some isolated places and fought bravely, as if to show what might have been had France possessed any great tank commanders other than de Gaulle and had their armoured forces been properly organized. But it was a purely panzer affair.

The 'Knights' of the *Panzerwaffe* were in the ascendancy and the word blitzkrieg spread alarm and despondency worldwide. However, instead of pressing on across the Channel, the Germans paused to celebrate and then endeavoured to crush Great Britain using only the Luftwaffe. Tank actions meanwhile moved to the perfect arena – the desert wastes of North Africa.

NOTES TO CHAPTER 4

1 DLM = *Division Légère Mécanique*, which comprised a tank brigade of two tank regiments, a motorized rifle brigade, a recce regiment, a towed artillery regiment, an engineer battalion and normal supporting units. The DLM's role was strategic reconnaissance and security. DCR = *Division Cuirassée Rapide*, which comprised two demi-brigades (one of medium tanks and one heavy), a motorized infantry battalion, an artillery regiment and an engineer company. This was the armoured division of the French Army.

2 As quoted in *To Lose a Battle*.
3 As quoted in *The Tanks*, vol. 2.
4 *ibid.*
5 As quoted in Duncan Crow, *British and Commonwealth Armoured Forces (1919–1946)*
6 Hitler's Generals
7 *ibid.*
8 *ibid.*
9 As quoted in Kenneth Macksey, *The Tank Pioneers*

5 TANKS ACROSS THE DESERT

The scene now changes to the barren Western Desert of North Africa, where tanks would once again prove themselves to be the dominant arm, in a series of hard-fought campaigns lasting over a period of three years. However, one must start even earlier, at the time of the Munich crisis of 1938, when it appeared very likely that Mussolini might pre-empt any declaration of war in Europe and invade Egypt. It was decided that the Mobile Force, formed in 1935 at the time of the Duce's invasion of Abyssinia, needed to be welded into a better balanced, armoured fighting force, so a very special officer was flown out from England to Egypt with the task of creating an armoured division.

A Trainer from England
Maj Gen Percy Cleghorn Stanley Hobart, 'Hobo' as he was known (but never called) by everyone in the RTC, had already shown himself to be a superlative armoured trainer on Salisbury Plain in the early 1930s. In 1937 he had been appointed Director Military Training at the War Office, an appointment about which he had grave misgivings because of the prevailing bad attitude towards mechanization and tanks in the British Army. His year as DMT had not been an easy one, yet he found even greater hostility on his arrival in Egypt. GOC in C, Lt Gen Sir Robert Gordon-Finlayson greeted him with the words, 'I don't know what you've come here for, and I don't want you anyway!'[1]

'Hobo' had made many enemies in the Army, mainly because he did not suffer fools gladly, was a passionate supporter of the tank and of armoured warfare and detested the pomp and circumstance of Army life.

Typically 'Hobo' did not let Gordon-Finlayson's hostility deter him. He immediately set about his task of transforming the Mobile Division into a formidable fighting force. Initially it was composed of the Cairo Cavalry Brigade (later called the Light Armoured Brigade), a tank group and a pivot group. The striking arm, the tanks, consisted of just two regiments – 1st and 6th Royal Tanks. The Cavalry Brigade comprised 7th and 8th Hussars, with light tanks, and 11th Hussars, an armoured car regiment since 1928, with Rolls Royce armoured cars. In the pivot group were 3rd Regiment Royal Horse Artillery and 1st Bn KRRC, the latter soon to be re-organized as a motor battalion. Their vehicles and equipment were all but worn-out, thanks to the parsimony of the British government over the years, the tanks in particular being in a very sorry state. Nevertheless, despite these handicaps, 'Hobo' decided to concentrate on teaching his new division dispersion, flexibility and mobility, getting them used to moving at speed and operating over wide frontages. He had to fight against a great deal of obstruction and ignorance, but his enthusiasm and determination never flagged. By August 1939 he had fashioned a force that would become world famous as the 7th Armoured Division, the immortal 'Desert Rats'.

Unfortunately, before he could take the Division into action, 'Hobo' was relieved of his command and ordered back to the UK. Once again, his quick temper and abrasiveness were the main cause, although on this occasion there had been right on his side. Gordon-Finlayson's place had been taken by Lt Gen 'Jumbo' Wilson, with whom 'Hobo' got along very amicably until one particular exercise, when a series of misunderstandings arose between them, due mainly to the fact that 'Hobo', like so many other successful armoured commanders, led from the front and so was never available at his HQ, where more orthodox commanders like Wilson expected to find him. This unfortunately led to a personal row, which ended in Wilson writing to Wavell, reporting that he had no longer any confidence in Hobart and requesting that a new commander be appointed to the armoured division. 'Hobo' left without further ado. Gen O'Connor, who had found no difficulties in working closely with Gen Hobart, wrote saying that the Mobile Division was the best-trained division he had ever seen.

Hobart's place was taken by Maj Gen Michael O'Moore Creagh (late 15/19 Hussars), but his influence was to remain long after his departure and many times his views were quoted – 'Hobo always used to say . . .'.[2] As Maj Gen Verney said of him, in the prologue to his history of the 7th Armoured Division: 'To his country the General's services had been considerable, to the Division he formed and trained they were immeasurable, and the long record of success in the years that followed stands as a tribute to their first commander.' 'Hobo' went back to the temporary obscurity of retirement, exchanging his major general's badges of rank for those of a lance corporal in his local Home Guard!

Operations under Wavell

7th Armoured Division formed one of the major components of the 30,000 British and Commonwealth troops stationed in Egypt pre-war, or hurriedly sent out during the build-up to war, and now available to the CinC Middle East, Gen Sir Archibald Wavell. Opposite this small force were two Italian Armies (5th and 10th), almost ten times its size, under Marshal Rodolfo Graziani, who was also Governor General and CinC of Libya. Graziani had taken over from the popular Marshal Italo Balbo, who had been killed when shot down by his own anti-aircraft guns as he came into land in Tobruk in June 1940.[3] Graziani had been in charge of Libya between 1930 and 1934, so he was well known and thoroughly disliked by the locals for his brutality. He had been ordered by Mussolini to invade Egypt, the Duce rightly reckoning that the loss of Egypt and the vital supply route through the Suez Canal would have a major effect upon Great Britain's ability to continue to wage war. However, Graziani did not earn the nickname 'The Reluctant Warrior' for nothing and showed markedly little enthusiasm for the task, especially as he had totally overestimated the strength of the British forces.4

Nevertheless, after much prompting, Graziani did at last move, and between 13th and 16th September 1940 his forces advanced to Sidi Barrani, some 60 miles inside Egypt but still 80 miles west of the most advanced British positions, at Matruh. However, that was quite far enough for Graziani, who halted, established a supply base and started to repair the coastal road which the British had destroyed, and to build a water pipeline up from the frontier. It was Graziani's intention to improve his lines of communication and supply and to concentrate on building a string of fortified camps inland from the coast, putting off any further advance until the cooler winter weather.

OPERATION 'COMPASS' But he was not left in peace for long. Wavell had already decided that it would only be a matter of time before the Germans joined the Italians in North Africa. In addition, he had received more reinforcements and thus felt strong enough to take the offensive against the Italians. Accordingly, he ordered the commander of the Western Desert Force, Gen Sir Richard O'Connor, to make a large-scale raid into Libya and, after some early successful patrolling against the Italian forts of Capuzzo and Maddalena, the British launched Operation 'Compass' on 9th December.

Born in 1889 O'Connor was a Cameronian who had served with great gallantry in WW1, winning the DSO and bar, the MC, and nine Mentions in Despatches. He had also served on the Italian front and as a result had been awarded the Italian silver Medal for Valour in 1918. His bravery and professional competence as a soldier were hidden by his gentle, shy manner. Short of stature, he possessed a cool, logical mind and had proved himself a highly professional and effective soldier both in war and peace. He had commanded the Peshawar Brigade from 1936 to 1938 and was Military Governor of Jerusalem 1938–9. A scholarly soldier, he nevertheless believed in commanding from the front like Rommel and Guderian, keeping his headquarters well forward and often reconnoitring on his own far behind enemy lines.

O'Connor's plan was to send 4th Indian Division, plus the heavy Matilda II tanks of 7th RTR, through a gap between two of the Italian fortified camps at Sofafi and Nibeiwa and then to assault Nibeiwa and Tummar camps from the rear. Meantime 7th Armoured Division and the Matruh garrison would screen this movement and prevent the Italians at Sofafi and Buq Buq from interfering, while the Navy bombarded Sidi Barrani and the RAF attacked Italian airfields to keep their planes grounded. This sea and air bombardment began on the night of 8th/9th December and was highly effective.

The ground attack began at 0715 hours on 9th December and three-and-a-half hours later the Matildas had broken through the rear of the Nibeiwa camp, knocking out a number of enemy tanks, while the infantry assaulted with fixed bayonets, capturing over 2,000 prisoners. The Italians fought bravely, their commander, Gen Pietro Maletti, being shot dead with a bullet throught the lung as he fired a machine-gun at the advancing British forces. That afternoon Tummar West and Tummar East were attacked and by the evening both had been taken in a similar manner. Meanwhile, 7th Armoured Division tanks had captured Azzizaya and cut the Sidi Barrani to Buq Buq track, capturing some 400 men and 60 vehicles in the process. The second phase of O'Connor's plan then came into operation, the capture of Sidi Barrani by 16th Infantry Brigade of 4th Indian Division. The attack began with a fierce artillery duel and lasted all day, but by 5pm it was all over and large numbers of prisoners and booty had been taken, including two complete enemy divisions caught between British troops.

O'Connor now decided to pursue the retreating Italians with the faster tanks of 7th Armoured Division, sending 4th Armoured Brigade due westwards above the escarpment, while 7th Armoured Brigade harried them along the coast road. Despite bad weather and supply difficulties they pushed the Italians back steadily, capturing Sollum on the 16th. Operation 'Compass' was thus a complete success and O'Connor had shown himself to be capable of getting the best out of his armour, even in these difficult conditions. Thanks to 'Hobo', the 'Desert Rats', as the 7th Armoured Division was now known – the name being taken from the jerboa emblem which their GOC, Gen O'More Creagh, had chosen for them[5] – was a highly effective fighting force, well experienced in the difficult art of desert warfare.

ON TO BEDA FOMM After such a swift and easy victory, both Wavell and O'Connor were determined to keep up the pressure and to push the Italians back into Cyrenaica. This was done most successfully, the coastal strongholds of Bardia and Tobruk being captured by 6th Australian Division (which had replaced 4th Indian Division), supported by the heavy Matilda tanks, so that by 22nd January, the British forces were within 20 miles of Derna. In Tobruk alone, some 25,000 prisoners were taken, plus 208 guns and 87 tanks. It was by now clear that the Italians intended to pull right out of Cyrenaica, so O'Connor decided upon a daring plan, which meant establishing an armoured roadblock behind the retreating enemy, well southwest of Benghazi in the Beda Fomm-Sidi Saleh area. To achieve this block, 7th Armoured Division was ordered to send a flying column through the desert, while the rest of the British forces kept up pressure along the coastal route. Combe Force, under the CO of 11th Hussars, was despatched and, despite the terrible going and several enemy air attacks en route, managed to reach the coast at Sidi Saleh and to cut off the Italian retreat on the morning of 5th February. Combe Force comprised just one squadron of 11th Hussars and one of the King's Dragoon Guards, 2nd Battalion Rifle Brigade, with nine Bofors guns, less than 2,000 men in total, with no tanks or artillery. Meanwhile, 4th Armoured Brigade was following up fast, the leading elements of 7th Hussars and 2nd Royal Tanks reaching Beda Fomm that afternoon, with just 20 cruisers and 36 light tanks still motoring. The two blocks had a paralyzing effect upon the Italians, who had never expected to find the enemy so far behind them. Instead of trying to outflank the tiny British forces, they launched a series of uncoordinated frontal attacks, all of which were beaten off with heavy loss.

It was a remarkable battle, which lasted until the early hours of 9th February, when the Italians finally surrendered. The small British force had by then captured 20,000 men, including six Italian generals, 216 guns, 112 tanks, 1,500 lorries and immense quantities of arms, equipment and stores of all kinds, not to mention all those of the enemy they had killed. All this was achieved at a cost to 7th Armoured Division of just nine killed and fifteen wounded. Small wonder that Anthony Eden coined a new version of Churchill's famous Battle of Britain phrase, saying, 'Never has so much been surrendered by so many to so few!' The small, well-trained, brilliantly led British force was ideal for this type of operation, while the entire campaign must rank among one of the greatest feats of arms of WW2. Thanks to O'Connor's unorthodox but highly effective command, two divisions, one armoured and one infantry, plus a battalion of Matilda tanks, had completely destroyed an entire Army of 10 divisions. Total British casualties during the campaign were under two thousand, while they took over 130,000 prisoners! O'Connor and the Desert Rats had certainly left their mark upon the desert war, but soon they would be up against a new opponent.

The Desert Fox

With the surrender of the 10th Italian Army the whole of Cyrenaica was in British hands and the road to Tripoli lay wide open. Yet, just two months later, the enemy were once again back on the Egyptian border and the dashing Gen O'Connor was 'in the bag'. What caused this sudden reversal of fortunes? It was mainly the arrival of just one man, the newly promoted Lt Gen Erwin Rommel, late GOC of the 7th (Ghost) Panzer Division and now commander of a new force, which from 19th February 1941 was called the *Deutsches Afrika Korps* (DAK).

The 'Desert Fox', as he soon became known by both sides, was in his element in the desert. A master tactician, who, as we have already seen, liked to lead from the front, issue his orders over the radio or in person and to dominate a battle by his very personality, Rommel was also a chivalrous and honourable man – witness that Winston Churchill said of him in the House of Commons in January 1942: 'We have had a very daring and skilful opponent against us and may I say across the havoc of war, a great General.' Rommel's reputation was such that Auchinleck, who replaced Wavell as British CinC Middle East Forces in early July 1941, foolishly caused a special order to be published:

TO: ALL COMMANDERS AND CHIEFS OF STAFF
FROM: Headquarters, BTE & MTE

There exists a real danger that our friend Rommel is becoming a kind of magician or bogeyman to our troops, who are talking far too much about him. He is by no means a superman, although he is undoubtedly very energetic and able. Even if he were a superman, it would still be highly undesirable that our men should credit him with supernatural powers.

I wish you to dispel by all possible means the idea that Rommel represents something more than the ordinary German general. The important thing now is to see to it that we do not always talk of Rommel when we mean the enemy in Libya. We must refer to 'the Germans' or 'the Axis Powers' or 'the enemy' and not always keep harping on Rommel.

Please ensure that this order is put into immediate effect and impress upon all Commanders that, from a psychological point of view, it is a matter of the highest importance.

(Signed) C J Auchinleck
General

The order merely increased Rommel's reputation instead of diminishing it.

Clearly the British thought more highly of him than did some of his seniors in the German Army. Gen Walther von Brauchitsch, CinC of the OKH, did not like Rommel's continual impatience with authority, while Franz Halder, the Army Chief of Staff, actively disliked him and called him an upstart. Rommel was prepared to flout any orders he did not agree with, banking on his popularity with Hitler to see him through. It is also not generally appreciated that Rommel was in fact the second choice to command the DAK. Originally Gen Baron von Funck had been sent out by von Brauchitsch to Africa after Graziani's defeat, to carry out a detailed recce and to command any German forces sent to the assistance of the beleaguered Italians. However, on his return he had to report to Hitler, who discovered that he had once been the personal staff officer of the disgraced Gen von Fritsch. He was swiftly replaced by Hitler's favourite.

Rommel held a number of military parades in Tripoli, as each element of his force disembarked. He even made the tanks of 5 Leichte's Panzer regiment drive around the town several times, so as to keep the British guessing on the true strength of the DAK. He also had his pioneers make scores of dummy tanks out of wood and cardboard, so as to fool enemy air recce.

Rommel's initial orders were to use the DAK as a blocking force to bolster up the shattered Italians and to prevent the British from advancing any further into Tripolitania. Despite the fact that, on its arrival, the DAK comprised just two divisions – 5 Leichte (retitled 21 Panzer Division on 1st

October 1941) and 15 Panzer Division – Rommel did not bother to wait until even this small force was completely assembled, and, firmly believing the old maxim about attack being the best form of defence, he began to advance on 31st March, a bare six weeks after the arrival of his first troops and well before 15 Panzer was anything like complete. To be fair he did also have the Italian Ariete armoured division (with only half its tanks) and four Italian infantry divisions, but the Germans had no previous desert experience and their tanks were still not fitted with suitable air or fuel filters. Nevertheless, Rommel was determined to disobey OKH's direct orders not to advance, gambling on speed and surprise to win the day.

Luck was also on his side, because, unbeknown to the Germans, Wavell had been forced to withdraw troops from Cyrenaica and send them to the assistance of Greece. The British front line was held by two under-strength divisions, with the newly arrived 2nd Armoured Division, commanded by Maj Gen M.D. Gambier-Parry, at the sharp end. They were having problems with their new cruiser tanks and comprised just one armoured brigade and half a support group.[6] Their reconnaissance regiment had only just converted from horses to armoured cars and none of them had the Desert Rats' battle or desert experience.

Consequently, when Rommel attacked at Mersa Brega on 31st March, 5 Leichte went through the enemy like a hot knife through butter, causing a general withdrawal. Gen Johannes Streich, the commander of 5 Leichte, fell in with his commander's plans to continue to attack whatever Berlin might order, and was so successful that Agedabia was captured on 2nd April. The DAK had advanced so quickly that they soon ran out of fuel and Rommel had to send part of 5 Leichte back to El Agheila, 40 miles to the rear, for fresh

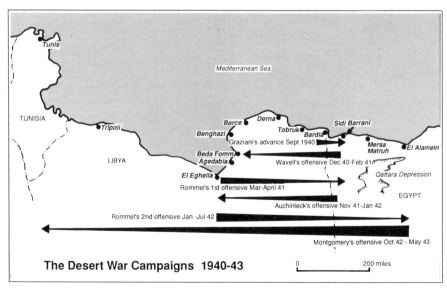

The Desert War Campaigns 1940-43

supplies. The DAK staff had reckoned this refuelling operation would take four days but, typically, Rommel allowed only 24 hours! The advance was resumed on the night of 4th/5th April, Rommel dividing his force into four blitzkrieg-type columns, sending them up the coast with the orders to keep going at all costs. He even persuaded the visiting Gen Kircheim to command one of them (Kircheim was subsequently, on 14th May 1941, awarded the Knight's Cross to the Iron Cross).

As they had done in France, the panzers spread confusion far and wide. They had Luftwaffe support – units of Fliegerkorps X had been arriving in Tripoli since mid-February, so there were some 50 Stukas and 20 Me 110s on call, and the panzers had access to long range Ju 88s and He 111s from Sicily. 3rd Armoured Brigade and the Indian motorized brigade were, for example, caught near Mechili and practically wiped out. The desert seemed to be full of German columns shooting up everything in sight, or halted waiting for more fuel to arrive so that they could press on, while their dynamic commander was everywhere. He even found time to write back to his wife, saying:

We've been attacking since the 31st with dazzling success. There'll be consternation among our masters in Tripoli and Rome, perhaps in Berlin too. . . . We have already reached our first objective, which we weren't supposed to get to until the end of May. The British are falling over each other to get away. Our casualties small. Booty can't yet be estimated. You will understand that I can't sleep for happiness.[7]

What Rommel did not tell her was that he had driven his small force forward mainly on the strength of his own personality, always at the sharp end, always urging his men on faster and faster. The story is told of the commander of a leading recce column, who halted for no apparent reason. A note fluttered down from a light aircraft overhead: 'Why have you stopped? if you do not move on at once, I shall come down. Rommel.' David Irving quotes a description by Rommel's aide, Lt Hermann Aldinger, of such a flight with the Desert Fox: 'The Storch lifts off for a quick look over the front lines and dispositions. The pilot gets a sign: "Go lower!" but no sooner is he down than the Italian troops (in error) are letting fly at it with all they've got. Bullets begin hitting his wings . . .' The pilot managed to avoid their fire and then Rommel saw a column of British troops, a possible counter-attack force, and decided he must warn his leading troops. They managed to land, the Storch losing half its undercarriage in the process. The German troops had an 88mm gun with them, but it was disabled: '. . . The general asks, "what transport have you got?" "A truck". "Then let's get to hell out of here. The British will be here in five minutes, they mustn't find us. We'll make a detour through the desert. I know the way."' Rommel regained his HQ safely and got on with the battles as if nothing had happened.

Rommel was very much a 'soldier's general', but it would be wrong to imagine that he was not as arrogant, as publicity-seeking or as difficult to handle as his future British opponent, Montgomery. In many ways they were very similar, although Rommel did not keep a photograph of his adversary stuck up in his command caravan as did Montgomery, nor did he specifically mention any of his many opponents by name in any of his diaries.

Tobruk was surrounded and cut off by 11th April, while the Germans and Italians drove the remnants of the British forces back towards Bardia and Sollum. Rommel had declared that his intention was to capture Cairo, but he was beginning to run out of steam, while the British were at least able to regain some control. 7th Armoured Division's Support Group held the frontier for some days, while 6th British Infantry Division and 7th Australian Division prepared a strong defensive position just west of Matruh.

Thus by 11th April, the British were back behind the Egyptian frontier wire, except for the small, stubborn force of two Australian brigades and the remnants of 3rd Armoured Brigade holed up in the battered fortress of Tobruk and ready to defend it against all comers. Apart from their determined stand, it had been a shattering defeat, Rommel having recaptured in just 12 days, all the ground Wavell had taken 50 to capture from the Italians. And to make matters worse, the British had lost their best field commander, Sir Richard O'Connor, plus Lt Gen Neame VC and Maj Gen Gambier-Parry, who had all been captured by the advancing enemy. They would spend the next three years as POWs in Italy, until the Italians surrendered. O'Connor was thus unfortunate to be unable to pit his wits against a worthy opponent like Rommel. He could certainly not be blamed for the fiasco in Cyrenaica as Neame was commanding and he was merely in a strange 'limbo' position as an advisor (Wavell's idea), but he certainly paid the price for reconnoitring too far forward without a proper escort. Neame and O'Connor had left Martuba to go back to XIII Corps HQ at Tmimi. However in the darkness their driver overshot the turning and instead of taking the track to Tmimi, drove on towards Derna. The two generals were asleep in the back of the car as they drove along, blissfully unaware of the danger. Wolfgang Everth who was commanding an armoured car company in 5 Leichte included the following description of what happened in a report he wrote later:

After the past strenuous days the generals dozed while a motorcycle patrol from the Commander's group overtook the staff car and stopped it. The English co-driver fired at once and killed one of our soldiers. The second soldier of the patrol fired a burst from his machine carbine – the British driver fell, the Generals raised their hands. When next morning in the POW area Gen O'Connor recognised the chief person involved, Feldwebel 'Kuttel' Borchardt, he presented him with his valuable camera with the words: 'Brave Soldier', but this would not give him pleasure for long, for two weeks later he fell at Tobruk.[8]

'Brevity' and 'Battleaxe' The Australian and other Commonwealth troops stubbornly defended Tobruk against all comers, so well that eventually Rommel was forbidden by Berlin to make any more attacks. Halder's deputy, Lt Gen Paulus, was sent out to make an on-the-spot report and instructed Rommel to regard the holding of Cyrenaica as his primary mission, regardless of whether or not he had Tobruk. OKH had rightly appreciated that the British would attack soon. Churchill was insistent that Wavell should begin an offensive to win back Cyrenaica and relieve Tobruk, and this led to the badly conceived 'Brevity' and 'Battleaxe' operations, which contained some of the bloodiest tank battles of the desert war and achieved very little except to give the Germans their own little 'Tobruk' in the form of the spirited and gallant defence of Halfaya Pass by a small garrison under Hauptmann Wilhelm Bach, who was awarded the Knight's Cross for his gallant action – on 15th June alone he knocked out eleven Matildas. Bach did not finally surrender until starvation forced him to do so on 17th January 1942, long after the rest of the DAK had been withdrawn.

Even before 'Battleaxe' began, the Eighth Army had lost an armoured commander who many informed historians consider would have been the greatest in the British Army. Lt Gen Vyvyan Pope CBE, DSO, MC was killed in an air crash in the desert in October 1941, when he was on his way to take command of XXXth Corps. This was to be the main armoured element of the newly formed Eighth Army and would together with XIIIth Corps form the main British striking force in the 'Battleaxe' operation. The one-armed Pope (he had lost his arm in France in March 1918 while serving with the North Staffords) did not have a chance to put his long-expounded theories of armoured warfare into practice, so we will never know his true potential. Of his senior staff, only Bill Liardet, then his AA and QMG survived, as he had stayed behind when the rest took off on their fatal flight. Liardet encapsulates Pope's thinking on the use of armour in a remark he makes in Ronald Lewin's biography of Pope, *Man of Armour*. 'VVP several times said to me that our biggest mistake in France and in the desert was to "penny packet" our armour. He said to me, "That is one thing I will never do. I will keep and fight the armour concentrated whatever happens."' How different might have been this period in the desert war had this been done!

'CRUSADER' One of the results of the failure of 'Brevity' and 'Battleaxe' was the replacement of Wavell by Gen Sir Claude Auchinleck, while the British and Empire troops in the desert were grouped together to form the Eighth Army under Lt Gen Sir Alan Cunningham. Almost immediately Auchinleck found himself under the same pressure from Churchill to mount another attack. The aims of the 'Crusader' operation were to relieve Tobruk and at the same time to destroy the bulk of the enemy armour and thus force Rommel to withdraw. The upshot was the major tank battle of Sidi Rezegh, in which both sides fought themselves to a standstill. This is how an RAF pilot who flew over the battlefield described the battle scene below him:

Guns were blazing on all sides as the land cruisers made for each other. It was impossible to pick out from our position which was which. Most of them were on the move, but there were several stationary and no longer firing. Several hundreds of them appeared engaged in a grim showdown. It was like looking down on some huge prehistoric arena with fire-breathing, scaly-sided monsters pitted against each other in a terrific struggle, lumbering slowly forward, swinging this way and that, each intent upon the destruction of the other. It must have been a concentrated hell of shell against shell and steel against steel.[9]

The casualties on both sides were extremely heavy. Although the Germans could be said to have won the battle at Sidi Rezegh, the eventual outcome of 'Crusader' was a territorial advantage to the British. In addition, Rommel had over-reached his lines of supply and was running short of everything. The elastic had stretched just that little too far and he was forced to order a general withdrawal, so that by the end of 1941 he was right back at El Aghelia, where he had started so confidently some nine months previously.

Just three weeks after he had withdrawn into Tripolitania, the Desert Fox was on the way forward again, bolstered up by the arrival of reinforcements. This time it was the British who were over-extended and vulnerable – witness the speed at which the DAK swept through the British positions until the front could be stabilized along the Gazala-Bir Hakeim line. For the next three months both sides built up their strength and then Rommel was off again, capturing Tobruk on 21st June 1942 (Hitler was so delighted that he made Rommel a field marshal) and driving the British right back to the El Alamein positions, well beyond the Egyptian frontier. This time, however, Rommel had really shot his bolt and his supply lines were once again seriously over-extended. He was short of everything – the 400 tanks with which he had started at Gazala were now down to under 50. Nevertheless, he attacked. By now he was also facing the new team of Alexander and Montgomery, the latter having issued an order that there was to be no withdrawal from the Alamein line in any circumstances. The Battle of Alam Halfa that followed was a watershed in the fortunes of the DAK. Rommel lost the battle, and was forced to withdraw a few miles and dig in. The British did not follow up, Montgomery sensibly deciding to build up his strength before making the major push. And, for the very first time in his military career, Rommel had to report sick; he flew home to Germany for treatment.

THE PANZERS AND THEIR COMMANDERS   Although the term 'Afrika Korps' is commonly used for the entire German forces in North Africa, these forces did in fact contain other elements. On 15th August 1941, for example, Rommel's command was raised to the status of a Panzergruppe, Rommel being promoted to full general at the remarkably young age of 49 (his 50th birthday was not until 15th November) By this time the DAK had been joined by a third division – 90 Leichte, while six Italian divisions (the Ariete, Trieste, Pavia, Bologna, Brescia and Savonia) were also put under Rommel's command. HQ Panzergruppe was at Beda Littoria, and although Rommel's command was, in theory anyway, under the direct control of the Italian CinC, it would always be commanded by a German and always kept intact. As the war progressed, other headquarters were formed, although the main German element remained as the DAK.

As this expansion took place, other Panzer generals arrived to serve under Rommel, and, while they took their cue from their commander, undoubtedly they individually had a major effect upon the battles that followed. Lt Gen Ludwig Cruewell, for example, took over as Commander DAK on 15th August

1941, remaining in command until 8th March 1942. Later, while command-ing the Italian front, his Storch light aircraft was shot down and he was captured, on 29th May 1942, during Rommel's second offensive. Brave and skilful, he was awarded Oakleaves to his Knight's Cross (won while command-ing 11 Pz Div in Russia) on 1st September 1941. It was he, rather than Rommel, who was the prime mover of the initial German successes during the 'Crusader' operations, Cruewell managing to get his Panzer forces deep into Cunningham's rear areas without detection and then to link up with the Italian Ariete and Trieste armoured divisions.

Another fine senior commander was Lt Gen Walther K. Nehring, who took over from Cruewell on 9th March 1942, remaining in command until he was wounded in the arm on 31st August 1942 during an air attack. Subsequently Nehring was to return to Africa, in November 1942, to assume command of all German forces in Tunisia. Later Stab Nehring changed its title to XC Korps, only to be absorbed into Panzer-Armeeoberkommando 5, which was formed to strengthen the command structure in Tunisia. Nehring remained in command until Generaloberst Jurgen von Arnim arrived on 9th December 1942. Nehring, who was later awarded both Oakleaves and Swords to his Knight's Cross, was without doubt both a brave and clever soldier.

The list of excellent panzer commanders at DAK level and below is a long one, the Germans quickly settling down to fighting in the desert, and, like the British, seeming to take to its hostile environment easily and to use its limited resources to the full. It was a tradition within the German Army to encourage individual initiative and independence on the battlefield, and this was most relevant during the fluid, mobile, fast-moving operations that typified desert warfare. Gustav von Vaerst, Wilhelm Ritter von Thoma, Gustav Fehn, Kurt Freiherr von Liebenstein, Heinz Zeigler and Hans Cramer all commanded the DAK, as did the ubiquitous Oberst Fritz Bayerlin (Stabschef of the Korps staff) who stood in twice on a temporary basis. They all used their initiative as and when required, but at the same time owed a great deal of their success to the well-established organization, tactics and war doctrine of the German Army, and, of course, to Rommel's overall dynamic leadership. The size of the panzer division was also just about right, its weapon systems were properly proportioned, so that the infantry element had the right amount of heavy weapons with which to hold the ground the tanks had captured, while its commander and staff had all the necessary means for command and control immediately available, so that they could carry out any tasks assigned to the division with the minimum of difficulty. Initially, British armoured divisions were lacking in all these respects.

In the main the DAK also fought an honourable war and this was recipro-cated. Desmond Young, in his book on Rommel, quotes one example which perhaps typifies the spirit of the desert war. Gen von Ravenstein, GOC 21st Panzer Division, was captured in November 1941 and taken to Cairo. There he was received by Gen Auchinleck, who told him, 'I know you well by name.

You and your division have fought with chivalry. I wish to treat you as well as possible.' For his part, von Ravenstein clearly was of a like mind. Before he left Cairo he heard that 'Jock' Campbell (then GOC 7th Armoured Division) had been awarded the VC and asked permission to write to him. The letter read:

I have read in the paper that you have been my brave adversary in the tank battle of Sidi Rezegh on 21–22 November 1942. It was my 21st Panzer Division which fought in those hot days with 7th Armoured Division, for whom I have the greatest admiration. Your 7th Support Group of Royal Artillery too made the fighting very hard for us and I remember all the many 'irons' that flew near the aerodrome around our ears. The German comrades congratulate you with a warm heart for your award of the Victoria Cross. During the war your enemy, but with high respect. Ravenstein.

BRITISH COMMANDERS   The Germans did not have a monopoly of brave armoured commanders, but it is clear that on the British side there was, until the arrival of Gen Montgomery, a decided lack of senior commanders who understood how to employ armoured forces properly. Monty brought out with him two new corps commanders, Sir Oliver Leese and Sir Brian Horrocks. To quote from Monty's Chief of Staff, Gen Sir Francis de Guingand: 'They were Montgomery's choice and I'm sure he never regretted it. They were both great Commanders, possessing drive and enthusiasm – in fact all the right qualities. Leese was more methodical and thorough, whilst Horrocks was more spectacular and colourful. I always used to think of him as Marshal Ney.'[10] Leese would take over XXX Corps from Gen Ramsden, while Horrocks took over XIII Corps after Gott was killed (see below). Monty's third corps commander was not his automatic choice, being Lt Gen Herbert Lumsden, a dashing 12th Lancer, whose corps was the designated 'corps de chasse' to provide the follow-up force once the breakthrough had been achieved at El Alamein. There was no love lost between him and Monty, who considered that he was not up to the job, so it was hardly surprising that he was replaced as soon as possible. This was not entirely fair, as Lumsden, who had been awarded an immediate DSO for his services in France as CO 12L, had been commander 28th Armoured Brigade and then 1st Armoured Division, before getting X Corps, and was an able armoured commander and an experienced desert warrior, who clearly resented Monty's tight personal control. Writing later in his memoirs about the dismissal Montgomery said: 'I also decided that as soon as X Corps was established in the Jebel I would bring Horrocks up to command it and would send Lumsden back to England. I had reached the conclusion that command of a corps in a major battle was above Lumsden's ceiling. On the other hand, he was a good trainer and as such he would be valuable back in England.' Monty then brought Gen Sir Miles Dempsey out to take over XXX Corps.

Gen Lumsden was not the only 12th Lancer to reach a high position in the desert. Maj Gen (later Lt Gen Sir) Richard McCreery had been chosen by Alexander as his Chief of Staff. As the history of the 12th Royal Lancers says: 'He was to come by his share of honours after other and later exploits, but it was in this unspectacular and unpublicized role that he showed himself stamped with the hall-mark of greatness.' McCreery would go on to command the Eighth Army in Italy.

At a lower level, 7th Armoured Division, for example, had a succession of able commanders, but the attrition rate was phenomenal. No fewer than eight GOCs followed 'Hobo', the first being Sir Michael O'More Creagh, who commanded during the defeat of the 10th Italian Army. He was followed by 'Strafer' Gott, who began his career with the division as its first GSO1. He went on to command XIII Corps and had been appointed to command the newly formed Eighth Army, but was killed when a German fighter shot down his aircraft on the way back from the front to Cairo. He survived the crash, but was killed by machine-gun fire while trying to rescue others from the wreckage. Montgomery was thus, like Rommel, second choice for the job which was to make him the most famous British soldier since Wellington. In the meantime the division had been taken over by the most famous Desert Rat of all – 'Jock' Campbell VC, DSO, MC – who had been responsible for conceiving the mobile harassing columns that then bore his name. He was killed when his staff car skidded and overturned near Halfaya Pass. Campbell had won his VC at the battle of Sidi Rezegh on 21st November 1941, commanding from an open, unprotected staff car, in which he stood, with a blue flag, forming up lines of tanks and then personally leading them into action. This is how Jake Wardrop, then a tank driver in 5th RTR, described his actions during the battle:

There were tanks and lorries all over the place, some blazing, guns firing and the whole place covered with a fine cloud of dust. On the landing ground there were planes burning, and others destroyed – what a mess! Nobody seemed to have much idea of what was going on and we milled around for a bit.

Just about that time Jock Campbell arrived and took over the whole show. He came running up in a car, shouted over 'Follow me' and we chased after him for about half a mile round the airfield and there they were – a long line of Mark IIIs and fifty millimeter anti-tank guns, so we went to town on them.

Campbell's sentiments were that enemy tanks should be charged at all times. Protests were met with the reply: 'That's what you are soldiers for – to die!' Indeed one officer summed up the situation very well, when he said that most of them were far more scared of 'Jock' Campbell than they were of the enemy!

Campbell was followed by Sir Frank Messervy, who had been commanding 4th Indian Division and, despite his undoubted personal bravery, was not really an armoured commander. He had the doubtful distinction of having his Div HQ captured during the 'Gazala Gallop', but managed to escape and walk back to British lines. He was followed by Callum Renton, known affectionately as 'Wingy' due to the loss of an arm during the battle of Sid Saleh. Next to command was probably one of the finest armoured commanders of all, John Harding (later FM Lord Harding of Petherton) who had been Chief of Staff to Gen O'Connor. A fearless and brilliant armoured commander, he was responsible for the division's breakout at El Alamein, but was wounded soon afterwards. He possessed great physical and intellectual courage and was strong-willed and persistent – Montgomery called him 'that little tiger'. When he was wounded, his place was taken for a short time by Brig (later Maj Gen) 'Pip' Roberts, who went on to command 11th Armoured Division for the Normandy campaign. The last commander of the Division in North Africa was Gen 'Bobbie' Erskine who went on after the war to be CinC East Africa during the Mau-Mau rebellion.

It was no different among the other divisions, where there were some excellent commanders, men like Gatehouse, Briggs, Birks, Richards and Roberts (a divisional commander when he was barely 37). However, unlike their opponents, the British did not have the same tried and tested organization and tactics to follow. Instead of using tanks as part of an all-arms team – which was at the heart of the success of blitzkrieg tactics – the British commanders were much more likely to use their tanks in unsupported 'cavalry charges', with the result that many were lost needlessly. Until the arrival of Montgomery there was no really strong central command, orders were usually a basis for discussion and, as an American historian, Dr Sherwood S Cordier, put it in an article in *Armor* magazine: '. . . lack of strong, central command fatally marred the efforts of British armies. Many reasons are advanced to explain this. Infantry and tank officers regarded each other with distrust if not downright antagonism. Even among tank officers, the holy odor of the horse clung to British armor, as reluctantly converted cavalrymen dubbed their command tanks "chargers" and rode into the fray with their whips out.'

'Monty'

In his book *From the Desert to the Baltic*, Gen 'Pip' Roberts tells of his first meeting with General Montgomery. Roberts was commanding 22nd Armoured Brigade at Alam Halfa and had been told to expect a visit from the new GOC in C Eighth Army one morning in August 1942. Roberts was at the time suffering from 'gyppy tummy' and had just returned from behind the nearest ridge with his spade, when he saw a large party arriving. He recognized Horrocks, Erskine and de Guingand, but not the 'little man with white knobbly knees, an Australian hat and no badges of rank', whom he took to be a newly arrived war correspondent. He concluded that Monty would be arriving later and was just about to inquire when the Great Man would appear when the man in the Australian hat said, 'Do you know who I am?' Roberts sensibly replied, 'Yes, Sir', reasoning that whoever he was it was better to know. 'And of course it was Monty!'

Monty for his part realized that he must take command of his Army and not allow his orders to be merely a 'basis for discussion' as had been the case before his arrival. As he says in his memoirs: 'I had taken command of truly magnificent material; it did not take me long to see that. The Eighth Army was composed of veteran fighting divisions. But officers and men were bewildered at what had happened and this had led to a loss of confidence, "Brave but baffled" the Prime Minister had called them.'

It would be wrong to consider Montgomery as a commander who had been trained in tank warfare at a lower level, as he had no previous experience of using tanks until he took over the Eighth Army. Although he afterwards on occasions used a converted M3 Grant tank as a command post, he had had no basic tank training, nor had he ever handled armour in the field, as had his opponent Rommel. Nevertheless, as the battle of El Alamein showed, he planned and prepared for the battle with meticulous thoroughness, ensured that he had an overwhelming superiority of men and material – in particular tanks[11] – and conducted the battle with firmness and resolution. Clearly Monty had an affinity with tankmen and even took to wearing their black beret, which suited him well and soon became his best-known trademark. As Lord Chalfont says in his biography of Montgomery: 'Photographs of Mongtomery in regulation headgear, in bush hat and in beret show the progression from a somewhat awkward-looking little man to the assured almost rakish figure which has passed into history.' Montgomery fully merits his place in this book as a great tank commander. Certainly no other British commander had used so much armour before in a major operation, nor had the undoubted success with armour that Montgomery achieved against one of the most skilled armoured soldiers of WW2.

By the end of the campaign in North Africa, Montgomery had: 'moulded Eighth Army in his own image; he had established the central points of his military creed – an effective chain of command and a devoted army.'[12]

SPRINGBOKS IN ARMOUR None of the Commonwealth countries had armoured divisions in North Africa, but the 6th Australian Divisional Cavalry Regiment served there and the South African Tank Corps produced some excellent armoured car regiments and reconnaissance battalions to fight in the Western Desert and Cyrenaica in 1941–2. Earlier, in the deserts and high mountains of Abyssinia, they had contributed greatly to the success of the campaign against the Italians. The strength of the armoured car regiments was based upon the South African Marmon-Herrington armoured car, designed by Capt D.R. Ryder. The first to go into action was B Squadron of the 4th SA Armoured Car Regiment, under the command of the 11th Hussars, which led the 7th Armoured Division's advance on Fort Capuzzo. The SA Armoured Car Regiment suffered badly at Sidi Rezegh, but continued to take part in operations right up to the capture of Benghazi in November 1942. Early the following year it was decided to disband the Tank Corps and to absorb its men into the newly forming 6th South African Armoured Division, which went on to fight in Italy.

El Alamein

On Friday 23rd October 1942, Operation 'Lightfoot', the second and most famous battle of El Alamein, opened. The massive artillery barrage that preceded the initial attacks began at 2140 hours. The German soldiers who faced this barrage described it as 'the Inferno', so great was the weight of artillery shells fired from over 1,000 guns. For his part, Monty was fast asleep in his caravan when the battle began. All his meticulous planning and preparation was over and he realized that he could not do anything to influence events, so might as well get some sleep, because, as he put it in his memoirs, he would probably be needed later! Montgomery was calm and confident, in charge of the situation and exactly in the right place, while his main opponent was still convalescing in Austria when the battle began. As soon as Rommel heard about the British offensive he rushed to Weiner-Neustad airfield and waited there anxiously for his specially converted Heinkel He III to arrive. Gen der Kavallerie Georg Stumme, who had been left in command, had in the meantime died of a heart attack, falling from his vehicle while visiting the frontline on 24th October. His place had been taken by the tall, ascetic Lt Gen Ritter von Thoma,[13] then commanding the DAK. Rommel returned on the following day and at 2325 hours on 25th October sent out a signal: 'I have taken command of the army again.'

The battle did not go well for the Germans. Rommel wanted to manoeuvre, but was restrained by the 'Victory or Death' signal he had received from Adolf Hitler: 'The German people, in company with myself, are following your heroic defensive struggle in Egypt with devout trust in your personal leadership and the bravery of the German and Italian troops who serve you. In your present situation you can have no other thought than to hold out, refuse to yield a step and commit to the battle every weapon and every soldier who can be released from other duties . . .'. FM Kesselring, CinC South (Italy) visited Rommel on 4th November and suggested that he explain to the Führer how outnumbered his forces were and that the only chance of retaining a foothold in North Africa would be to carry out a fighting withdrawal. Rommel had already decided to disobey Hitler's order, even before Kesselring's visit, 'My men's lives come first', he had told his Chief of Staff, Siegfried Westphal. In the end Hitler approved a withdrawal, but not before the DAK had suffered badly, being at one point down to only 21 battleworthy tanks.

Although some of Montgomery's armour was used in the breakthrough battle, the armoured divisions did not really come into their own until the Afrika Korps was forced to give ground. Thereafter they were always on the move, pressing the enemy back towards Tunisia. However, Rommel and his men fought every inch of the way, defending every suitable position, inflicting casualties and never letting the withdrawal become a rout. Rommel's part in this fighting withdrawal was paramount and he used every method he could devise to slow up and weaken the advancing British forces: 'Now the pursuit became a nightmare for the enemy – dummy minefields sown with scrap metal alternated with the real thing, arranged with fiendish ingenuity to lull and kill and destroy and maim. Abandoned buildings were booby-trapped with explosives that detonated when lavatory handles were flushed, or when crooked pictures were straightened . . .'.[14] Hitler promised to restore the depleted DAK to its original strength, but his promises were always empty ones, the campaign in North Africa taking a very definite second place to 'Barbarossa' and the Führer's personal battle with the hated Russians.

Operation 'Torch'

While the Panzerarmee Afrika was carrying out its stubborn fighting withdrawal through Cyrenaica and Tripolitania, a new threat had appeared behind them in the shape of the Allied landings on the coasts of Algeria and Morocco. Three task forces, totalling some 107,000 troops, were involved, under the overall command of Gen Dwight D Eisenhower. The western task force, which had the job of occupying French Morocco, was commanded by Gen George S. Patton, who was thirsting to get into a real shooting war. The plan was for the three task forces to strike simultaneously – Gen Ryder in the east landing at Algiers, Gen Fredenhall in the centre at Oran and Gen Patton at Casablanca. Patton's orders were to secure the port and its adjacent airfields and maintain communications between Casablanca and Oran in conjunction with the centre task force. A secondary task was to build up forces with a view to securing Spanish Morocco if that became necessary. Patton's force, which had sailed from Norfolk, Virginia (the others sailed from the UK), contained some 24,000 men, while their potential enemy in Morocco was estimated at up to 100,000 French and a similar number of Spaniards.

Almost from the outset of the planning stage, Patton fell out with Rear Adml Hewitt, commander of the western naval task force, who went so far as to say that unless the Army sacked Patton the US Navy should pull out. Although they patched things up to some degree, Patton did not help matters by announcing at the final briefing: 'Never in recorded history has the navy put the army ashore at the planned time and place. But if you manage to land me anywhere within 50 miles of Fedala, and a week of D Day, I'll go in and win!'

As Gen Essame pointed out in his book, *Patton, the Commander*, Patton's message to his troops when they were safely on board the troopships and unable to breach security was vintage Patton prose:

We are now on our way to force a landing on the coast of North West Africa. We are to be congratulated because we have been chosen as the units of the United States Army to take part in this great American effort.

Our mission is threefold. First to capture a beach-head, second to capture the city of Casablanca, third to move against the German wherever he may be and destroy him. . . .

We may be opposed by a limited number of Germans. It is not known whether the French Army will contest our landing. It is regrettable to contemplate the necessity of fighting the gallant French, who are at heart sympathetic, but all resistance, by whomever offered, must be destroyed.

When the great day of battle comes, remember your training and remember that speed and vigour of attack are the sure roads to success. And you must succeed, for to retreat is as cowardly as it is fatal. Americans do not surrender. During the first days and nights after you get ashore you must work unceasingly, regardless of sleep, regardless of food. A pint of sweat will save a gallon of blood.

The eyes of the world are watching us. . . . God is with us. . . . We will surely win.

Patton's comments about being landed in the wrong place unfortunately proved all too prophetic. An unknown coastal current had made a nonsense of naval navigation and the fleet found itself in the early hours of 8th November about six miles from its correct position, with a much longer run-in to the beaches. The surf was much heavier than expected and many landing craft were swamped and their occupants drowned. Many landed in the wrong places and all found themselves under heavy artillery and machine-gun fire. To make matters worse, the French battleship *Jean Bart* opened fire, followed later by an attack on the convoy by seven French destroyers. This latter event took place precisely when Patton was trying to get ashore. It resulted in him losing all his shore-going baggage and delayed him getting ashore. When he did land he found much to complain about. The assault waves had gone through, but the follow-up troops, who should have been unloading supplies and sending them forward, were too busy digging foxholes in order to escape from the enemy fire. No doubt Patton had to 'kick a lot of ass' in order to get things organized, personally going up and down the beach berating the soldiers and sailors and galvanizing them into action by the force of his personality. He had to repeat the process the following day, when he discovered that only a fraction of the supplies that had been brought ashore the previous day had been moved forward. While Patton was sorting out the beach-head, his leading troops had fought their first tank *v* tank action – not much of a contest, as it involved an American force containing seven M3 light tanks and a French detachment with 18 WW1-vintage Renault Ft 17s. The M3's 37mm guns soon made short work of the enemy tanks and put the infantry to flight.

The other two landings had a much easier time and by the evening of the 9th only Patton's objectives remained to be taken. Fortunately, the French decided to surrender just before Patton's planned all-out attack was due to take place, which saved a great deal of unnecessary bloodshed. In his diary Patton recorded that the hours from 7.30 to 11 on 11th November (his 57th birthday) as his troops moved forward into Casablanca: '. . . were the longest of my life.' Patton soon discovered that the easy part was over and that he was now forced to become a diplomat and work out peace terms which would satisfy both sides and leave French honour untarnished. Remarkably, this is exactly what he managed to do, the conference finishing in an atmosphere of relief and mutual cordiality. It had been agreed that the Americans would take over only what they needed to continue the war against the Axis, while the French troops would be confined to barracks but not disarmed, POWs would be exchanged and no-one punished for helping either side. Essame says that Patton behaved like 'the good and generous soldier, but politically naive man he was', which is probably as accurate a summation as any. In other words 'forgive and forget', with the Stars and Stripes and Tricolor flying side by side, a policy which would lead to many problems as the French commander (Gen Nogues) was playing a double game, being in touch with both Vichy France and the Germans, while appearing to be the friend of the Allies.

Patton versus Rommel

It must have been a great relief for Patton to leave this nest of intrigue and double-dealing when, in February 1943, he was ordered by Eisenhower to take command of II Corps in Tunisia from Gen Fredendall, who had lost control when the Germans suddenly attacked in the area of Kasserine Pass and Gafsa, while still holding the Eighth Army at bay along the Mareth Line. *Fruehlingswind* ('Spring Breeze'), the first offensive, was launched through the Faid Pass against Sidi bou Zid on 14th February by von Arnim's 10th and 21st Panzer Divisions. *Morgenluft* ('Morning Air') followed two days later when the DAK attacked in strength through Gafsa. Rommel's aim was to cause maximum casualties and confusion among the green American troops. If their luck held, then the German forces might even be able to cut right behind the Allied lines and destroy their main bases at Bone and Constantine. However, there was little love lost between von Arnim (then Commander of the Pz AOK 5 in Tunisia) and Rommel, who were complete opposites – the aristocratic von Arnim from the established officer class hated the 'upstart Swabian'. In addition, there was little co-ordination between the two armies (Heeresgruppe Afrika was not formed until 23rd February), so there was never much chance of the Axis actually achieving their major aims.

Nevertheless, there was a desperate situation at the front. American soldiers had panicked at their first taste of the German blitzkrieg and Eisenhower had no hesitation in sending Patton to do the job no other American general in the theatre was capable of doing – to get a grip on the American troops, stabilize the situation and then prepare them for an offensive to retake Gafsa on 17th March. Patton put his finger on the root cause of the problem, namely indiscipline among the easy-going, green GIs. His arrival in the corps area has been likened to 'Moses descending from Mount Ararat', but instead of the Ten Commandments he brought as his text severe discipline of the kind only he could administer, as he motored around all the units of the Corps, 'displaying the largest stars his aides could produce, escorted by scout cars and half-tracks bristling with machine guns and to the accompaniment of screeching sirens, armed to the teeth, he swooped down on every single battalion of his four divisions.'[15]

This was the visible face of Patton, the one that got all the publicity. However, at the same time he was running his staff ragged, making them work long hours getting supplies for the corps – new tanks, vehicles, equipment, uniforms and rations. Patton made sure that whatever was required was available precisely where it was needed. He also instituted an all-out drive on training and preparation for battle, so that everyone would be ready when the offensive began. Eisenhower's representative at HQ II Corps, Gen Omar Bradley, was then appointed as Patton's deputy (their positions would be reversed later in the war), bringing together for the first time these two outstanding soldiers. In his autobiography FM Alexander says of them: 'Both were good soldiers. Patton was a thruster, prepared to take any risks; Bradley . . . was more cautious. Patton should have lived during the Napoleonic Wars – he would have been a splendid Marshal under Napoleon.' Patton was certainly thirsting for action, but it was necessary to restrain him until a co-ordinated plan could be worked out with the British. Montgomery would put in a major assault on the Mareth Line, break through and push Rommel back to Tunis, while Patton would provide support by tying down as many German and Italian formations as possible.

When the battle began Eisenhower had the greatest difficulty in stopping Patton from continually leading his troops from the front. Typical was his action on 7th April, when he discovered that one of his tank/infantry battle groups was held up by a minefield and that the commander was reluctant to move forward. After berating him on the radio without success, Patton drove forward and personally led the way through the minefield and on until they were only some 45 miles from Gabes. After ordering the commander to 'keep going for a fight or a bath', Patton reluctantly returned to his headquarters. Later, during a similar incident in an anti-personnel minefield, he sacked the commander on the spot and sent him to the rear.

On the other side Rommel was behaving in much the same way. Capt Alfred Berndt (Rommel's chief aide) wrote to Rommel's wife, 'You should have seen their eyes light up as he suddenly appeared, just like the old days, among the very foremost infantry and tanks, in the midst of their attack, and hit the dirt just like the riflemen when the enemy's artillery opened up! What other commander is there who can call on such respect!'

'OLD GRAVEL VOICE' At the same time as Patton took over operational command of US II Corps, Maj Gen Ernest N. Harmon took over as CG of 1st Armored Division. Gen Bradley was later to write of him: 'The profane and hot-tempered Ernest N. Harmon brought to corps the rare combination of sound tactical judgement and boldness that together make a great commander. More than any other division commander in North Africa, he was constantly aggressive; in Europe he was to become our most outstanding tank commander.' Ernie Harmon was a West Point graduate in 1917, finishing the war as a young cavalry captain, gaining battle experience in the St Mihiel and Argonne offensives. Between the wars he took part in the Olympic Military Pentathlon of 1924 and made the momentous decision to transfer from the cavalry to the under-manned, only partially equipped, Armored Force. He prospered in the new force and, as it expanded was promoted steadily, until in 1942 he was selected to command 2nd Armored Division.

His transfer to 1st Armored in February 1943 came about in an unusual way. Eisenhower sent him to investigate and report on the British complaints about bad leadership at HQ US II Corps, which Harmon found to be correct and so reported, the outcome being that Patton replaced Fredendall.

Harmon then went back to 2nd Armored, then training in Morocco. However, the following month he was on his way back again to Tunisia to take over the 1st.[17] 'Old Gravel Voice', as he was affectionately known, did not initially find life easy under Patton and quickly crossed swords with him, after deciding to step up the tempo of operations and attack the Germans more effectively.

The End in Africa

It was only a matter of time before the Axis forces would be swamped by the pressure from both flanks. The link-up between the two fronts was achieved and the enemy forced into a tight perimeter around the coastal plain in the Tunis-Bizerta area. Both the Eighth and First Armies had been reinforced. The reinforcements to the First Army had included IX Corps, commanded by Gen John Crocker, although only one of the two armoured divisions (6th) was sent out initially, the other (11th) and Corps HQ did not get there until mid-February. At one stage it looked as though 'Hobo', who had formed and trained 11th Armoured Division, would command the division under his young former brigade major, but at the last minute the 57-year old Hobart was once again denied his chance to lead an armoured division in battle, being removed by the War Office and retained in UK instead, in order to train the newly forming 79th Armoured Division.

Rommel, sick in body and mind, was not there when the end came, having flown back to see Hitler and beg him to rescue his gallant 'Africans'. The Führer refused and then would not allow Rommel to return – Germany could not afford to lose its great folk hero to the ignominy of a POW cage. Hitler made amends by awarding him the Diamonds to his Knight's Cross.

Patton also was not in at the kill, having handed over his corps to Bradley on 16th April, in order to return to Rabat to join in planning the invasion of Sicily, an operation in which he would be commanding an army.

Only Monty was there at the end, his Desert Rats having the great satisfaction of being the first troops into Tunis. Organized resistance ended on 12th May, some 248,000 Axis troops being taken prisoner. The last message from the DAK read: 'Ammunition shot off. Arms and equipment destroyed. In accordance with orders received the Afrika Korps has fought itself to the condition where it can fight no more. The German Afrika Korps must rise again. Heia Safari! Cramer, General Commanding.' About the same time Alexander sent a signal to Churchill: 'Sir, it is my duty to report that the Tunisian campaign is over. All enemy resistance has ceased. We are masters of the North African shores.'

It is perhaps only right therefore to let Montgomery, who had fought so long and so hard, to have the last word:

One of the big lessons I learnt from the campaign in Africa was the need to decide what you want to do and then to do it. One must never be drawn off the job in hand by gratuitous responsibility.

91

My great supporter throughout was Alexander. He never bothered me, never fussed me, never suggested what I ought to do, and gave me at once everything I asked for – having listened patiently to my explanation of why I wanted it. But he was too big to require explanations; he gave me trust. My upbringing as a child had taught me to have resource within myself. I needed it in the desert campaign. I was also taught to count my blessings, and this I certainly did.[18]

NOTES TO CHAPTER 5

1 Quoted in *The Tanks*, Vol. 1

2 *ibid.*

3 Balbo was also very popular with the British, the RAF dropping a wreath, with a note of condolence, on the following day.

4 There were plenty of Italian spies in Cairo, but in their efforts to please their masters they were prone to exaggeration, so Graziani had really no inkling of the true situation.

5 In fact the symbol was the Greater Egyptian Jerboa (*Jaculus orientalis*), which, after much searching, Mrs Creagh and Mrs Peyton (wife of Gen Creagh's GSO3) had found in the Cairo Zoo. They drew its likeness on a sheet of hotel notepaper!

6 A Support Group in those days comprised the division's infantry battalions and artillery.

7 B.H. Liddell-Hart, *The Rommel Papers*

8 As quoted in George Forty, *Afrika Korps at War*

9 *The Second Great War* (edited by Sir John Hammerton)

10 F. de Guingand, *Operation Victory*

11 Montgomery had an army of 195,000 men while Rommel had only 104,000, of which one-third were Italians. Rommel had only half as many tanks (527 to 1029) and while there were 849 of the new 6pdr anti-tank guns in the Eighth Army, Rommel had just 24 of the famous 88s available. Even in the air the Desert Air Force was superior in numbers and quality of aircraft.

12 Alun Chalfont, *Montgomery of Alamein*

13 Von Thoma would be captured by the British a few days later, having decided to desert. David Irving, in his book *The Trail of the Fox*, tells how von Thoma had put on all his medals, denounced Hitler's 'Stand Fast' as lunacy and driven off in a tank 'to the focus of the battle'. Col Bayerlein had driven after him and 'an hour later found a cemetery of blazing tanks, corpses and wrecked anti-tank guns.' From 200 yards away he had seen the general's tall, gaunt figure standing erect near a flaming tank, his little canvas satchel in his hand, as the British tanks converged on him.'

14 David Irving, *Trail of the Fox*

15 Maj Gen H. Essame, *Patton, the Commander*

16 H.W. Schmidt, *With Rommel in the Desert*

17 To quote from 1st Armored's history: 'The Division was tired, frustrated and depressed, its reputation in higher headquarters was suffering, and in response to Alexander's request and his own misgivings, Patton determined to give the Division a new commander to build it up again.'

18 *Memoirs*

6 THE RUSSIAN FRONT

Hitler was so impressed by the speed and effectiveness of his panzer divisions and by their superlative commanders that he undoubtedly allowed their performance in Poland and France to colour his judgement in deciding to attack his erstwhile ally Russia. Of course, this was only a contributory factor, as the Führer had been looking eastwards for the *lebensraum* (living space) the German people needed from as early as 1928.[1] Ever since the Nazi-Soviet non-aggression pact had been signed in August 1939, he had also become more and more convinced that sooner or later the Soviets would abandon the pact and join his enemies. War with Russia was thus inevitable and to postpone it for too long would just make the task all the more difficult, although as far as he was concerned the outcome was never in doubt. Russia's poor performance against Finland had further convinced him that the Red Army was no match for the Wehrmacht, despite its vast reserves of manpower. On paper, the Soviets had an overwhelming superiority of at least four to one, but there was a great deal wrong with the Soviet armed forces, as Hitler knew, and this must have further coloured his judgement. All these factors caused him to make the fatal decision that, above all others, would cost Germany final victory and bring about the fall of the Third Reich. At first, though, all went well for Hitler, as the German armies exploited the Soviet difficulties and deficiencies.

Soviet Problems

Foremost among the Soviet problems was the effect of the terrible purge that Stalin had instituted in 1937. This had led to the removal and execution of a number of those who had supported the 'reactionary, decadent, capitalistic' theories of mobile warfare such as those expounded by Liddell Hart. So able men like Tukhachevsky and Kalinovsky were put to death, leaving a grave shortage of experienced armoured officers which had still not been filled by 1940. To quote from an article which appeared some years ago in the Red Army magazine, *Soviet Military Review*: 'When the German forces attacked the USSR, the Soviet Army was in urgent need of experienced commanders of a higher echelon, who understood the nature of contemporary war. Many of the officers promoted to high command posts in 1937–1940 did not meet the requirements of the times: some of them lacked military knowledge, others combat experience.'

One such over-promoted officer was Gen Dmitry Pavlov, self-styled Russian Guderian, who had been so scornful about the performance of tanks in Spain. It was thanks to his influence that the mechanized units formed after the Revolution had been broken up and the tanks spread out in 'penny packets' to support infantry divisions on the French model. The poor showing of the Red Army in the Russo-Finnish war came as a great shock and forced a sudden volte-face upon the Soviets. A new policy for reversing the decline in armoured formations was hastily put into action, but was far from complete when the Germans attacked. The reorganization was started by the new Chief Marshal of Armoured Forces, Pavel Alexandrovich Rotmistrov, who has since become recognized as one of Russia's leading tank experts. Rotmistrov was born into a peasant family in 1901, in the village of Skovorovo in the province of Kalinin. He became a member of both the Soviet Army and of the Communist Party in 1919, and fought in the Civil War. Graduating from the Frunze Military Academy in 1931, he served as a brigade, corps and army commander, displaying great bravery and leadership especially while commanding 5th Guards Tank Army in the Kursk battle (see later). At a meeting in 1939 he expressed his views on how armour should be used: '. . . tanks must be employed in masses. The best situation for a tank commander is to be in command of large groups – a brigade, a corps, an army. These are splendid instruments in the offensive. A concentration of a thousand tanks – this is the dream of every tank commander!'[2] Thus, a major reorganization was still in train when the German assault came, and too few of the new mechanized corps were in existence.

When the Germans attacked, a very large proportion of the Red Army – 15 of its armies – was stationed in the frontier districts of the Soviet Union, and were thus ripe for immediate attack and encirclement by the Germans. Hitler's Directive No 21, of 18th December 1940, which spelt out for the first time his decision to attack Russia, contained the words: 'The bulk of the Russian Army stationed in Western Russia will be destroyed by daring operations led by deeply penetrating armoured spearheads. Russian forces still capable of giving battle will be prevented from withdrawing into the depths of Russia.' Stalin apparently ignored all warning signs about the impending German attack, including well-founded information from many diplomatic sources, and appears to have completely misread what was about to happen.

At the start of the Great Patriotic War, Russia had far too many different types of tanks in service. The policy to standardize on just three models – light, medium and heavy – had yet to take effect. Many of the tanks in front-line service were old models, obsolescent and virtually useless, while there was a general shortage of modern tanks. For example, of the 2,794 tanks built by USSR in 1940, only 115 were T34s (then Russia's latest and most powerful medium tank). In addition, repair and recovery were not at all well organized, while all too many of the various types of tanks were notoriously difficult to keep on the road. Tanks were not the only problem either; the Red Army lacked adequate signals equipment, was short of field and anti-tank artillery, and was, in main, poorly trained at all levels. Thus, although the Red Army could boast having 4½ million men under arms in June 1941, with over 20,000 tanks and over 14,000 aircraft, much of this apparent strength was merely useless cannon-fodder.

German Dissent

Guderian first heard about 'Barbarossa', the code name for the invasion plan, when Lt Col Freiherr von Leiberstein, his Chief of Staff, and Maj Fritz Bayerlin, his First General Staff Officer, returned from a conference at OKH in late 1940. He tells in his autobiography how they spread out a map of Russia before him and explained what Hitler had in mind. Guderian was amazed. 'I could scarcely believe my eyes,' he wrote, 'Was something which I had held to be utterly impossible now to become fact? . . . I made no attempt to conceal my disappointment and disgust.'3 Guderian goes on to explain how all Hitler's senior soldiers had warned him over and over again about starting to fight a war on two fronts. Guderian's staff officers were, however, quite surprised by his attitude, having been convinced by the Chief of the Army General Staff, Gen Franz Halder, that the Soviets would be beaten in a campaign lasting a mere eight to ten weeks. Three army groups would attack on three different axes and with three differing objectives. 'Looked at from a professional point of view this did not appear at all promising,' Guderian comments. He arranged for his views to be conveyed to the OKH, but they produced no effect whatsoever, so great was the unshakable optimism at OKH and OKW alike. Like the good soldier he was, Guderian therefore got on with the job of preparing his panzer forces for the inevitable attack, commenting wryly that 'Our successes to date, however, and in particular the surprising speed of our victory in the West, had so befuddled the minds of our supreme commanders that they had eliminated the word "impossible" from their vocabulary'.4

Clearly Guderian was not the only field commander to disagree with his Führer, although he was perhaps the only one brave enough to voice his comments. Others have done so in retrospect, although, to be fair to them, they may not have been in such a privileged position as Guderian. Erich von Manstein, architect of the final 'Fall Gelb' plan that had worked so successfully in France and Belgium, was not privy to the planning of 'Barbarossa'. As he explains in his memoirs, he had only been appointed to command LVI Panzer Corps in February 1941, which had for him: 'fulfilled a wish I had cherished even before the campaign in the west – to command a mechanised army corps.' Thus at this relatively low level he did not find out about the campaign until he received his own operation order in May 1941, and was then far more concerned with the immediate commitments of the panzer group to which his corps belonged than to query high strategy. It is clear from his comments that he considered Hitler's major mistake was in under-rating the resources of the USSR and the fighting qualities of the Red

Army. The toughness of the Soviet system, their apparent indifference to suffering, casualties and living conditions, made them a much more formidable enemy than the Germans realized. To Hitler they were just despised *Untermenschen* (sub-humans), to be beaten, raped and pillaged into submission. When the Germans first attacked they were in some regions welcomed with open arms by the people, who were genuinely pleased to be freed from 'the yoke of Communism'. However, instead of fostering this, the German follow-up forces deliberately set about alienating the local population by their harsh and repressive measures.

Operation 'Barbarossa'

The frontage on which the Germans would launch their attack was some 2,000 miles in length, stretching from the Baltic at Memel down to the Black Sea. In the centre were the Pripet Marshes, which roughly divided the front into two halves. The main German attack was to be to the north of the marshes; there Army Group North (26 divisions) and Army Group Centre (51 divisions) would attack, while south of the marshes was Army Group South (59 divisions). Army Group North, commanded by FM Ritter von Leeb, had Leningrad as its main objective. An artilleryman and one of the old school (Hitler had once called him an 'incorrigible anti-Nazi'), he had been promoted field marshal in July 1940, after his army group in France had played a steady but unspectacular part in the victory. He had had a single panzer group of three divisions under Gen Erich Hoepner, who was considered by some to be every bit as good an armoured commander as Guderian. He had done well in Poland and France, and is described by Brett-Smith in his book *Hitler's Generals* as being an outspoken, honest, no-nonsense character, and 'not one to appeal to a leader whose military abilities were lower than his own'. Later in his career, when 4th Panzer Group was enlarged to become 4th Panzer Army, he became an army commander, but was dismissed for supposed failure in the attempt to take Moscow in 1942. Army Group North was opposed by the Soviet North West Front (8th and 11th Armies) under Col Gen F.I. Kuznetsov, which contained an almost equal number of divisions, including four tank divisions.

Army Group Centre commanded by FM Fedor von Bock, which contained nine panzer divisions divided into two Panzer groups, was to drive along the axis Minsk-Smolensk towards the ultimate prize of Moscow. Initially, however, they would surround and destroy the Russian West Front (3rd, 4th and 10th Armies) under Pavlov, which contained 38 divisions (including eight tank divisions). The panzer groups were II, commanded by Guderian, and III, under Hoth, so clearly it was the strongest of the three army groups, although not the largest numerically. This left Army Group South under FM Karl Rudolf Gerd von Rundstedt, which, although it totalled 59 divisions, contained 14 Rumanian and two Hungarian divisions, plus five panzer divisions in von Kleist's Panzer Group I. Opposing them were the South West Front

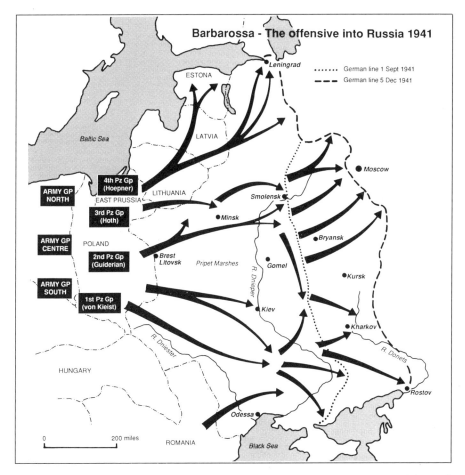

Barbarossa - The offensive into Russia 1941

```
....... German line 1 Sept 1941
- - - German line 5 Dec 1941
```

(5th, 6th, 12th and 26th Armies) under Gen M.P. Kirponos, comprising 56 divisions including 16 tank divisions, and the South Front (9th Army) under Gen I.V. Tulenev, down to the shores of the Black Sea, with 16 divisions including four tank divisions. Army Group South's objective was Kiev.

The Assault

The assault began at 0315 hours on 22nd June 1941 – exactly a year after the French had signed the surrender at Compiègne. It achieved almost total tactical surprise, despite the fact that the German build-up must have been blindingly obvious to everyone on both sides of the border. Stalin had prohibited any reinforcement or other action that could be construed as aggressive, not wanting to provoke the Germans. Guderian watched the opening barrage from an observation tower south of Bohkaly, some nine miles northwest of Brest-Litovsk, where his Panzer Group Command Post was located. It was still dark when he got there at 0310 hours. He recalled: 'At 0315 hrs our artillery opened up. At

97

0340 hrs the first dive-bomber attack went in. At 0415 hrs, advance units of the 17th and 18th Panzer divisions began to cross the Bug. At 0445 hrs the leading tanks of the 18th Panzer Division forded the river.'5

Guderian goes on to mention that the tanks were equipped with water-proofing that had been developed for Operation 'Sea-Lion' (the invasion of England that never came about), which enabled them to schnorkel in depths of up to 50ft of water and to remain submerged for some 20 minutes.

Guderian himself crossed at 0650 hours in an assault boat, but had to wait until 0830 hours before his command vehicles and staff arrived and he could press on, following in the tracks of his leading panzers. He recalls that he soon reached a bridge over the Lesna, which was most important to the advance of his XLVII Panzer Corps who were on the left wing. He found nobody there except for some Russian pickets, who took to their heels when Guderian's HQ group arrived. The leading tanks arrived at 1025 hours and crossed, followed by the divisional commander Gen Walter Nehring (later to command the DAK under Rommel). Guderian was fortunate to have men of his calibre, but almost everyone in his Panzer Group was of an extremely high standard, from the highest – his four Corps commanders, von Geyr (XXIV), Schroth (XII), Lemelsen (XLVII) and von Vietinghoff (XLVI) – down to the individual tank crews and Panzergrenadiers. A measure of their success can be gauged by the fact that they advanced all the way to the Dnieper in just seven days.

As always, Guderian was up at the sharp end, dodging Russian tanks and constantly under fire. At one stage, while visiting 18th Panzer Division's forward tank platoons (fortunately in a Panzer IV), he unexpectedly found himself in the middle of a crowd of Russian infantry, who were busy dismounting from their lorries. He ordered his driver to speed up and drove straight through the surprised Russians, who did not have time to fire their weapons. Guderian reports in his memoirs that he must have been recognized, because later the Soviet press announced his death. He felt duty bound to inform them of the mistake via the German radio!

By the beginning of the autumn of 1941 it must have appeared to Hitler and his victorious forces that Russia was finished. When the Führer spoke in Berlin on 2nd October, he told the German people that the enemy was 'already beaten and would never rise again!' Within three weeks of the opening of the campaign, von Leeb's Army Group North was moving rapidly through the Baltic states towards Leningrad; Army Group South was advancing towards the Dnieper River and Kiev, capital of the Ukraine; Army Group Centre had done even better, having reached Smolensk, only 200 miles from Moscow. And not only had a great amount of real estate been taken, the Russians had also lost enormous numbers of men, tanks, guns, aircraft and all the rest. Nevertheless, a fair number of Russian soldiers had been able to escape from the German attacking columns, as there were large gaps in between them. However, in the first two weeks, over 300,000 prisoners were taken and 3,000 tanks destroyed or captured. The new armoured divisions had not had a chance to form, instead all that could be done was to make up independent tank battalions and brigades under the Supreme Command, the new tactical doctrine stressing that they should be used en masse and not split up into smaller units. Marshal Pavlov paid the price for his incompetence, being executed in late 1941, when Rotmistrov took his place. Pavlov's tactical doctrine had led to chaos, as Gen von Mellenthin describes in his book *Panzer Battles*: 'At first the Russian tank armies had to pay heavily for the lack of experience, and in particular the lower and middle commands showed little understanding or aptitude for armoured warfare. They lacked the daring, the tactical insight, and the ability to make quick decisions. The initial operations of the tank armies were a complete failure. In tight masses they groped around in the main German battle zone, they moved hesitantly and without any plan.'

The Germans also took over many of the areas in which tank and tank component plants were located, so they had had to be evacuated, and to be moved even as far as the Urals and Siberia to escape enemy bombing. This meant that extended lines of communication were needed to bring the finished tanks forward. Nevertheless, despite all the problems, the new T34 medium tanks and the KV1 and KV2 heavy tanks were battle-winners. (They were named, somewhat inappropriately, after FM Klimenti Voroshilov, head of the Red Army in 1937 after the Purge, who had listened to Pavlov's comments about tanks in Spain and been responsible for the disastrous 'penny-packeting' that followed.) T34 was far superior to any German tank then in service, while the KV1 was also very effective, although there were insufficient numbers of either tank to have a great effect upon the early battles. The other Russian tanks were destroyed in vast numbers – sometimes a single German anti-tank gun accounting for up to thirty tanks in an hour.

In the north, von Leeb's Army had initially made good progress towards Leningrad, with Hoepner's 4th Panzer Group well out in front, however, by September they were being delayed by heavy rain. In the centre, Guderian's 2nd Panzer Group and Kleist's 1st had completed their encirclement of Kiev, capital of the Ukraine. Further south, good progress was being made in the Crimea. It was by then becoming clear to everyone, Hitler included, that the lightning campaign which he had so fondly envisaged would be impossible, so he ordered a general reorganization, which affected most of the armoured formations. He decided, for example, that the siege of Leningrad could be left to the infantry and artillery, plus suitable air support, so 4th Panzer Group was switched to reinforce Army Group Centre. Despite the fact that thousands died of starvation, the garrison and people of Leningrad held out against everything the Germans produced against them.

RUSSIA'S MOST FAMOUS SOLDIER   The man who was initially entrusted with the defence of Leningrad was to become Russia's most famous soldier of the Great Patriotic War: Marshal Georgy Konstantinovich Zhukov. Born in 1896 in a small village just outside Moscow, son of the village shoemaker, he joined the Imperial Army in 1915, as a trooper in the 10th Novgorod Dragoons. A brave and energetic NCO, he quickly rose through the ranks, winning two decorations during WW1. After the war he joined the Red Army, in October 1918, and the Communist Party in the following year. He also became a firm supporter of tanks, but fortunately escaped the Great Purge and went on to lead the successful Soviet counter-offensive against the Japanese in Manchuria in July–August 1939. During the Russo-Finnish War he was Chief of Staff of the Red Army, so once again was able to avoid the disgrace suffered by many of the field commanders for their poor showing against the tiny Finnish army. It was about this time that he became a favourite of Stalin, who made him Chief of the General Staff in February 1941. Zhukov was to become a living legend, as the 'Saviour of Moscow', when he was given the task of organizing the defence of the Russian capital. Wily, tough, uncompromising, he also had under him two of Russia's best generals – Ivan Koniev and Andrei Yeremenko, plus a brilliant Chief of Staff, Vasily Sokolovsky. All three were to win great honours as the war progressed, Koniev, for example, demonstrating that the Red Army could succeed with blitzkrieg tactics even in terrible winter conditions when he went onto the offensive in the early months of 1944 in the Ukraine. Koniev's blitzkrieg was only possible because the T34 tank could keep going in waterlogged, muddy conditions that stopped almost every other form of transport. Popular with his troops, Koniev had a formidable reputation which was partly based on his exploits during the Civil War in command of an armoured train.

MOSCOW: THE TIDE TURNS Kiev was captured on 26th September. Well over half a million Russian soldiers were taken prisoner and many more killed (including the commander of the South West Front and his staff) because they had been ordered by Stalin to stay put and defend the city to the bitter end. Guderian comments that the German Army would later suffer the 'direst calamities' because of just such similar interference from 'higher levels'. The main task for Army Group Centre was now to capture Moscow before the onset of winter. Both 3rd and 4th Panzer Groups would take part in Operation 'Typhoon', together with 2nd Panzer Army, as Panzergruppe Guderian was now called. In his autobiography *Reminscences and Reflections* Zhukov explains that by regrouping their forces the Germans now had assembled a superior force for 'Typhoon': 'They had 40% more men, 70% more tanks, 80 % more mortars and guns, and twice as many planes.' Initially the battle went well for the Germans, but by early October they were running out of steam and suffering heavy casualties. Zhukov quotes Guderian as saying how the battles near Orel and Mtensk had failed because: 'A large number of Russian T34s was engaged in the battle, causing considerable losses to our Panzers. The superiority that our Panzers had so far was now lost and seized by the adversary. This wiped out the chances of a rapid and unintermittent success.'

Despite all their efforts, the Germans failed in their attempts to take the

Russian capital, even though they got to within 29 miles of the city centre. Zhukov organized a spirited defence in depth, no doubt assisted by the worsening weather and the difficulties the Germans were experiencing in keeping their tanks serviceable. By mid-November Guderian, for example, had only 50 running tanks left out of the 600 with which he had started out on 'Barbarossa', while the combat strength of his infantry companies was down to under 50 men. There was also a severe shortage of winter kit,[6] fuel and vehicle spare parts. He was not alone. All the other panzer formations were in much the same state, and so, as Bryan Perrett comments in his book *A History of Blitzkrieg*, '. . . orders from the Führer to seize particular objectives with "fast moving" units were greeted with jeers of derision, since they bore no relation to the reality of the situation.' Zhukov had strong personal reasons for not allowing the Germans to reach Moscow, as he had, in the nick of time, been able to rescue his mother and his sister and her children from the outlying village of Strelkovka and bring them to the capital. 'I asked myself what would happen to them if the fascists came to the village. What would they do to a Red Army general's relatives? Shoot them, surely. "First chance I get", I thought, "I'll have them brought to Moscow".' Events proved him correct – his mother's house was burnt to the ground along with the rest of the village, while all their friends were beaten or hanged.

Shelter at night became vital to the continued existence of both armies, so battles would develop towards last light as each side fought for what buildings were available. Entire German units would, on occasions, allow themselves to be cut off by Russian counter-attacks, rather than give up the shelter afforded by a particular town or village. Of course there were many brave actions fought. Two Russian tankmen who became Heroes of the Soviet Union at that time were Snr Sgt Lyubushkin and Jnr Political Officer Ilya Barmin, who was commanding a tank company in 28th Tank Brigade of 16th Army. Lyubushkin distinguished himself on 6th October 1941, in the village of Voinovka, where his tank was crippled by enemy gunfire and he was wounded but continued to fight, setting fire to four German tanks. Lyubushkin died in battle on 30th June 1942. Barmin, through his personal example, so inspired his men that this company destroyed 10 enemy tanks. He went missing on 10th December 1943. There are many such stories. As Marshal Zhukov says in his autobiography: 'It is impossible to list all the heroes who distinguished themselves during the heroic defence of Moscow in October 1941. Whole military units who displayed mass heroism – not only individual soliders – won fame in the battles for the Motherland. Such hero units were at every sector of the front.'

Zhukov goes on to comment on the various reasons historians give for the German failure to take Moscow – weather and climate, for example, and mud and the lack of roads. As to the first, he comments: 'Warm clothes and uniforms are also a weapon. Our country fed and clothed her soldiers. But the Nazi army was not prepared for the winter.' As to the second, he tells how he watched thousands and thousands of Moscow women work through the appalling weather digging anti-tank ditches and trenches, putting up barricades, carrying sandbags, etc: '. . . Mud stuck to their feet and to the wheels of the barrows in which they carried earth. Mud stuck to the blades of the spades, making them unwieldy in the feminine hands. . . . No! it was neither rain nor snow that stopped the fascist troops near Moscow. The grouping of picked Nazi troops, over one million strong, were routed by the courage, iron staunchness and valour of the Soviet troops which had the people, Moscow and their country behind them.'

The news was no better for the Germans further south. Von Rundstedt, who had been forced to abandon his plan to outflank Rostov, had taken it by frontal attack in mid-November. He was then counter-attacked and decided to withdraw, much to Hitler's annoyance. He resigned when Hitler tried to countermand the order. He was replaced by von Richenau from the 6th Army,[7] and was thus the first of the 'Hitler-induced casualties' among the German senior field commanders. He was followed, in mid-January 1942, by von Leeb, whose place as Commander Army Group North was taken by von Kuechler. Lower down the scale, Hoepner was dismissed, together with a number of corps and divisional commanders. But, without doubt, the most serious loss was that of Guderian.

The mud, the frostbite, the casualties to men and tanks, had all reached such limits that Guderian considered his men had done enough – 'I frequently cannot sleep at night', he wrote, 'and my brain goes round and round while I try to think what more I can do to help my poor soldiers who are out there without shelter in this abominable cold.'[8] He explained the situation to Hitler's adjutant, Schmundt, whom he had asked to see, telling him to pass on everything to Hitler. However, the Führer phoned Guderian the following night, commanding him to hold fast, refusing to countenance any withdrawal, but promising to send reinforcements. Nothing happened, so Guderian decided he must take the initiative. He wrote to his wife that he was getting increasingly depressed by the enormous weight of responsibility, which, 'in spite of all the words, no-one can take off my shoulders'. Realizing that he must take the bull by the horns, Guderian requested an interview with Hitler and, on 20th December, flew to see him in East Prussia. Guderian recalls that, for the first time, he saw 'a hard, unfriendly expression' in Hitler's eyes, which immediately made him suspect that some enemy had turned Hitler against him. They argued for some minutes, Guderian pointing out all the problems, Hitler dismissing them out of hand, saying, for example, that there was no shortage of winter clothing, but then being proved wrong when the quartermaster general was sent for and forced to admit that Guderian was speaking the truth. The unsatisfactory evening ended inconclusively, but it was clear that Guderian was now out of favour. Therefore, when von Kluge, who had replaced Bock as Commander Army Group Centre, and who disliked Guderian intensely, accused him of withdrawing without permission and reported it to Hitler, the Führer swiftly dismissed him from his command.9 In actual fact, Guderian had been so incensed by von Kluge's threat to report him to Hitler, that he had already requested that he be relieved of his command. Guderian was transferred to the OKH officers' reserve pool, where he would remain for the next 12 months.

Stalingrad

'All available forces will be concentrated on the main operations in the southern sector, with the aim of destroying the enemy before the Don, in order to secure the Caucasian oilfields and the passes through the Caucasus Mountains.' This extract from Hitler's Directive No 41 encapsulates the Führer's plans for 1942 – not just to destroy the Red Army, but also to take control of the Soviet infrastructure, including the capture of the oilfields, in order to gain precious fuel for his panzers. Within this overall strategy the capture of Stalingrad was not essential, although 'every effort will be made to reach Stalingrad itself, or at least to bring the city under fire from heavy artillery, so that it may no longer be of any use as an industrial or communications centre'.10 However, before the Germans could launch their main assault, Marshal Timoshenko's South West Front launched in early May a two-pronged attack to recapture Kharkov, but this was halted near Izyum with heavy losses. Semyon Konstantinovich Timoshenko was one of the 'old guard' and a close advisor to Stalin, who had been commanding the all-important approaches to Moscow before Koniev and Zhukov and was then switched to command the South West Front. His chief political advisor was Nikita Khruschev, later to become first secretary. The state of the Russian tank forces at the time can perhaps be judged by a remark made by the then Chief of Staff of 4th Tank Army: 'We are very aptly named – we have only four tanks!'

The following month, Army Group South began the drive, code-named 'Fall Blau', towards Stalingrad and the Caucasus. Army Group South was divided into two halves – on the right, Army Group A (17th Army and von Kleist's 1st Panzer Army) and on the left, Army Group B (6th Army and Hoth's 4th Panzer Army). The Russians unfortunately committed their splendid T34 tanks in 'penny packets' and after only 48 hours the two German Groups met, encircling a large number of prisoners and then driving on unhindered. As Bryan Perrett puts it: '. . . once more the German columns rolled across the empty steppe. Superficially, all was as it should be; the Russian line had been broken and the whole apparatus of 'Blitzkrieg' was in top gear, the tanks of the leading battalions covering mile after mile under a glorious summer sun . . .'11 But the Panzer leaders were not to be left to get on with the job unfettered, indeed Directive No 41 had warned: 'It must not happen that, by advancing too quickly and too far, armoured and motorised formations lose connection with the infantry following them.'

All might have gone well had not Hitler started to interfere, first dismissing the commander of Army Group B (von Bock) because he was going too slowly, then moving 4th Panzer Army south to help 1st Panzer Army to cross the Don. This left Army Group B too weak to take Stalingrad, while the clutter of vehicles now in the Army Group A sector made supply and traffic problems worse and worse. Von Kleist clearly did not need any help – his soldiers even had time to bathe in the Don because there were no enemy to be seen. He wrote later: 'The 4th Panzer Army was advancing . . . on my left. It could have taken Stalingrad without a fight at the end of July, but was diverted south to help me in crossing the Don. I did not need its aid and it merely congested the roads I was using. When it turned north again, a fortnight later, the Russians had gathered just sufficient forces at Stalingrad to check it.'[12]

Hitler then switched part of Hoth's force back to rejoin 6th Army, announcing to Halder on 30th July that 'the fate of the Caucasus will be decided at Stalingrad'. As the German force approached the city, the Luftwaffe carried out a very heavy raid, reducing many of the mainly wooden buildings to ashes. So began an eight-month siege of the city – 'the war of the rats' (*rattenkrieg*) as the Germans called it. The superior armoured tactics of the panzer forces were of little use in the street fighting that followed, actions being mainly confined to individual tanks and hand-to-hand fighting between small groups of infantrymen among the rubble of ruined buildings. As in the defence of Moscow, thousands of the citizens of Stalingrad came out to build fortifications to defend their city. At the same time, Russian partisans, operating from the Caucasian mountains, sowed fear in the German rear areas and caused them substantial losses.

First to arrive at the outskirts of the city was XIV Panzer Corps, which had been sent ahead while the infantry recovered from the bitter four-day battle to capture a crossing over the Don. Paulus had succeeded in destroying two complete Soviet armies, but further strong Russian forces still remained to the north. XIV Panzer Corps, under Gen von Wietersheim, was now some 35 miles ahead of the rest of the German force, at the end of a narrow supply route and had some anxious moments until they were relieved on 2nd September, when the real battle began. Defence of the Stalingrad Front was under the overall command of Gen V.N. Gordov, who had replaced Marshal Timoshenko when he was pulled out of front-line command to become an advisor to Stalin at the Kremlin. The responsibility for the defence of Stalingrad itself rested upon Gen Vasily Ivanovich Chuikov, who at the age of only 42 was commanding the 64th Army. Stalingrad was then a sprawling city of some half a million inhabitants, which straggled along the western bank of the Volga for about 18 miles. Its factories produced tanks, guns, tractors, vehicles and many types of weapons. However, in the eyes of the German field commanders, it was not the vital target Hitler clearly considered it to be – much more important was the capture of the Maikop oilfields, which 1st Panzer Army had reached on 9th August, while the ultimate prize of the Baku oilfields was still some 300 miles away and becoming ever more remote as German strength was dissipated on secondary objectives.

By early September the defenders had been squeezed back into a small perimeter, only some 30 miles by 18 miles. XIV and XXIV Panzer Corps of 6th Army had been joined from the south by Hoth's 4th Panzer Army, in a ring of steel around the city. Chuikov, cut off from the rest of the Soviet forces, bravely declared, 'We shall either hold the city or die here.' The Germans broke into the centre of the city and even came within 800 yards of Chuikov's headquarters. However, it was by now obvious that Stalin would never permit the city that bore his name to be lost. He was as determined that it should be held as Hitler was that it should be taken. 'It was clear,' wrote Zhukov, 'that the forthcoming battle was of the utmost military and political importance. With the fall of Stalingrad, the enemy command would be able to cut off the south of the country from the centre. We might also lose the Volga, the country's most important waterway which carried a constant flow of goods from the Volga area and the Caucasus. The Supreme Command was sending to Stalingrad everything it could possibly spare at the time.' It was inevitable that both sides would therefore expend far more men and material in the battle for Stalingrad than it was worth, both sides becoming conveniently blind to real tactical and strategic considerations. As Brig Peter Young commented: 'Stalingrad became the Verdun of the Second World War'.[13]

Undoubtedly the vital battle for Stalingrad marked a major turning point in the war. It also led to a number of senior command changes within the German Army. The first to go was FM List, whose Army Group A, which had been weakened by the loss of Hoth's 4th Panzer Army, lacked the strength to capture the still-distant oilfields, the River Terek being the limit of their advance. An impatient Hitler had sent Col Gen Alfred Jodl to find out what was happening, becoming beside himself with rage when Jodl returned and explained that he agreed entirely with List, who wanted a complete regrouping as his forces were too weak. Jodl nearly got the sack, List did and was swiftly followed by the Army's Chief of Staff Halder, who had supported him. Rommel, hearing the news in Africa, wrote to his wife, 'I hear that Field-Marshal List is retiring. I thought particularly highly of him, as you know.' Casualties at Stalingrad were heavy on both sides, but the Russians were able to replace theirs while the Germans were not, save for a handful of engineer battalions and an under-strength panzer division. The bitter fighting continued in October, with the Germans capturing some of the key strongholds and even raising the Nazi flag over the city centre.

While the battle for the city was in progress the Russians were busy completing preparations for a massive counter-stroke. Zhukov again: 'By November, the Supreme Command would have mechanised and armoured formations equipped with the highly effective and manoeuverable T34 tanks, which would allow us to set our troops more exacting targets.' The 'targets' were to be the weakest link in the German front, the Rumanian Third Army to the northwest of the city. Operation 'Uranus' began on 19th November, when, advancing behind a massive barrage, waves of over 500 T34s swept through the Rumanians and then virtually annihilated XLVIII Panzer Corps, whose commander, Lt Gen Ferdinand Heim, was first sentenced to death by Hitler, later pardoned when it was found that his corps had been too weak, jailed instead and then finally released as a private soldier! The Russians were led by Gen Nikolai Fedorovich Vatutin, who was later involved in the Kursk battle and also in a similar pincer movement in early 1944 in the Ukraine, which resulted in massive German losses. Vatutin was assassinated soon after the battle, on 1st March 1944, by Ukranian nationalists.

At the same time, another Russian attack was coming up from the southeast and, when it met up with Vatutin's thrust, Paulus's 6th Army and that part of Hoth's 4th Panzer Army which had joined him were effectively sealed into Stalingrad. Paulus wanted to break out, but Goering boasted that the Luftwaffe could keep him supplied by air – a boast which failed miserably, despite the great bravery shown by all the aircrews of the transport aircraft. Hitler therefore decided to relieve 'Fortress Stalingrad' by land and sent for one of his most brilliant generals, Erich von Manstein, architect of past successes, to command Army Group Don with the aim of relieving Stalingrad and restoring the original front. But it proved impossible to get closer than 30 miles from the trapped 200,000 in Stalingrad. In the end the Germans surrendered on 2nd February, having suffered some 120,000 casualties. It was a major disaster for Germany. The Soviets claimed the capture of 91,000 prisoners, including some 24 generals, while three Panzer divisions (14th, 16th and 24th) were lost.

Hitler appears to have been more upset that Paulus surrendered just after he had been promoted to field marshal than about anything else: 'That's the last field marshal I shall appoint in this war,' he is reputed to have said, '. . . he could have got out of his vale of tears and into eternity (by suicide), and been immortalized by the nation, but he'd rather go to Moscow. What kind of a choice is that?'[14] Zhukov wrote that the Nazi debacle at Stalingrad had prompted jubilation around the world and went on to say: 'For myself personally, the defence of Stalingrad, the preparation of the counter-offensive and participation in deciding the main aspects of the operations in the south were of special importance as now I had accumulated far more experience in mounting a counter-offensive than I had at Moscow in 1941, where limited forces did not permit a counter-offensive with the aim of encircling an enemy grouping.' Zhukov had undoubtedly shown himself to be a great commander. Soon he would follow his Stalingrad triumph with victory in the greatest armoured battle in history. Chuikov would continue as a tough and uncompromising army commander, his Eighth Guards Army spearheading Zhukov's advance through Poland and then going on to bridge the Oder on 3rd February 1945, after covering 220 miles in under two weeks. It was Chuikov who negotiated the surrender of Berlin and its garrison on 2nd May 1945 and it was his troops who found the bodies of Adolf Hitler and Eva Braun, still smouldering after being burnt in petrol-soaked carpets.

In February 1943, Hitler relented and recalled Guderian to active duty, as Inspector-General of Armoured Forces. In his normal forthright way, Guderian replied that he was prepared to accept the job in view of the needs of Germany and the panzer forces, but only if he had a direct link to the Führer and would not be subordinated to the Chief of the Army General Staff or the Commander of the Training Army! He must also be able to exert influence over the development of armoured equipment and be able to have control over the training and organization of tank units in the Waffen-SS and Luftwaffe, as well as those of the Army. He would also have to control all the tank units in the Training Army and all their schools. Hitler agreed and, when Guderian went to see him, 'mentioned that he had re-read my pre-war writings on armoured troops and had noticed that I had even then correctly prophesied the course of future developments.' For his part, Guderian thought Hitler had aged greatly, that his manner was less assured, his speech was hesitant and that his left hand trembled.

Kursk

Stern, harsh, ruthless, prepared to accept casualties, provided the end was achieved; that perhaps encapsulated Zhukov's method of command. Kursk would require an even more ruthless approach by this formidable commander.

The after-effects of the Russian offensive in the early months of 1943 on a front line from Rostov northwards to Orel, combined with the subsequent German counter-attacks, in which Manstein had made use of the new Tiger tanks to great advantage (its 88mm gun was capable of ripping the turret clean off a T34, giving rise to the phrase, 'The T34 raises its hat whenever it meets a Tiger!'), had left an enormous salient sticking out around Kursk. Manstein was determined to cut off this salient or 'bulge' and destroy the Russian forces it contained. This was the aim behind Operation 'Citadel', which developed into the largest tank battle ever fought, involving over 6,000 tanks, over two million men and some 4,000 aircraft.

Manstein's plan was basically quite simple. Model's 9th Army (Army Group Centre) would attack the bulge from the north, coming from the direction of the German-held Orel Salient, while Hoth's 4th Panzer Army plus Operational Group Kempf (both Army Group South) would attack from the south, from the Kharkov salient. The Germans had small numbers of new tanks, both the already-proven Tiger and the equally new, but yet untried, Panther, which owed much of its design to the T34 and would be plagued by mechanical problems initially. Model's 9th Army comprised six panzer divisions, two panzergrenadier divisions and 12 infantry divisions (eight of which were designated to take part in the attack). In the south, Manstein had an even more powerful force totalling 22 divisions, containing eight panzer divisions. 'Citadel' thus consumed the major proportion of available German armour – some 2,500 tanks and SP guns out of a total of about 3,500 on the Eastern Front.

On the Russian side, the Central and Voronezh Fronts occupied the bulge, Gen Konstantin Konstantinovich Rokossovsky commanding the troops in the north and Gen Nikolai Vatutin those in the south. Rokossovsky, undoubtedly another great tank commander, was born in 1896, of Polish/Russian parentage. Orphaned in his early teens, he was drafted into the tsarist army at the start

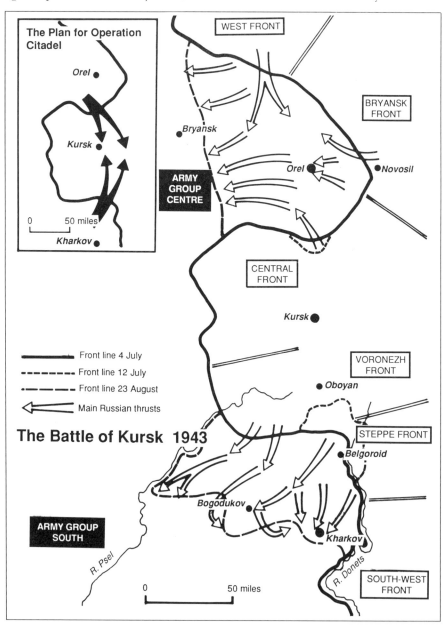

The Plan for Operation Citadel

Orel

Bryansk

Kursk

0   50 miles

Kharkov

WEST FRONT

BRYANSK FRONT

Bryansk

ARMY GROUP CENTRE

Orel ●Novosil

CENTRAL FRONT

Kursk ●

VORONEZH FRONT

● Oboyan

──────► Front line 4 July

- - - - - - ► Front line 12 July

-·— — —·► Front line 23 August

◄═══ Main Russian thrusts

The Battle of Kursk 1943

STEPPE FRONT

●Belgoroid

ARMY GROUP SOUTH

Bogodukov ●

Kharkov

R. Psel

0   50 miles

R. Donets

SOUTH-WEST FRONT

of WW1, ending up as a cavalry sergeant. He joined the Red Army in 1917 and rose to command a cavalry division in 1930. He was a corps commander at the time of the Great Purge, was beaten and thrown into jail, but released and 'rehabilitated' in March 1940. Rokossovsky's career never looked back after that. He commanded first a cavalry corps, then 9 Mechanized Corps in the Ukraine and, later, 16th Army in the battle for Moscow. It was he who had offered surrender terms to Gen Paulus at Stalingrad and, after they had been rejected, finally defeated the German 6th Army. A very strong character, he was one of the few generals to argue with Stalin and win his point. He was twice awarded the title of Hero of the Soviet Union. On meeting Rokossovsky in May 1945, Monty described him as being 'an imposing figure, tall, very good-looking and well dressed . . . a bachelor and much admired by the ladies.'

Behind these two Fronts was the powerful GHQ strategic reserve – the Stepnoi Front, under Gen Ivan Stepanovich Koniev. Another remarkable commander, Koniev was born in 1887 of peasant stock, served as a private soldier in the tsarist army and joined the Communist Party and the Red Army in 1918. An infantryman, Koniev did not have much to do with tanks until the Great Patriotic War, when he rose swiftly to division, corps and army command. He took over the defence of Moscow from Timoshenko in September 1941, only to be replaced by Zhukov in the following month, after Stalin blamed him for letting large Soviet forces become trapped. However, Zhukov managed to persuade Stalin to let him keep the popular Koniev as his deputy, and he was given the Steppe Front for the great autumn offensives of 1943. From May 1944 until the end of the war he commanded the First Ukrainian Front – 1,200,000 strong with 17,000 guns and mortars, 3,300 aircraft and 3,500 tanks. He found an original solution to the problem of committing tank armies to action in the course of an offensive, seeking to commit them within the limits of the tactical zone of defence and sometimes even within the limits of the enemy main line of defence. Employment of complete tank armies in a breakthrough or even to effect a breakthrough of the enemy tactical defence zone helped decrease losses in infantry, particularly when there was a shortage of close-support tanks. It also increased the rate of advance in the first day of operations, resembling blitzkrieg tactics, but on a far larger scale. He commanded the First Ukrainian Front in 1945, joined up with Zhukov's forces to encircle Berlin and later commanded the Russian occupation forces in Austria. It was ironic that, after the war, he should have a hand in getting Zhukov dismissed during the Khrushchev era.

The Russian defensive plan was based upon a series of eight concentric defensive zones, crammed with anti-tank, anti-infantry and anti-aircraft weapons. Never before had the Red Army organized such a powerful defensive system.

They were aided in all this by knowing exactly what the Germans were planning, thanks to good intelligence and a spy network. Thus the Soviet GHQ had reliable information that the enemy would probably attack between the 3rd and 6th July. When the battle began, the Central and Voronezh fronts contained more than 1.3 million men, some 20,000 artillery guns and mortars, 3,600 tanks and SP guns and some 3,130 aircraft, giving them a considerable superiority over the Germans. To quote from a supplement issued with the *Soviet Military Review* on the 30th anniversary of the battle:

> The Kursk battle was one of the greatest engagements in the Great Patriotic War . . .. It lasted for fifty days – from July 5 to August 23, 1943. During this time both sides consecutively committed to action over 4 million men, about 70,000 guns and mortars, nearly 13,000 tanks and self-propelled guns and up to 12,000 aircraft. The results of the battle had enormous international repercussions, exerting a decisive influence on the development of major military and political events.

A TIGER ACE   At first the German attacks made good progress, but they were soon bogged down within the lines of Soviet defences, many tanks becoming separated from their supporting infantry, who then had to fight hand to hand in order to reach them again. There were, as in all the tank battles in Russia, many heroic incidents, and Kursk saw the blossoming of the career of one extraordinary man, who was to become Germany's most famous Tiger-tank commander (at a single-tank level), Unterstürmführer Michael Wittmann. Wittmann had already been awarded the Iron Cross 2nd Class in Greece as an armoured car commander, then the Iron Cross 1st Class in Russia when commanding an assault gun in 1941. Sent to the SS Junkerschule at Bad Tolz, he was promoted and rejoined the Leibestandarte. In his Tiger tank, as a section commander in 13th (Heavy) Tank Company of the 1st SS Panzer Regiment, he knocked out 30 Soviet tanks, 28 anti-tank guns and two complete artillery batteries during the Kursk battle. He survived the battle and by early January 1944 his 'score' was 66 tanks, for which he was awarded the Knight's Cross. A few days later, he knocked out another 19 T34s and three heavy assault guns, was promoted to SS Oberstürmführer and received his Oakleaves. Wittmann went on to even greater achievements in northwest Europe.

THE GREATEST TANK BATTLE OF WW2   In the north, as Model's forces smashed their way forwards, Rokossovsky put in a strong armoured counter-attack, but when this failed to make much impression, ordered his tanks to be dug in and to fight from hull-down positions, stopping Model's advance and destroying some 400 tanks. On 11th July, Operation 'Kutuzov', a counter-attack by five Soviet armies, broke through to the north of the German salient around Orel, threatening their rear. In the south, a vast tank battle was taking place that day, after a week of bitter fighting. Hoth's Fourth Panzer Army was endeavouring to break through in the area of Prokohrovka and unexpectedly collided with 5th Guards Tank Army advancing in the opposite direction. This resulted in a:

> sudden, frenzied armoured joust involving many hundreds of tanks fighting in the narrow reach of land between the River Psel and the railway embankment. . . . As Hausser's SS Panzer Corps resumed its advance, Rotmistrov's tanks met it head-on in a furious high-speed charge, the T34s

rolling across the sloping ground and in a nightmarish mechanized re-enactment of the Light Brigade at Balaclava, passing through the entire German first echelon and throwing the battle from the outset into milling confusion. Though outgunned by the awesome Tigers, the Soviet T 34s closed the range and used their 76mm guns to devastating effect: tanks, literally locked together, blew up in mutual death or were separately blown apart, ripping entire tank turrets off and flinging them yards away from the mangled wrecks.[15]

It was a battle from which the Germans would never totally recover. They lost over 300 tanks, including more than 70 Tigers, in that one engagement, while over half of Rotmistrov's 5th Guards had also been destroyed. However, Rotmistrov had won an important victory and it was the beginning of the end for the Germans in Russia.

The Russian Counter-offensive

The Kursk battle marked the end of the major German assaults in Russia and the start of the Soviet counter-offensive. The Allied landings in Sicily and then Italy meant that Hitler would now have to fight on two fronts, splitting his forces and removing some of his best divisions from the Eastern Front. However, that should not be allowed to detract from the way in which the Red Army had managed to seize the initiative, re-equip and motivate its soldiers to drive the Nazi invaders from Soviet soil. Their tank units played a major part in the counter-offensive, with men like Gen Ivan Danilovich Chernyakhovsky playing a major part. One of the youngest Soviet wartime commanders, he was born in 1906 in the town of Uman into the family of a railway worker. He joined the Red Army in 1924 and became a member of the Communist Party in 1928. He served as a deputy commander and then commander of a tank division during the German invasion, losing many tanks to the advancing panzers. After service on the Leningrad front, he took over a tank corps and then the 60th Army, being awarded the title of Hero of the Soviet Union on 17th October 1943. At the remarkably young age of 38, he was given command of the Belorussian Front for the major Soviet advances in 1944, and was awarded, for the second time, the Gold Star medal on 29th July 1944, for displaying great personal courage and bravery. Chernyakhosky was fatally wounded by enemy shellfire, near the town of Mehlsack in East Prussia in February 1945 and was buried at Vilnius. A bronze bust was erected to him in his home town, the name of the town of Insterburg was changed to Chernyakhovsky in his honour, while various other memorials were raised to him in other places.

Another tank hero was Gen Andrei Grigorevich Kravchenko, who had joined the Red Army in 1918 and served on the staff of a motorized division and then a tank division during the Finnish War. Kravchenko was commanding a tank brigade during 'Barbarossa', then went on to command a brigade of the new T34 tanks in the battles to save Moscow. Recognized as an aggressive and capable operational commander, he advanced rapidly and was given command of first the 2nd and then the 4th Tank Corps in 1942. Actions during the Stalingrad battles won for his corps the coveted title of 'Guards', so it was fitting that they should be chosen to spearhead the Soviet advance across the Dnieper river after Kursk. His task was to cross the Desna, another major river which had to be crossed before the Dnieper could be reached. There was not time to build bridges, so Kravchenko was ordered by the front commander, Gen Vatutin, to find a ford. A search of the river produced a potential ford, in the vicinity of the village of Letki, where the river was 300 yards wide and over 6 feet deep – twice the normal fording depth of a T34! Nevertheless, it was the only possible crossing place, so the tank crews had to make the best of it and use their inventiveness to make their tanks waterproof, having no tried and tested schnorkel gear as the Germans had used on the Bug at the start of 'Barbarossa'. To quote from an article on the crossing which appeared in *Armor* magazine in 1988: 'All cracks, openings, hatches, engine louvres and the turret race, were caulked with oakum, soaked in grease or tar. Other potential openings were sealed with tarpaulins, oiled and battened down. Air could reach the engines through the turret hatch, but exhaust fumes had to be fed through exhaust pipes made from tarpaulin sleeves, which carried the gases to the water surface.'[16] The banks were prepared with an approach road of brushwood and the crossing began on 4 October 1943 (less than 24 hours after Kravchenko had been given his mission) the tanks being personally led by the corps commander.

Some tanks were flooded, their crews having to sit in the icy water until rescued, however, by 0800 hours the next morning, 71 tanks had crossed. 'Andrei Grigorevich, what people your tankers are!' exclaimed the commander of the 38th Army, Gen Chibisov, when he visited the crossing site, 'I have never seen more courageous soldiers than I see at this time. The people are hours in the cold water without getting out. And such a risk the drivers take driving to the opposite bank!'[17] It was a remarkable achievement, but this still left the Dnieper which was wider and deeper than the Desna. Kravchenko's recce forces managed to find two damaged barges which the Germans had sunk when they withdrew. They were raised and repaired. Each would take three tanks, while the two heavy ferries which the corps engineers made from pontoon bridging sections would carry more. During the night of 5th/6th October, Kravchenko got 60 of his tanks across the second obstacle, and was then in a good position to support the infantry and artillery, who were already across. Boosted by the arrival of the tanks, they succeeded in repelling every German counter-attack and enlarging the bridgehead. Kravchenko's corps went on to be the first into the centre of Kiev, his tireless and aggressive performance earning him the highest Russian award of Hero of the Soviet Union.

In January 1944, 4th Guards Tank Corps was combined with 5th Mechanized Corps to form the 6th Tank Army, the last Army to be created during the war. Under the continuing brilliant leadership of Gen Kravchenko, 6th Tank Army went on to fight in many more successful battles, winning the 'Guards' designation and finishing the war fighting through the Balkans and Carpathian mountains. They were then transferred to the Far East and, in August 1945,

Kravchenko attacked across the Greater Khingan mountains and deserts of western Manchuria against the Japanese Kwantung army. In another lightning campaign he chased the Japanese to the shores of the Pacific Ocean, being awarded the title Hero of the Soviet Union for a second time.

Although the German panzer commanders in general conducted brilliant rearguard actions, they were driven remorselessly out of Russia – Leningrad was relieved in January 1944 and Manstein's Army Group Ukraine had to abandon Odessa in April 1944 and Sevastopol in May. Hitler was so infuriated by these losses that he relieved both von Manstein and von Kleist, replacing them with Model and Schoerner. For all his brilliant achievements Manstein was decorated with Swords to his Knight's Cross, but at the same time Hitler told him, 'The time for operating is over. What I need now is men who stand firm.' He was not going to find them, particularly when, in the early summer of 1944, the Red Army launched a massive assault comprising three fronts, under the overall command of Marshal Zhukov, driving Army Group Centre back into Poland. Hitler's dream of *lebensraum* in the east was in ashes. And there was worse to come.

NOTES TO CHAPTER 6

1 Writing in *Mein Kampf*, Hitler had said: 'And so we National Socialists consciously draw a line beneath the foreign policy tendency of our pre-war period. We take up where we broke off six hundred years ago. We stop the endless German movement to the south and west, and turn our gaze towards the land in the East. . . . If we speak of soil in Europe today, we can primarily have in mind only Russia and her vassal border states.'

2 As quoted in John Milsom, *Russian Tanks 1900–1970*

3 Heinz Guderian, *Panzer Leader*.

4 *ibid.*

5 *ibid.*

6 Because Hitler and his staff had been so convinced that the campaign would be over in a few short weeks, insufficient quantities of winter clothing and equipment were available. Men were still dressed in thin cotton denims and suffered severely from frostbite or froze to death. Anti-freeze was also in short supply so engines had either to be run at regular intervals all night, with a resulting increase in fuel requirements, or crews had to light slow fires under vehicle sumps!

7 A colourful character who belied his typical Prussian appearance, being a controversial figure and very much an extrovert. While he was commanding 6th Army he made every junior commander during the drive to Kharkov write on his millboard, 'Pursuit without rest'. Richenau's career was cut short by a heart attack the following month (January 1942) at the age of 57.

8 *Panzer Leader*

9 Their quarrel did not end here. In July 1943, Kluge actually challenged Guderian to a duel with pistols (with Hitler as his second!), but nothing came of it.

10 H.R. Trevor-Roper, *Hitler's War Directives 1939–1945*.

11 Bryan Perrett, *A History of Blitzkrieg*

12 Matthew Cooper & James Lucas, *Panzer*

13 *Atlas of the Second World War* (edited by Brig Peter Young)

14 John Toland, *Adolf Hitler*

15 John Erickson, *Decisive Battles of the 20th Century – Kursk*

16 As quoted in 'Red Army Tank Commander' by Lt Col Richard Armstrong, from *Armor* November–December 1988

17 Extract from an article by Col N. Svetlishin on Marshal Konev in *Soviet Military News*

7 THE UNDERBELLY OF EUROPE

Winston Churchill and President Roosevelt met at Casablanca in January 1943, in order to plan how to conduct the next stages of the war once the Axis forces in North Africa had been defeated. One of their major decisions was that, until conditions were favourable for a cross-Channel assault, they would continue operations in the Mediterranean by mounting an offensive against the 'soft underbelly' of Europe, namely Italy. However, as a prelude, and perhaps also by way of a rehearsal for the main assault, they would first mount an amphibious operation against Sicily. This was bound to undermine Italian morale, while helping to clear Axis aircraft from one of the most dangerous stretches of the Mediterranean by denying them bases; and, at the same time, making it easier for Allied bombers to reach the mainland.

Sicily: Operation 'Husky'

The operation – Operation 'Husky' – would be undertaken by two task forces, each basically comprising one army, with the newly formed and relatively inexperienced US Seventh Army under Gen Patton as the western task force, while Gen Montgomery's battle-hardened Eighth Army was in the east. They would be under the overall command of Gen Eisenhower, as Supreme Commander Mediterranean Theatre with Gen Alexander as his deputy. The Americans needed a major success after their relatively poor showing in Tunisia and Patton was the ideal person to lead them to victory. On the British side, while 'Monty' had already more than proved his prowess, it was clear that he was not going to take a back seat or allow himself to be upstaged.

So the stage was set for fireworks, especially after Montgomery, in his usual direct way, had told Alexander that he disagreed with the plan as proposed. Monty said that the only way the operation could be made to work successfully was for his task force to be increased in size at the expense of Patton's and given operational priority, with the Americans taking on a supporting role protecting his left flank, while his Desert Rats did the real fighting. The British planners and Alexander saw this as sensible, because the Eighth Army had proved its reliability, while the Americans not unnaturally saw it as 'the bombastic and swollen-headed Montgomery undermining Patton's chances of success'.[1] Fortunately, Patton, like the good soldier he was, accepted the changes with good grace, but no doubt was secretly determined to put one over on Montgomery should the opportunity present itself. Operation 'Husky'

114

was therefore bound to produce high drama, irrespective of how well the enemy performed! As Gen Essame put it in his book about Patton: 'Seen as a clash of highly original and brightly contrasted personalities it has human interest outshining the other scenarios of World War Two.' Two strong-willed, ambitious and publicity-seeking men would soon be vying with one another and, while competition can be a spur to greater efforts, this time it would not entirely help the Allied cause.

It did not make matters any easier for Patton and his Americans that Gen Alexander initially both agreed with Monty and found it difficult to control him. Gen Alanbrooke realized this and wrote in his diary that Montgomery was 'a difficult mixture to handle, brilliant commander in action and trainer of men, but liable to commit untold errors, due to lack of tact, lack of appreciation of other people's outlook. It is most distressing that the Americans do not like him and it will always be a difficult matter to have him fighting in close proximity to them. He wants guiding and watching continually and I do not think Alex is sufficiently strong and rough with him.'[2]

THE AXIS FORCES FM Albert Kesselring was Supreme Commander Mediterranean and in his defence of Italy he would show himself to be one of the greatest of the German commanders. Born in 1885, he served originally in the artillery before transferring to the Luftwaffe. Kesselring knew Italy well and used this knowledge to conduct a brilliant retreat. In his memoirs Alexander says of him: 'Every time we attacked Kesselring in Italy we took him completely by surprise; but he showed great skill in extricating himself from the desperate situations into which his faulty Intelligence had led him.' The Allies, thanks to Ultra, knew of the most secret German codes and knew what was going to happen before the Axis made any major move.

In Sicily the Italian commander was Gen Alfredo Guzzoni, who had as his German advisor Gen Frido von Senger und Etterlin, a cavalryman and a first-class soldier, who had fought with great success in Russia as a corps commander. He was an Oxford graduate, where he had studied before the war and, in addition, he was a Benedictine lay brother. The other senior German officer was Gen Hans-Valentin Hube, the commander of XIV Panzer Corps, who had two of his divisions in Sicily. He would be sent from Southern Italy by Kesselring on 13th July, three days after the Allied landings, to command all German troops on the island. Originally an infantryman, Hube had lost an arm in WW1 and had already served with distinction in Russia. He would return there to take part in the Cauldron battles in March 1944, commanding 1 Panzer Army and being awarded the Diamonds to his Knight's Cross.[3] He was killed in an air crash in April 1944. In his command in Sicily he had 15 Panzer Grenadier Division under its deputy commander Col (A/Maj Gen) Ernst Gunther Baade and the 1st Parachute Panzer Division 'Hermann Goering', under Gen Paul Conrath.

Baade was an extremely colourful and eccentric character, who was the son of a Brandenburg landowner, an expert horse breeder and an international show-jumper (as was his wife). In the desert he had commanded the DAK combat group which broke into the Free French fortress of Bir Hakeim. He also had been known to command desert patrols in a kilt and to signal to the British (on their own radio sets!) after a patrol: 'Stop firing, on my way back, Baade'.[4] He had fought in Poland, France, Russia and North Africa, and after Sicily he would go on to fight bravely at Cassino, then to command a Panzer corps on the Western Front in 1945, only to be killed in an air raid on the last day of the war. Conrath, on the other hand, was an entirely different character and his division did not fight well in Sicily, giving a cumbersome and slow performance. A number of his commanders had to be changed quite early on.

THE ASSAULT   The leading elements of both task forces got ashore with little difficulty, but the complementary airborne assaults went awry and the Axis forces were given time to organize their defence. Eighth Army was soon bogged down in heavy fighting around Catania, while Patton, displaying his usual panache, pressed on as fast as he could up the western side of the island towards Palermo. The bickering between the two armies reached its climax when Alexander gave the British priority over a central route that had been allocated to Bradley's II (US) Corps. This was the last straw and Patton flew back to see him protesting violently that he must be allowed to operate more freely. It would appear that only then did Alexander appreciate the depth of American feeling and changed his mind, from then on almost taking a back seat and allowing both his strong-willed army commanders to run their own battles.

Eventually it became a race to see who could reach Messina, in the northeast corner of the island, first. Even though the Americans had a longer distance to travel, against equally tough opposition, they had Patton behind them urging them on. Clearly many of his commanders would rather face the enemy than the wrath of their battling commander, who was determined to get there before his rival – and did so, driving triumphantly into Messina on the morning of 17th August. 'The best damn ass-kicker in the whole US Army!' is how Patton described himself and his approach certainly worked; his army quickly became battle-hardened and learnt more in the short Sicilian campaign than would have seemed possible. 'The Seventh Army showed the world what the American soldier could do when well led.'[5] At the same time, the Eighth Army reinforced its already high reputation. And the Germans too enhanced theirs, Gen Hube's defence of the Etna Line and his withdrawal across the straits being described by some historians as a tactical masterpiece.

THE PATTON 'INCIDENT'   The Sicilian campaign not only proved Patton's ability in battle, it also highlighted his impetuosity and quick temper, when he was involved in a series of incidents while visiting wounded soldiers in hospital. On the first occasion, Patton went to the 15th Evacuation Hospital, shortly after witnessing the carnage in the Mount Troina area, where 1st Infantry Division took heavy casualties over a four-day, desperate battle. (Patton later sacked both the divisional commander and his deputy.) After visiting some wounded, talking to them and presenting medals, he came across a private from 1st Division who appeared uninjured and, when Patton asked him why he was in hospital, replied that he just could not take any more fighting. Patton cursed him roundly and finished up smacking the soldier on his face with his gloves, then storming out, whilst cursing all cowards and malingerers. This encounter prompted him to send out a memorandum to all his commanders which read:

It has come to my attention that a very small number of soldiers are going to hospital on the pretext that they are nervously incapable of combat. Such men are cowards and bring discredit to the Army and disgrace to their comrades who they heartlessly leave to endure the danger of battle while they themselves use the hospital as a means of escaping. You will take measures to see that such cases are not sent to hospital but are dealt with in their units. Those who are not willing to fight will be tried by Court Martial for cowardice in the face of the enemy.

That might have been the end of it, had not Patton decided to visit another hospital (93rd Evacuation) a few days later. The drama of the previous occasion was repeated, Patton finding another soldier who told him that he was suffering from nerves. Patton was enraged and called the soldier a 'god-damned coward and a yellow son of a bitch'. He also threatened to shoot him, drawing one of his pistols and waving it under the soldier's nose. He then ordered Col Currier, the CO of the hospital, to see that the man was sent back to his unit immediately. Finally he struck the now weeping soldier with such force as to knock his steel helmet across the ward. The hospital CO then intervened and Patton again stormed out.

Patton at first tried to shrug off the incidents. 'Sorry to be late Brad', he said on arriving at Gen Omar Bradley's HQ shortly afterwards, 'Stopped off at a hospital on the way; there were a couple of malingerers there; I slapped one to put some fight back into him.'[6] No doubt he then forgot completely about the incident; however, that was not to be the end of the matter. It was the hospital CO's unofficial report to Gen Eisenhower which did the real damage, as Eisenhower explains in *Crusade in Europe*: 'The story spread throughout the hospital and among neighbouring units with lightning speed. I soon received an unofficial report from the surgeon commanding the hospital and only a few hours thereafter was visited by a group of newspaper correspondents who had been to the hospital to secure the details.'

Patton was vilified in the press. In the end, it was only because of Eisenhower's conviction that Patton should be 'saved for service in the great battles still facing us in Europe', that he was able to survive. However, this was not before he had paid penance in public, being made to deliver a personal apology to the staff of the 93rd Hospital. Patton then voluntarily did the same to each of his divisions, trying to explain what had motivated him to strike the soldier, namely that he had only been trying to, as he put it, 'slap some sense into him'. He expressed his anger and frustration at the way he had been treated in his diary, writing: 'My command so far has disposed of 177,000 Germans, Italians and French – killed, wounded and prisoner, of which they have killed and wounded 21,000. Our average loss has been one man for 13½ of the enemy. It would be a national calamity to lose an Army commander with such a record.' Later he wrote in a letter to his wife Beatrice: 'During the last few days I have not written as I have been feeling a bit anti-social. . . . The thing that hurts me is that as far as I can see, my side of the case has never been heard. It is like taxation without representation. . . . However, I am sure that my move is to make no move.'7

It has to be said that, had Eisenhower allowed Patton to be disgraced by this incident, then the US Army would have lost its greatest tank commander. Fortunately for the Allied cause he did not do so, but he clearly felt that Patton could not in future be trusted without closer supervision and should not be promoted above army commander. He was probably right, but for the wrong reasons, as George Patton was essentially a field commander, and would have hated the political nuances of higher Allied command. He was in his element as a field commander.

Italy

The campaign in Italy that followed the capture of Sicily was an extremely hard-fought and difficult one, particularly because of the nature of the country, which was exceptionally mountainous in the centre, with only narrow coastal plains which were criss-crossed by innumerable rivers. Like the XIV Army's brilliant campaign in Burma, it suffered from being upstaged, in its case by the landings in northwest Europe. One of the major strategic aims of the campaign was to tie up as many enemy divisions as possible, so that they could not be used against the Allied invasion of Normandy. By the time Rome fell in early June 1944, 26 German divisions were in Italy and there were still 23 there when the war ended, so this aim was achieved. Alexander was, however, thwarted continually by having divisions withdrawn, first for D Day and then for Operation 'Dragoon', the Allied invasion in Southern France, when seven divisions were taken away from Italy.

ALLIED COMMANDERS Basically there were two Allied armies employed. Gen Mark Clark's US Fifth Army landed and operated on the west coast, while Montgomery's Eighth Army landed and fought in the east. Monty would himself be taken away, in late December 1943, to command 21st Army Group, which was then preparing for the Normandy landings, his place being taken by Gen Sir Oliver Leese.8 Eisenhower would also go at the same time, handing over as Supreme Commander Mediterranean to Gen 'Jumbo' Wilson, while Alexander became CinC of the Allied Armies in Italy. Leese, who had been brought into the Eighth Army by Monty to command XXX Corps, had already shown his ability, both in North Africa and in spearheading the invasion of Sicily. A capable and popular commander, Leese typified the modern general, 'driving along crowded and muddy roads, which the enemy may actually be shelling as he drives, waving and calling to the men'.9 Mention must also be made of Alexander's Chief of Staff from January 1944, Gen (later FM) Sir John Harding, who had already shown his prowess as a fast-thinking armoured commander in the desert. Italy would be his 'finest hour'. Alexander later wrote of him: 'I was fortunate to have such a fine soldier and capable staff officer, and, besides, a delightful companion who was liked and trusted by all the many nationalities that composed my armies during the Mediterranean campaign.'[10] In December 1944, when Alexander became Supreme Allied Commander in the Mediterranean, he appointed Harding to command 13th Corps.

The Allied invasion plan was for a two-phase landing. The first, Operation 'Baytown', was on 3rd September, with Eighth Army units landing on the 'toe' of Italy. It was followed six days later by Operation 'Avalanche', the US Fifth Army landing in the Gulf of Salerno. This was the day after the Italians had surrendered, and for the remainder of the war in Italy the Germans were only able to count upon those Italian units which were part of Gen Graziani's Army of Liguria, a mixed German and Italian force, while the remainder were disarmed and took no further part in the fighting.

The Allies were able to advance quite speedily through southern Italy, but then found themselves held up south of Rome by the onset of winter, which significantly added to the Germans' determined resistance. 'General Mud' certainly played a major part in halting the campaign until the following spring. Alexander's plan was then for a two-pronged attack, to destroy the enemy south of Rome and then liberate the capital, joining up with those forces that had broken out of the Anzio beachhead. This was achieved in June 1944. The next major German defence line, the Gothic Line, was astride the Apennines and this, plus once again 'General Mud', succeeded in delaying the Allies' final advance until the following spring. Despite the fact that Alexander now had only 17 divisions against 23 of the enemy, he achieved a hard-fought and well-deserved victory, reaching the Austrian border in early June 1945.

ALLIED ARMOURED FORCES In view of the nature of the ground, armoured operations were extremely difficult for both sides in Italy. Neither of the two Allied armies ever contained more than two armoured divisions (although there was more armour available in the independent armoured brigades). For example, from Salerno to the Volturno (reached in October 1943), US Fifth Army had US 1st Armored and British 7th Armoured, but then lost the Desert Rats, who were sent home to take part in the Normandy landings. The same thing had happened to the US 2nd Armored, who had been in Patton's Seventh Army in Sicily. Eighth Army contained no armoured divisions until the arrival of the 5th Canadian Armoured Division (5 CAD), which replaced 7th Armoured Division, but went to Eighth Army instead of US Fifth. They were followed by the British 6th Armoured Division in March 1944 during the battles for Cassino, under the command of Maj Gen V. Evelegh (later to hand over to Gen Gerald Templer who found fame after the war during the operations in Malaya). Finally in May 1944, the South African 6th Armoured Division arrived and went under the command of Fifth Army, so each Army had only two armoured divisions for the rest of the war.

Special mention must be made of the American 1st Armored Division, which had been the first US armoured division to go overseas and to fight against the Germans in North Africa. The 'Old Ironsides' fought throughout the Italian campaign, being the first Allied troops to enter Rome, and saw more days of actual field service than any other US armoured division. They landed in Italy under a great armoured commander, Maj Gen Ernest N. Harmon, who left them in July 1944 to command a corps, his place being taken by Maj Gen Vernon E. Pritchard, who remained in command until the end of the war. Harmon had taken over the division from Maj Gen Orlando Ward, after the debacle at Kasserine Pass. He wrote about the forthcoming campaign: 'I am also tremendously interested in the problem of the use of tanks in Italy and am looking forward to it with a very serious mind for I feel that we are going to be under a tremendous handicap as to terrain'.

Worthy of mention also is Gen Geoffrey Keyes, who was Patton's Chief of Staff in the early days of 2nd Armored Division. He had activated and commanded 9th Armored Division, but was taken away to become Patton's deputy commander for the 'Torch' operation and remained as his deputy for the invasion of Sicily. It was Keyes who had commanded the 'Provisional Corps' which Patton had formed for the sweep to take Palermo. He commanded US II Corps in Italy and after the war went on to command both US Seventh and Third Armies. A contemporary wrote of him to me: 'He was the "brains" behind Gen Patton . . . but sadly he shunned publicity so little is known of this great armor commander.'

GERMAN ARMOUR It was for the most part definitely not good tank country, but that does not mean that armour was not used skilfully during the campaign, nor that there were no able Allied tank commanders. However, it was the Germans who had, on balance, more powerful armoured forces in Italy, although the numbers of panzer and panzergrenadier divisions varied considerably at various stages of the campaign. Rommel was for a time considered by Hitler for the post which eventually went to Kesselring, the command of all forces in Italy, but the Führer finally preferred to put Rommel in charge of strengthening the Atlantic Wall against the forthcoming Allied invasion.

At the time of the Allied invasion of Italy, the German forces were divided under CinC South (Kesselring) and Army Group 'C' (Rommel), with a total of 19 divisions, which included the following Panzer and Panzergrenadier divisions:

Under Kesselring	*Under Rommel*
LXXVI Pz Corps (containing	162 (Turco) Inf Corps
16 Pz Div & 29 PzGren Div)	(containing 18 Pz Div)
XIV Pz Corps (containing 26 Pz Div	LI Mtn Corps (containing
3 & 15 PzGren Div)	Adolf Hitler Pz Div)
	LXXXVII Corps (containing
	24 Pz Div & 90 PzGren Div)

By the time of the final Allied offensive in April 1945, neither XIV or XXVI Pz Corps had any Pz or PzGren Divs under command, while there was just 26 Pz Div and 29 and 90 PzGren Divs left within the remaining corps. The two panzer corps commanders were initially Hube and Herr. In October 1943 Hube handed over to Gen von Senger und Etterlin, who continued to command XIV Corps for the rest of the campaign. Gen Traugott Herr, who had been commanding 13th Panzer in Russia, also remained in Italy throughout the entire campaign, becoming commander of 10th Army in October 1944, his place in LXXVI Pz Corps being taken by Gen von Schwerin. Perhaps the highspot of von Senger's military career was during the Cassino battles, when the 100,000 men of his corps successfully defended their key positions, thus seriously delaying the Allied advance. It was also von Senger who, on 4th May 1945, arrived at Mark Clark's headquarters as the German liaison officer charged with ensuring the terms of capitulation.

COMMONWEALTH ARMOUR The Canadian government had authorized the formation of 1st Canadian Armoured Division early in 1941, and it formed in March, redesignated as 5 CAD and sailed for the UK in the autumn. It had been agreed that 30th Corps HQ would be exchanged for 1st Canadian Corps and 7th Armoured Division with 5 CAD, and this took place at the end of 1943. After its arrival in Italy the division had four different GOCs in as many months. Brig B.M. Hoffmeister took over from Maj Gen E.L.M. Burns, who succeeded Gen Crerar as Corps Commander.

Bert Hoffmeister was a militia infantry officer (Seaforths) in 1939 and commanded the battalion for the landings in Sicily. . . . Taking command of 5CAD in the spring of 1944, he trained the formation for the operations in the Liri Valley in May–June . . . After regrouping after the Liri Valley 5th Armoured was outstanding, in my opinion, at the Gothic Line. . . . Bert commanded the division for the rest of the war, in Italy and finally in Holland. His command was distinguished – imaginative, courageous, thorough. He was an outstanding leader as well as commander, the best of Canadian generals I would say, at least as divisional commander.'[11]

The 6th South African Armoured Division was commanded by Maj Gen Evered Poole throughout its service in Italy. It went into the line at Cassino, and later took part in operations to capture Florence and breach the Gothic Line. The Springboks suffered from a lack of infantry and had to have the British 24 Guards Brigade attached throughout their year of operations. The division's achievements were considerable and due in no small measure to the calibre of its GOC.

The 2nd New Zealand Division which fought in Italy, was a 'new model' division with some 4,500 vehicles and 20,000 men. The GOC was Lt Gen Sir Bernard Freyberg VC, whom Churchill likened to a salamander, because he 'thrived on fire'. He inspired his men by commanding from the front, but although he was a very brave and first-class leader, he cannot be classed as a great armoured commander.

POLISH ARMOUR It would also be unthinkable not to mention the Polish 2nd Corps in Italy and their bloody victory at Monte Cassino, after so many other units had tried and failed to take the monastery. In their assaults they were valiantly supported by the Sherman tanks of the Polish 2nd Armoured Brigade. By the end of the battle over a quarter of the corps' infantry were casualties.

A HOTSHOT GUNNER   To close on Italy, it is worth remembering that a tank commander is only as good as the rest of his crew, so a good tank gunner is worth his weight in gold. Cpl 'Alfie' Nicholls of B Squadron, 9th Queen's Royal Lancers, was one such gunner. His pre-war hobby had been poaching the local squire's pheasants on his way to work, using a .22 rifle which he concealed down one of his trouser legs. In later years he reckoned that the experience he acquired then was of the greatest value to him later on in perfecting his skill in tank gunnery. In one day during the Battle of Alamein he knocked out nine German tanks and 14 during the entire battle. Gen Montgomery, who had been listening for part of the time to the tank's wireless, gave an immediate order that Nicholls should be given the MM. His reputation as a brilliant shot was to continue through the rest of the war in North Africa and then Italy. His OC, Major Derek Allhusen, told me:

In B Squadron's last tank battle of the war, just south of the River Po, east of Ferrara, against the remnants of the 26th Panzer Division, Alfie's shooting was seen at its most brilliant when three German Mark IV tanks came along a road across our front at about 800 to 1,000 yards distance at high speed. He scored a right and a left and the third tank hit hard with smoke pouring out of its engine disappeared out of sight to be found by us the next day. This was to be the final example of his great skill as a tank gunner. During the war he had been responsible for the destruction of some 40 to 50 German tanks.

NOTES TO CHAPTER 7

1   W.G.F. Jackson, *The Battle for Italy*

2   Quoted in Maj Gen H. Essame, *Patton, the Commander*

3   Hube was one of only 27 members of the Wehrmacht to be awarded oakleaves, swords and diamonds to the Knight's Cross. Other Panzer commanders to receive this award were FM Rommel; Oberst Adalbert Schulz, CO 25 Pz Regt; Gen Hermann Balck, of 4 Pz Army; Gen Hasso von Manteuffel, of 5 Pz Army; and Lt Gen Dr Karl Mauss, comd 7 Pz Div. Two SS pz comds, Dietrich and Herbert Gille, also received the award.

4   Quoted in *Hitler's Generals*.

5   Quoted in *Patton, the Commander*.

6   *The Patton Papers*, Vol. 2.

7   *The Patton Papers*.

8   Leese would hand over in October 1944 to Gen McCreery, who had been commanding X (Br) Corps.

9   Said by Harold Macmillan and quoted in Christopher Tunney, *A Biographical Dictionary of World War II*

10   FM Earl Alexander of Tunis, *Memoirs 1940–1945*

11   Quoted from a letter written by Dr William McAndrew of the Directorate of History, National Defence HQ, Ottawa, to the author.

8   D DAY

Between 12th and 15th May 1943, a conference, code-named 'Trident', was held in Washington, and attended by Roosevelt, Churchill and their senior advisors, at which the invasion of France was agreed provisionally for 1st May 1944.

The Build-up

In preparation for the invasion there followed an immense build-up of troops, vehicles and equipment in the UK, until Great Britain was bursting at the seams with some three million men. These included many American formations direct from the USA, Allied divisions taken from Italy, 'home-grown' British divisions and British Commonwealth, French and Polish elements. These forces included a large proportion of tanks and other AFVs, although those in the assault formations were 'specialized armour' rather than normal armoured units, which would follow once the initial beach-head was captured. The assault force basically comprised the US First Army and the British Second Army, plus airborne formations from both nations. The overall grouping for the opening phase was as follows:

	US First Army Group		*British Twenty-first Army Group*		
Follow-up Armies	US Third Army		First Canadian Army		
Assault Armies	US First Army		British Second Army		
Follow-up Corps	VIII (two divs)	XIX (two divs)	VIII (three divs)	XII (three divs)	
Assault Corps	VII 79 Inf Div	V 2 Armd Div	XXX 49 Inf Div	I	
Follow-up Divs	9 Inf Div 90 Inf Div	2 Inf Div 29 Inf Div	7 Armd Div	51 Inf Div	
Assault Divs	4 Inf Div	1 Inf Div	50 Inf Div	3 Cdn Inf Div	3 Br Inf Div
Assault areas	Utah	Omaha	Gold	Juno	Sword

SPECIALIZED ARMOUR   Before dealing with the main armoured forces, a word about the specialized armour. The driving force behind the vast proportion of these strange devices, which were the product of many inventive minds, was one man, arguably the greatest British trainer of armoured soldiers ever, namely, Maj Gen Percy Hobart. He had already proved his prowess pre-war on Salisbury Plain, again in Egypt with the Mobile Division and yet again when he was responsible for the formation and training of the soon-to-become-great 11th Armoured Division. However, his finest achievement was undoubtedly his work with 'Hobo's Funnies', as the specialized armoured vehicles came to be called. In 1943, at the age of 57, he was switched from 11th Armoured (on the grounds that he was too old to command them in action) to reorganizing 79th Armoured Division and given the task of preparing the 'Funnies' which would spearhead the invasion. He took to this latest challenge with all his customary enthusiasm, and although for the most part his division fought in 'penny packets', his eagle eye was everywhere and his contribution to the Allied success in Normandy was enormous. Strange tanks, such as those fitted with deep-wading screens, mine-clearing flails, flamethrowers and tankborne searchlights, joined more conventional armoured bulldozers and armoured engineer-assault vehicles.

79th Armoured Division played a major part in the success of D day and went on being used as far as the crossing of the Rhine, when it had a strength of 21,000 all ranks and 1,566 tracked vehicles (compared to the 350 AFVs and 14,000 men in a normal armoured division). Liddell Hart rightly described them as the 'tactical key to victory', while Nigel Duncan, in his book about the division, captures their jaunty mood: 'The inverted triangle with its ferocious Bull's Head, the divisional sign of "Hobo's Funnies", was better known and more widely distributed in Second Army's area than any other. Inspired by its divisional commander, it pursued its way with gaiety tempered with the resolution to be defeated by no difficulty whether of Nature's or man's creation.'[1]

BRITISH AND COMMONWEALTH ARMOUR   Until early 1942, British armoured divisions, like those in both Germany and the USA, had been 'armour heavy', comprising two armoured brigades and just one infantry motorized battalion, plus a support group of three artillery regiments and an infantry battalion, with additional divisional troops which contained an armoured car regiment and a battalion of engineers. This enormous force contained nearly 15,000 men (including first-line reinforcements) and over 4,500 vehicles, including 561 AFVs (340 tanks, 58 armoured cars, 163 carriers and scout cars). By 1942 the all-armoured formation was dead, battle experience having shown that a smaller, better-balanced force was far preferable. One of the armoured brigades was replaced by an infantry brigade, the support group split up and artillery, engineer and other supporting arms and services divided between the brigades, while the armoured car regiment was replaced by a more powerfully equipped armoured reconnaissance regiment. Armoured car regiments were still vital for longer range recce, so they became corps troops, while for close recce within infantry divisions units of the newly formed Reconnaissance Corps were employed. Thus, by 1944, the AFV content of armoured divisions had shrunk to 306 tanks, but their motorized infantry had increased. The main tank in these formations was the Cromwell (75mm gun), with a stiffening of Sherman Fireflies (17-pdr gun) or later, Challengers (also 17-pdr).

It was the same within infantry divisions, where, in 1942, tank brigades were substituted for one of the three infantry brigades – a policy which Lt Gen Le Q. Martel, who was then Commander Royal Armoured Corps, described as 'the absorption of the armoured forces into the rest of the army'. However, this did not work, as it was found that there were insufficient infantry reserves, so the 'mixed' division was abolished. However, the tank brigade remained as close support to the infantry division, mainly being equipped with the better armoured and slower Churchill tank. Thus, a fair proportion of the British armour used in Northwest Europe was made up of these independent armoured brigades. The actual number of British armoured divisions to be used in Northwest Europe was small – 7th Armoured, under Maj Gen W.E.J. Erskine, 11th Armoured (Maj Gen G.P.B. Roberts), and the specially formed Guards Armoured (Maj Gen A.H.S. Adair) being the sum total. To these must be added independent tank brigades, supporting the infantry formations.

Gen 'Bobbie' Erskine had commanded the Desert Rats during their memorable advance from Tripoli and throughout their short stay in Italy. His division had been brought back to add a leavening of battle-experienced soldiers to the British forces for the Normandy campaign. With the benefit of hindsight, although this was of considerable help to those units assisted, it did not prove to be such a good idea for the Desert Rats. To start with, 7th Armoured were upset to lose their tried and trusted Sherman tanks and to receive in their place Cromwells, which many considered to be inferior. A number of their best officers and NCOs were then posted to other formations in order to pass on their knowledge and experience, which must have been most unsettling for those who remained.[2] It was clear once the fighting had started that the approach of these veterans was understandably more cautious and deliberate than that found among those who had never been in action before. This led Montgomery to feel that 7th Armoured were not making sufficiently rapid progress. He replaced Erskine with Maj Gen G.L. Verney, who had been commanding 6th Guards Tank Brigade. At the same time, commanders of 22nd Armoured Brigade and the CRA 7th Armoured also changed, together with over a hundred other officers and men. As the division's history points out, 'It was therefore, a rather different Division, still much under strength . . . that was to carry on the Normandy fighting.'

GOC 11th Armoured, Maj Gen 'Pip' Roberts, was a remarkable soldier, whose three DSOs and other decorations for gallantry give an indication of his bravery and prowess. He commanded 11th Armoured from Normandy to the Baltic and his division was considered to be one of the best in Northwest Europe. In his book *The Forgotten Victor*, John Baynes describes the 37-year-old 'Pip' Roberts as being 'the outstanding British armoured leader of the war.' Maj Gen Allan Adair's Guards Armoured Division earned for itself and its commander an equally fine reputation.

At corps level, mention should be made of three proven armoured corps commanders – Crocker, O'Connor and Horrocks. Gen Sir John Crocker, who had commanded 3rd Armoured Brigade in France in 1940, returned in the vanguard of the liberating armies as commander I Corps. Both the Guards Armoured and 11th Armoured were part of VIII Corps, one of the follow-up corps, under the command of Gen Sir Richard O'Connor, who had escaped from POW camp in Italy during the winter of 1943 and rejoined the fray, his determination and enthusiasm undimmed by his arduous period of captivity. Another armoured commander, who had also proved himself in the desert, Gen Sir Brian Horrocks was still recovering from his wounds, but would later take over command of XXX Corps from Lt Gen G.C. Bucknall, when Monty sacked Bucknall after warning him to 'get on or get out', at the same time as replacing GOC 7th Armoured, who were spearheading the advance of XXX Corps. Chester Wilmot said of Horrocks, when he first took over the Corps, 'Within a few days his fresh and fiery spirit had transformed the corps. A tall, lithe figure, with white hair, angular features, penetrating eyes and eloquent hands, he moved among his troops more like a prophet than a general.'[3]

Within 2nd Canadian Corps was the 4th Canadian Armoured Division. The division had been organized and commanded by Maj Gen 'Worthy' Worthington, but was taken to France by Maj Gen George Kitching, who commanded 4th CAD during its first operations in Normandy. He also would fall foul of Monty, being blamed somewhat unfairly for the delay in closing the Falaise gap and thus allowing numerous German panzer forces to live to fight another day. He was replaced by Maj Gen Harry Foster and then by Maj Gen Christopher Vokes, whom Montgomery described as 'a plain cook' – noted for personal bravery and plain speaking, but not for tactical brilliance.

Also part of the 2nd Canadian Corps was the 1st Polish Armoured Division, under the great Maj Gen Maczek, which was to take part in the battle of the Falaise pocket. The Poles were not the only foreign armour in 2nd Canadian Corps, there were also armoured brigades from the free Belgians and Czechs. US ARMOUR Of the 16 US armoured divisions to be activated in WW2, most saw service in Northwest Europe in one or more of the five separate campaigns into which the US Army 'officially' divided the Northwest Europe campaign. These were: 1. Normandy, 2. Northern France, 3. Rhineland, 4. Ardennes-Alsace and 5. Central Europe. It is perhaps easiest to show these in the form of a table (opposite).

The armoured divisions were divided between the corps of First and Third US Army; for example, Third Army's initial order of battle contained 4th, 5th, 6th and 7th Armored, plus 2nd French Armoured Division. Among the armoured division commanders there were a number who would eventually emerge as great tank commanders: Ernie Harmon and 'Tiger Jack' Wood, together with more junior commanders such as Cols Creighton W. Abrams and Bruce C. Clarke, who had as yet to prove themselves.

'Well, I have an Army and it's up to me. "God show the right." As far as I

Division	Campaigns	Division	Campaigns
2nd Armored	1,2,3,4 & 5	10th Armored	2,3,4 & 5
3rd "	1,2,3,4 & 5	11th "	3,4 & 5
4th "	1,2,3,4 & 5	12th "	3,4 & 5
5th "	1,2,3,4 & 5	13th "	3,4 & 5
6th "	1,2,3,4 & 5	14th "	3,4 & 5
7th "	1,2,3,4 & 5	16th "	3 & 5
8th "	2,3,4 & 5	20th "	3 & 5
9th "	2,3,4 & 5		

can remember, this is my twenty-seventh start from zero since entering the US Army. Each time I have made a success of it, and this one must be the biggest.' So wrote Patton in his diary on 26th January, having arrived in the UK that morning. His Army HQ arrived by sea from the USA at Glasgow docks three days later and Patton was there to greet them, 'aglitter with gleaming brass and boots'. Together they went by rail to Peover Camp, near Knutsford in Cheshire, where they were soon joined by the units which made up the 253,500 men in 'Georgie's Boys', as Third Army was soon called. Patton made visits to all his units, treating them to his 'off the cuff' speech. There are many versions of this, but the message was always the same, the need to fight, to kill the enemy and for everyone to do their duty no matter what their job might be. The enlisted men loved his profanity: 'There's one great thing you men can say when it's all over and you're home once more. You can thank God that twenty years from now, when you're sitting around with your grandson on your knee and he asks you what you did in the war you won't have to shift him to the other knee, cough and say, "I shovelled shit in Louisiana".'[4]

In the opening chapter of this book I included Ernest Swinton's 'Tank Tips', so I think it is interesting to include some of Patton's 'Fighting Principles', which he issued in a Letter of Instruction to all his Corps, Division and Separate Unit Commanders on 6th March 1944 (see overleaf).

Patton goes on to cover Orders, and then deals with administration. His earthy remarks on the supply service getting the things asked for 'to the right place at the right time', on visiting the wounded personally, on awarding decorations promptly and on maintaining perfect discipline are straight from the heart, as are his comments about reports from stragglers being viewed with scepticism – they '. . . seek to justify themselves by painting alarming pictures'. He also talks about the need for keeping in good physical shape – 'Fatigue makes cowards of us all. Men in condition do not tire.'

He closes this first Letter of Instruction with the words, 'Do not take counsel of your fears.' It was followed by a series of such Letters of Instruction, but at the same time, Patton was everywhere, visiting his units and making sure that his messages got across.

'1. COMMAND, Leadership. (1) Full Duty. Each, in his appropriate sphere, will lead in person. Any commander who fails to obtain his objective, and who is not dead or severely wounded, has not done his full duty.

(2) Visits to the front. The Commanding General or his Chief of Staff (never both at once) and one member of the general staff sections, the signal, medical, ordnance, engineer and quartermaster sections should visit the front daily. . . . The function of these staff officers is to observe, not to meddle . . . your primary mission as a leader is to see with your own eyes and to be seen by the troops . . .

Execution. In carrying out a mission, the promulgation of the order represents not over 10% of your responsibility. The remaining 90% consists of assuring, by means of personal supervision on the ground, by yourself and your staff, proper and vigorous execution.

Rest periods. Staff personnel, commissioned and enlisted, who do not rest, do not last. . . . When the need arises, everyone must work all the time, but these emergencies are not frequent; *unfatigued men last longer and work better under high pressure.*

Location of command posts. The farther forward the CPs are located the less time is wasted in driving to and from the front. . . .

2. COMBAT PROCEDURE. Maps. We are too prone to believe that we acquire merit solely through the study of maps in the safe seclusion of a Command Post. . . .

Plans. Plans must be simple and flexible . . . They should be made by the people who are going to execute them. . . .

Reconnaissance. You can never have too much reconnaissance. Use every means available before, during and after battle. Reports must be facts, not opinions; negative as well as positive. . . . information is like eggs: the fresher the better'.

Third Army did not start to move over to France until 5th July and Patton spent the three weeks waiting in the UK, fretting that the war would be over before he could get a 'piece of the action'. On landing, at an airstrip near Omaha beach, he promised the waiting newsmen that he would '. . . personally shoot that paper-hanging son of a bitch just like I would a snake!'5 The delay in sending Third Army over to France had been deliberate, as Patton's force was to be used for the breakout. However, it also assisted in the smoke-screen of subterfuge designed to make the Germans think that the main Allied assault would be in the Pas de Calais area, as it was unthinkable to the Nazis that the Allies would not use Patton – in their opinion the best Allied general – to command the main attack force. Patton would have to endure a further wait, while Bradley, somewhat ponderously, made certain that conditions were right to launch the American assault.

Chief Marshal of Armoured Forces, Pavel Alexandrovich Rotmistrov started the new policy of building up the Soviet Union's armoured formations. (CAFM)

Soviet armour in flames. Outclassed in all respects, such Soviet tanks as this BT 1 fast tank, with its two machine guns, was easy meat for the German Panzer 3s and 4s. (TM)

General der Panzertruppe Heinrich von Vietinghoff, who commanded XLVI Corps, talking here with Maj Gen Walter Kruger (*left*). Considered by many to be one of Germany's best tank generals along with Guderian, Hoepner, Hoth, Schmidt and Reinhardt. (HS)

Brave defender of Stalingrad, Gen Vasili Ivanovich Chuikov, was commanding the 64th Army at the age of only 42. 'Stalingrad became the Verdun of the Second World War', commented historian Brig Peter Young. (CAFM)

Greatest general and tank commander of the Soviet Army, Marshal Georgi Konstantin Zhukov. A brave and energetic soldier, he became a living legend after organising the defence of Moscow. (CAFM)

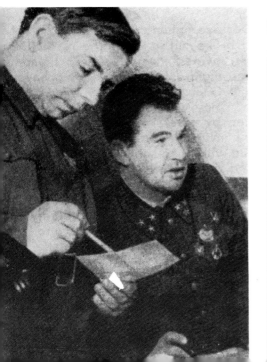

Gen Erich von Manstein (*left*), architect of the 1940 *Fall Gelb* plan for the invasion of France, was not privy to the planning of Operation Barbarossa, because he was serving at too low a level. Manstein would prove to be one of the greatest German generals of WW2. (IWM)

A Soviet tank company listen to an address by the OC, as they prepare for the next attack while safely hidden in a forest leaguer. The tanks are KV IAs. (TM)

Lt Gen Ferdinand Heim, whose XLVIII Panzer Corps was virtually annihilated by masses of T 34s in Operation Uranus. He was sentenced to death by Hitler, later jailed instead and reduced to the rank of private soldier. (HS)

Field Marshal Wilhelm List, who was dismissed by Adolf Hitler, for failing to push on as deep into the USSR as the Fuehrer wanted or to capture the Soviet oilfields. He is seen here inspecting panzer troops in Bulgaria in happier days in April 1941. (TM)

Even Gen Heinz Guderian had his ups and downs with his beloved Führer, being dismissed after protesting about the terrible conditions under which his poor soldiers had to fight. He was recalled to active duty in February 1943 and became Inspector of Armoured Troops, but was dogged by ill-health and professional jealousies within the higher army echelons. He was appointed Army Chief of Staff in July 1944 and lasted until 28th March 1945, when he was again dismissed after an epic shouting match with Hitler. (IWM)

This Soviet tank commander is explaining to the crews of his platoon of T 34s, the tactics of a new advance in a forested area on the Eastern Front. The original caption explains how, in a 40-day period in early 1945, over 800,000 Germans were killed and 350,000 taken prisoner. (TM)

Gen Konstantin Konstantinovich Rokossovsky, one of the Red Army's most brilliant tank commanders, is seen here inspecting a knocked out German heavy tank destroyer called 'Ferdinand'. He is standing on the ground in front of the group, while Maj Gen Fedorovid Telegin, leans on the barrel of the gun. At the time the photograph was taken (July 1943), Rokossovsky was commanding the Central Front. (CAFM)

The original caption reads: 'Hitlerites clamour all over the world that their retreat is planned. Here is one of the many illustrations for the German reports on planned retreat!' Such grim scenes were all too commonplace as the 'Red Steamroller' got into its stride. (TM)

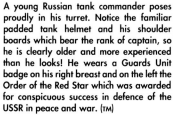

A young Russian tank commander poses proudly in his turret. Notice the familiar padded tank helmet and his shoulder boards which bear the rank of captain, so he is clearly older and more experienced than he looks! He wears a Guards Unit badge on his right breast and on the left the Order of the Red Star which was awarded for conspicuous success in defence of the USSR in peace and war. (TM)

Posthumous Heroine of the Soviet Union, Mariya Vasil'yevna Oktyabr'skaya deserves a special place in this book. After her husband was killed, she applied to the authorities to build a tank from her own personal savings to fight in against the Nazis. This she did, first as a driver mechanic then as a Guards Sergeant, and was badly wounded near Krynka on 18th January 1944 after knocking out two enemy guns. She died two months later and is buried at the Wall of Glory in Smolensk. (CAFM)

Operational briefing in Sicily. Montgomery briefs Alexander, whilst Patton and others look on. Gen Alexander, Eisenhower's deputy, was in overall command of 'Operation Husky', as the attack on Sicily was called. Alexander did not appreciate the depth of feeling existing amongst the US commanders and their desire to do well after the generally disappointing showing in North Africa. (IWM)

Another first rate panzer commander was Gen Hans Valentin Hube, who commanded XIV Pz Corps and initially had two of his divisions in Sicily. Despite having lost an arm in WW1, Hube served with distinction in both Russia and Italy. Here he is seen in his command vehicle at the 'sharp end' naturally! (HS)

'The Little Tiger', as Montgomery called Gen (later FM) Sir John Harding, was one of the most successful British armoured commanders. Here he leans on the barrel of a Panther tank turret which the Germans had incorporated into their defensive positions in both the Hitler and Gothic Lines. With him are Alexander and Leese (pointing). Gen Sir Oliver Leese was a capable and conscientious commander, who was well liked by his troops. (IWM)

Maj Gen 'Tiger Jack' Wood, who commanded the 4th Armored Division, was one of the finest US armoured commanders of WW2. However, he was relieved of his command on 3rd December 1944, supposedly on the grounds of ill-health. It is far more likely that he fell out with Patton, who continually expected his armoured divisions to press on regardless. According to one history of 4th Armored, when Wood was ordered to spearhead the penetration into the Alsace-Lorraine and close the Belfort Gap, he protested that his troops were 'not robots and needed a rest'. He always 'roared back' when Patton roared at him – hence his nickname. (PM)

Maj Gen Evered Poole, was GOC 6th South African Armoured Division, which achieved a great deal in Italy and had a high reputation, due in no small measure to his ability. (IWM)

Despite the infamous 'slapping incident', Patton was a warm-hearted man; despite his warlike reputation, he was easily moved to tears by the carnage of war. He admired bravery above all things and abhored cowards. Here he talks to some wounded infantrymen at Agrigento aerodrome, Sicily, 25th July 1943. (US)

Gen Frido von Senger und Etterlin, was a cavalryman and a first class panzer commander. He was initially the German advisor to the Italian commander in Sicily. (IWM)

Another brilliant panzer general in Italy was Gen Traugott Herr, who became commander of 10th Army. (IWM)

Gen Bert Hoffmeister was probably the best Canadian armoured commander of WW2, commanding 5th CAD in Italy and then in Holland. (CFPU)

Rommel on the Atlantic Wall. The Desert Fox was given a new challenge of organising the defence of the Channel coast against the coming Allied onslaught. In the event his 'Atlantic Wall' was breached, thanks to the success of the Allied cover plan, which convinced the Germans that the main assault would come in the Pas de Calais area and that Normandy was merely a diversion. (TM)

Patton addresses one of his units. Old 'Blood and Guts' went around every single unit in his US 3rd Army, giving his famous pep-talk to the troops. They loved his down-to-earth approach and revered their great commander. Here he speaks to men of the 10th Infantry Regiment, 5th Infantry Division, during training in County Down, Northern Ireland, 30th March 1944. (US)

One of the toughest Nazi SS panzer commanders was Sepp Dietrich. Hitler once said of him: 'he's a man who is simultaneously cunning, energetic and brutal'. He was one of the only 27 winners of the 'Brilliants' to the Knight Cross of the Iron Cross, but was also sentenced to life imprisonment by the Allied War Crimes Tribunal for his part in the Malmedy massacre. (CM)

The most famous of all Tiger tank commanders was SS Obersturmfuehrer Michael Wittmann, whose four Tigers held up the entire 7th Armoured Division and practically annihilated their advanced guard, knocking out 25 tanks, 14 carriers and 14 half-tracks. (TM)

Monty admires 'Pistol Packing' George Patton's Colt .45 'Peacemaker' in his right hand holster, with its ivory handle. GSP often wore two six shooters, the other being a Smith & Wesson .357 Magnum. They were not, as some thought, pearl-handled revolvers. 'Godammit' said Patton, when someone asked, 'my guns are ivory handled. Nobody but a pimp from a cheap New Orleans whorehouse would carry one with pearl grips!' (IWM)

Maj Gen Jacques Philippe Leclerc, commander of the French 2nd Armoured Division, which was part of Patton's 3rd Army. They were given the honour of liberating Paris. Leclerc was a dashing commander, very much in the Free French image, determined to make up for their poor showing in 1940. (GF)

A tough-looking group of American tank crewmen, belonging to 1st Platoon, B Company, 37 Tank Battalion, 1st Armored Division, pose in England on one of their Shermans, at Devizes, Wiltshire, May 1944.(GF)

This group of British commanders seen here with Montgomery, near Nijmegen in September 1944, includes Maj Gen G.L. Verney (GOC 7th Armoured Division) on right, who replaced Gen Bobbie Erskine during August 1944, when Monty decided to make a number of staff changes within the Desert Rats, as he was unhappy with their cautious performance. Also in the photograph (second from left) is Gen Dick O'Connor, who later was to have problems with his autocratic C in C. (IWM)

Gen 'Pip' Roberts, brilliant young commander of 11th Armoured Division, is seen here, north of the Seine, talking to Brig Roscoe Harvey, commander of 29th Armoured Brigade. (IWM)

A gaunt looking FM Erwin Rommel outside his headquarters in the chateau at La Roche-Guyon, on the Lower Seine. Rommel was seriously injured when his staff car was shot up by an RAF aircraft near Livarot, on 17th July 1944, while on his way back to his HQ after visiting front-line troops. (IWM)

Patton's Ghosts read about their exploits in *Stars and Stripes*, 14th November 1944. Third US Army went further, faster than any Army has done before or since, during their breakneck advance through Europe. (US)

Col Bruce C. Clarke, CO Combat Command 'A', 4th Armored Division, who earned his reputation defending St Vith in the Ardennes battle. Clarke went on to become a senior commander in the US Army, his final job being in command of the NATO Central Army Group at the time of the Berlin airlift. (PM)

Maj Gen Maurice Rose, CG 3rd Armored Division, was another of the great US Armor commanders, who some described as being 'Hollywood's idea of a soldier'. Sadly he was killed in action in late 1945 near Paderborn. (TM)

Commander of the 'Super Sixth' Maj Gen Bob Grow. Quieter and less spectacular than his Army Commander, GSP, or his fellow armored division commanders like 'Tiger Jack' Wood, Bob Grow was nevertheless a first class commander and his Sixth Armored gained an enviable reputation in NW Europe. (US)

Commanding Fifth Panzer Army on the left flank during the Battle of the Bulge, was Gen der Panzertruppe Hasso von Manteuffel, seen here in his ACV. He first entered the army as a 3rd Hussar at Rathenow in 1916, commanded the 7th Panzer Division in Russia, then the Gross Deutschland Division, before being promoted directly to command 5th Panzer Army. (HS)

On the last lap. A Soviet tank platoon gets ready to marry up with a platoon of mechanised infantry, before an attack. These T34 tanks are the upgunned T34/85, which was first introduced in December 1943. Its powerful 85-mm gun, well-sloped armour and wide tracks, made it a higly effective AFV which went on in service for over 20 years. (CAFM)

Victory in Berlin. The awesome Josef Stalin heavy tanks are seen here in front of the Brandenberg Gate in Berlin, shortly after the Nazis had capitulated. (CAFM)

The two greatest Soviet armoured commanders were undoubtedly Zhukov and Rokossovsky, seen here at the command post of 65th Army, near Warsaw, October 1944. They each commanded Fronts during the final assault on Germany. (CAFM)

'Not fit to fight in'. Both the US Army and the US Marine Corps used tanks and LVTs in their island hopping operations, such as here on Leyte in the central Philippines. However, AFVs were only used in small numbers. (US)

Allied Flag Raising Ceremony in Berlin. Gen Eisenhower, Marshal Zhukov, Field Marshal Montgomery and Gen Koenig were the principal figures in the ceremony held on 20th August 1945. In the background is the Kammergericht courthouse building which is where the Military Governors of each zone will meet to decide the policies for the governing of Germany as a whole. (TM)

The British and Indians made the best use of tanks to spearhead their re-capture of Burma from the Japanese. Here Shermans lead a lightning drive in the southern Mandalay area, which captured Meiktila after a 70-mile 'Blitzkrieg' sweep from their Irrawaddy bridgehead. (TM)

North Korean Blitzkrieg. On the 25th June 1950, fifty North Korean T34s spearheaded the invasion of South Korea and had similar success to the German attack ten years earlier in France. (SD)

North Korean tanks and infantry advance through a barrage, as they smash their way through the South Korean defences. (SD)

Fortunately, the Americans were able to hold the Pusan perimeter and build up their forces. Then they advanced northwards, passing knocked-out North Korean tanks, 18th August 1950. (US)

M46 Pattons, with their 90-mm guns were too powerful for anything the Chinese or North Koreans could produce. Here, two Pattons cover a road in the gutted town of Chorwon. (US/SD)

First US tanks into action in Korea were light M24 Chaffees, as seen here. Unfortunately, they were no match for the thick-armoured and better-armed T34/85s. (SD)

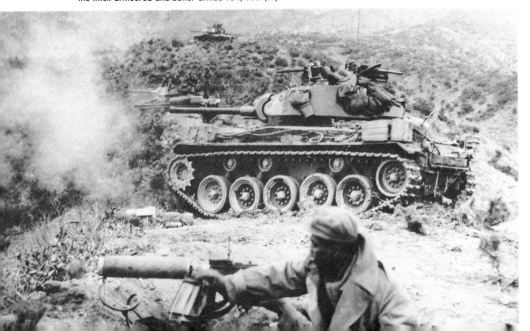

By far the best tank in service in Korea was the British Centurion Mark III, armed with a 20-pdr gun. Here a Centurion belonging to the 8th Hussars gives a lift to a section of Northumberland Fusiliers, as it climbs up the bank of the Imjin River. (IWM)

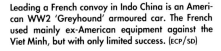

Chaffees were also used with limited success, but at least they were light enough to negotiate the terrain. (ECP/SD)

Leading a French convoy in Indo China is an American WW2 'Greyhound' armoured car. The French used mainly ex-American equipment against the Viet Minh, but with only limited success. (ECP/SD)

B Sqn 1st Armd Regt RAAC, pull into a squadron leaguer during Operation Barracuda. The RAAC had tanks in Vietnam from 1968, which performed with their usual excellence in all conditions. (SD)

Aussie tank commanders discuss their next move, whilst one of their Centurions stands ready. (AWM/SD)

M48 tanks from Co C, 34th Armor moving in line during a search and destroy mission at Filhol Plantation, 18th January 1967. (US/SD)

L Troop, 3rd Squadron, 11th Cavalry manoeuvre up a hill during Operation Junction City Phase II, some seven kms NE of Lai Khe, 13th April 1967. (US/SD)

LTC Creighton W. Abrahams, one of the most successful small unit commanders of US Armor in World War 2. Abrams went on to a highly successful post-war career, culminating in taking over in Vietnam from Gen Westmorland in 1968. Like a number of other famous US commanders his name has been given to an AFV, this time to the latest US main battle tank, the M1 and the others in this series (to date M1A1 and M1A2). (PM)

M113s from K Troop, 3rd Squadron, 11th Armored Cavalry Regiment, prepare to move out during a search and destroy mission, January 1971. (US/SD)

During the 1965 Indo-Pakistan War, Lt Col Tarapore, CO of 17 Horse (The Poona Horse), was posthumously awarded the Param Vir Chakra (Indian equivalent of the VC), for his bravery and leadership during the capture of the Phillora sector in Pakistan. (IA)

During the 'Lightning War' in 1971, 2nd Lt Arun Khetarpal of the Poona Horse was posthumously awarded the Param Vir Chakra for his bravery during the battle of the Basantar River. (IA)

An early Israeli armoured column, led by a machine-gun carrying jeep, followed by home-made armoured cars, known as 'sandwiches' because of their construction (see text). Note their open tops which allowed the crews to fire on the move. (DE)

Maj Gen Haim Bar-Lev was another brilliant tank commander, who had the distinction to command the first tank versus tank action near Rafa in 1949. (DE)

'Father' of the Israeli Armoured Corps was Maj Gen Yizhak Sade, who commanded 8th Armd Bde, its very first operational armoured formation. Born in Poland, he emigrated to Palestine in 1920 and joined the Haganah. He was the first to appreciate the importance of mobility. (DE)

Maj Gen Avraham 'Bren' Adan was one of the first students at the Israeli Armour School. Adan, who was born in Israel in 1926, was among the first tank commanders in the IDF. He commanded 82nd Tank Battalion in the Sinai campaign, took command of the Armoured Corps in 1969 and greatly distinguished himself in the Yom Kippur War while leading the 162nd Division. (DE)

'Advance now, out!' A typical Israeli tank commander. (DE)

Col (later Brig Gen) Uri Ben Ari, talking over his radio during operations in the lightning Sinai campaign of 1956, when he led the 7th Armd Bde. He then went on to become Commander of the Armoured Corps. (DE)

An IDF reserve unit 'bombing up' its modified Centurions shortly before the outbreak of the Six Day War. (DE)

Maj Gen Israel Tal, the most famous Israeli armoured commander ever. 'Talik' took command of the Israeli Armoured Corps in 1964 and made an immediate impact on professional standards. A 'giant amongst leaders', he was responsible for much of the design of the Merkava main battle tank. (IDF)

'Talik' gives out orders to a group of his commanders during the Six Day War. (IDF)

Maj Gen Dan Laner, who directed the battle on the Iraqi front during the Yom Kippur War, is seen here with Gen Bar-Lev and the instantly recognisable Israeli Defence Minister Moshe Dyan. (DE)

Col 'Gonen' Gorodish watches Gen Elazar giving orders over the radio during the Six Day War, while Col 'Men' Aviram sits in front of them. Aviram commanded an armoured brigade during the Six Day War. (DE)

Advancing into central Sinai. A tank company of Pattons advances at speed during the Yom Kippur War as they head for the Canal to attempt to halt the Egyptian breakout. (DE)

An Israeli Merkava company inside a Palestine camp in the Lebanon. (DE)

A Desert Rat tank commander in his turret during Operation 'Desert Sabre' (UKLF)

Tank crews belonging to one of the armoured regiments of 7th Armoured Brigade, getting acclimatised during the build-up towards Operation 'Desert Storm'. (UKLF)

Within Patton's 3rd Army was a single French armoured division, under the command of Maj Gen Jacques Philippe Leclerc. This division would rightfully be given the privilege of liberating Paris. Leclerc was a brave and resourceful soldier, who had been captured by the Germans in May 1940 at Lille, but managed to escape and join the Free French in the UK. He was sent out to Africa to become military governor of Chad and Cameroon, creating a Free French base in French Equatorial Africa. In December 1942 he led a force from Chad 1,500 miles across the desert to join the Eighth Army in North Africa, arriving in January 1943. Gen Brooke described him as 'the best type of French soldier . . . hard-bitten, capable and of great charm', while an American war correspondent likened him to 'a sophisticated d'Artagnan come to life again in the twentieth century.'

THE DEFENDERS Since the summer of 1943, Rommel had been in northern Italy, commanding Army Group B, and it was apparently Hitler's wish that he should take over as the commander of all German forces in Italy. Then, in late October 1943, the Führer changed his mind and appointed Kesselring instead. Rommel was earmarked to command a new HQ, formed from the staff of Army Group B, to be known as 'Army Group for Special Employment' and placed under direct control of OKW. It would have a vital role to play in the defence of the Channel coast against the coming Allied invasion.

THE DESERT FOX IN NORMANDY Rommel's orders were to make detailed tours of inspection of the coastal defences in the west and to prepare operational studies on each area, covering the employment of forces for defence and counter-attack. He was ordered to make specific recommendations on the employment of armour in the operational zones. His task was not an easy one, especially as the new HQ cut across the existing command structure for defence in the West, which was under the control of FM von Rundstedt. However, as the US Army's official history points out: 'The particular selection of Rommel undoubtedly had an additional morale motive. For the long neglected west garrison troops the appointment of a commander with Rommel's reputation in combat was a stimulant and a dramatization of the new importance assigned to the west.'

After his first round of inspections, Rommel wrote in his diary: 'Generally speaking the troops are not working hard enough on the construction of defences. They just don't realise how urgent it is. Everywhere there's a tendency to hive off reserves, and this will lead to the weakening of the coastal front.' He thus made it his business to see that the defences were strengthened, writing to his wife about the situation in Normandy: 'There's still a lot to do, because many a man here has been living a soft life and hasn't thought enough about the battles that are coming.' Very soon new obstacles started to appear – mines on the beaches and 'Rommel's asparagus', sharp stakes interlaced with barbed wire to protect against airborne landings. 'The main battle line is to be the beach', that was how Rommel began his first directive to his commanders. The Allied landing craft would first have to get through a network of underwater mines and obstacles, while behind the beaches would be a heavily mined Death Zone, covered by strongpoints, with panzer divisions immediately to the rear, their tanks and artillery dug in ready to pound the beaches or sweep in to clear the enemy the moment he landed.

Unfortunately, however, there were many who differed from Rommel's views. Guderian, for example, considered that the bulk of the available armour should be kept in reserve, well away from the beach defences, so that the panzers could be switched quickly once the main landing area had been determined and thus not become embroiled too early with minor or diversionary landings. This was also the view held by von Rundstedt and his senior panzer commander, Gen Baron Leo Geyr von Schweppenburg. It took no account of the Allied air supremacy which Rommel had already experienced in North Africa. Baron von Schweppenburg was just as worried by Rommel's 'Everything in the shop windows' plan, as Rommel was by the thought of their precious panzers having to move without air cover. 'Neither man budged in his views. Both were Swabian, both with a personal pride bordering – as the American interrogators later said of Geyr – 'upon the ridiculous'; and both obstinate to the point of pig-headedness.'[6] It was clearly a recipe for disaster.

GERMAN ARMOUR At the time of the Allied invasion there were only six panzer divisions and one panzergrenadier division stationed in northern France, and most of them were located too far away from the sea to take any immediate action, so the opportunity to deal with the invading force on the beaches would thus be lost. The number of panzer divisions rose to 10 quite quickly, but all were employed in typically un-panzerwaffe-like 'penny packets', particularly in the Caen area. These panzer divisions were: 2nd, 9th, 21st, 116th and the Pz Lehr division; 1st, 2nd, 9th, 10th, 12th SS Panzer divisions and the 17th SS Pz Grenadier division. Their total approximate tank strength was just over 1,500. Some of these divisions were still recovering from fighting in Russia, while others had to date no combat experience. The divergence of views as to where and how the armour should be employed did not help the situation, nor did the fact that both von Rundstedt and Hitler still considered the Pas de Calais area to be the most likely for the main Allied landing, and this would lead to a slow response when they realized, all too late, that they were wrong. However, Hitler did establish a special reserve for Rommel's use only, of 1 SS Pz Corps, under command of SS General Josef 'Sepp' Dietrich, who had been the head of the SS Lieberstandarte Adolf Hitler regiment during the early days and was among Hitler's most loyal and trusted followers. 'I've always given him the opportunity to intervene at sore spots,' Hitler is said to have remarked about Dietrich, 'he's a man who is simultaneously cunning, energetic and brutal.'[7] His brutality would become self-evident when, in 1946, he was given a life sentence for his part in the massacre of captured American troops at Malmedy. He was awarded the Knights Cross of the Iron Cross, and like Rommel, was one of only 27 winners of the Diamonds to that award.

It did not really help to have this special corps (comprising 21st Panzer

Division, the Panzer Lehr Division and 12th SS Panzer Division), 'outside' the rest of the panzer force which came under command of Gen von Schweppenburg's Panzer Group West (later called 5 Panzer Army). Its divisions were a mixed bag, the closest to the beaches being the worst equipped, namely, 21st Panzer Division. The division had been reformed in Normandy in mid-1943, after the original division was destroyed in the fall of Tunisia in May 1943. It included a number of DAK veterans, but was equipped with a motley collection of captured French tanks, with just a few Pz Kpfw IVs. Their commander was Lt Gen Edgar Feuchtinger, who had worked on Hitler's secret-weapons programme before taking command and showed little tactical ability in the battles in Normandy. The Panzer Lehr Division was quite a different story, being formed from the staff of the Panzer training schools. It was one of the strongest panzer divisions in the German army, with 109 tanks, 40 assault guns and 612 half-tracks – double the normal Pz division total. Its commander, Lt Gen Fritz Bayerlin, who was an old friend of Rommel's, had rejoined the German Army in the 1920s, became Guderian's Operations Officer in Russia in 1941, then Rommel's Chief of Staff in North Africa, where he was wounded late on and evacuated to Europe. Command of 3rd Panzer Division followed, then the Panzer Lehr. 12th SS Panzer Division 'Hitler Jugend' was composed of Hitler Youth, recruited from the SS military fitness camps; it was well up to strength with some 177 tanks and 12 assault guns. SS Lt Gen Fritz Witt was commanding, but was killed by Allied naval gunfire on 16th June, his place being taken by SS Maj Gen Kurt 'Panzer' Meyer, aged 33 and the youngest divisional commander in the German forces in 1944. Always in the thick of the fighting, a brave but fanatical Nazi, he was tall, handsome and totally dedicated to the Führer – 'You will hear a lot against Adolf Hitler in this camp' he told Milton Shulman when he interrogated him after the war, 'but you will never hear it from me . . . he was and still is the greatest thing that ever happened to Gemany.'[8] Bold, tough, and arrogant, he was the archetypal Nazi stormtrooper.

The Landings

The basic Allied landing tactics were slightly different between the American and British beaches. The Americans planned to have two waves of DD tanks, one at H– 5 minutes, the next at H, with the first wave of infantry landing at H + 1 minute, with successive waves every seven minutes from H + 30. Directly after the first wave of infantry, at H + 3, frogmen and combat engineers would deal with the beach obstacles. The British planned to use a much higher percentage of tanks – including, of course, the 'Funnies'.

THE 'FUNNIES', KEY TO SUCCESS   On the British beaches, the DD tanks were very successful; 13th/18th Hussars, for example, were launched some 5,000 yards out and swam ashore to cover the disembarkation of the assault troops and their progress inland. In the centre, on the Canadian front, they had only 1,000 yards to swim in, but were hampered once on the beach by obstacles of all types. In the western sector the sea was so rough that it was impossible to launch the DD tanks, so the 47th/7th Dragoon Guards and Sherwood Rangers were brought to the beach by landing craft and successfully supported 50th Division as they pushed six miles inland. The other 'Funnies' also did their job superbly well. As Montgomery wrote in his Foreword to the 79th's history: 'The Division is composed of units and equipment which have no parallel in any other Army in the world, and the skilful use of this equipment enabled us to obtain surprise in the tactical battle.'

In the American sector things did not go as well. Off Omaha beach, at H–50, two companies of DD tanks of 714st Tank Battalion were launched 6,000 yards offshore and almost immediately began to founder. Only five of the 32 tanks launched ever reached shore, the rest sinking in the heavy seas. Because of the lack of armoured support, movements of the infantry were able to be checked by small numbers of enemy. However, in general terms the Allies had no difficulty in getting ashore, holding and enlarging their beach-head.

THE GERMAN RESPONSE The German response was unlike anything one might have expected from the Panzerwaffe. The uncertainty as to whether the Allied landings in Normandy were really the main attack, the problems of dual command, the harm done by the Ultra interception, all combined with the strength of the Allied air, sea and ground attacks to cause almost complete paralysis. Only 21st Panzer Division was close enough to take any immediate action, yet it received no proper orders to leave its location on the banks of the Orne River, outside Caen. Feutchinger's division (he had gone to Paris on the eve of D day) advanced one armour group about 0630 hours, lost some tanks to British fire, but then held firm, effectively preventing the British from capturing Caen, although the division was now down to fewer than 70 battleworthy tanks. During the overcast morning, when air action was restricted, Hitler refused to release either the Panzer Lehr or Hitler Jugend divisions, so when they did move, in the afternoon after the skies had cleared, both suffered from Allied air attacks, which got progressively more severe – US Ninth Air Force fighters and bombers alone flew 3,000 sorties on D Day, mainly in the US zone of operation. Soon the Allied mastery of the air was so total as to prevent the Germans from moving safely except at night. One can well imagine the problems this caused. It made it all the easier for the Allies to build up superiority on the ground until they were far too strong to be pushed back into the sea. However, the German commanders, initially anyway, did not appear to be unduly worried by the Allied success. They were still convinced that the beach-head could be contained and the enemy defeated and that, in any case, this was not the main threat but merely a strong feint before the main invasion at Pas de Calais.

Rommel does appear to have grasped the seriousness of the situation, but he was too far away to make an immediate impact upon the battle. He had gone on leave to his home in Herrlingen on 4th June, and did not know about the invasion until he received a telephone call from his Chief of Staff, Gen Hans Speidel, at about 0600 hours on 6th June. Other senior German commanders were also away from Normandy and there appears to have been much indecision among those who remained, in particular at Rommel's HQ. The heavy bombing and naval bombardment had torn great gaps in the beach defences, Rommel's minefields and the Death Zone, as the Allies consolidated their foothold, but had Rommel been present it is certain that he would have taken positive action – 'If people had listened to me', he wrote later to his wife, 'we would have counter-attacked with three panzer divisions on the first evening and we would probably have defeated the attack.'[9]

When he did get back, at about 2200 hours, he immediately set about trying to restore the situation, but was hampered by the still widely held conviction that the Normandy landing was only a feint. This 'waiting for the real invasion' would continue to cloud German tactical thought for many days. And, instead of a clear-cut chain of command, the troops at the sharp end had to try to make sense of a mass of conflicting orders from a variety of headquarters. Undoubtedly the Germans had been caught on the wrong foot in every respect, but had some positive action been taken quickly enough the situation might have been retrieved. Three days later the Germans had still not mounted a properly organized panzer attack, so the Allied troops were able to push forward with confidence, defeating every piecemeal counter-attack the Germans mounted, until the chance to drive them out was lost for ever. 'Hitler's much-propagandized Atlantic Wall had been breached within a few hours. The once vaunted Luftwaffe had been driven completely from the air and the German Navy from the sea, and the Army taken by surprise. The battle was far from over, but its outcome was not long in doubt. "From June 9 on," says Speidel, "the initiative lay with the Allies".'[10]

NOTES TO CHAPTER 8

1 Nigel Duncan, 79th Armoured Division Profile Book, No 3

2 In *Normandy to the Baltic*, Montgomery explained, 'During the planning period, therefore, I set about putting across to the troops under my command a sound battle technique. This process was facilitated by the fact that I had 7 Armoured, 50 and 51 Divisions and two Armoured Brigades who had had considerable experience in the Eighth Army; by exchanging officers between these formations and those less experienced I endeavoured to spread our available experience as much as possible.'

3 As quoted in Philip Warner, *Horrocks, the General Who Led from the Front*

4 Martin Blumenson, *Patton Papers*, Vol. 2.

5 George S. Patton, *War as I Knew It*

6 David Irving, *Trail of the Fox*

7 As quoted in *The SS*, by the Editors of Time-Life Books

8 As quoted in *Hitler's Generals*

9 *Trail of the Fox*

10 William L. Shirer, *The Rise and Fall of the Third Reich*

9 NORMANDY TO BERLIN

Their foothold in Normandy secure, the Allies sought to break out of the beach-head area. Montgomery's basic strategy for the land battle in Normandy was to draw the main enemy strength onto the British Second Army on the eastern flank, in order that the Allies might more easily gain territory in the west and make the ultimate break-out on that flank, using the American First Army for this purpose. He did not consider the taking of ground in the Caen area to be so pressing, 'the need *there* was by hard fighting to make the enemy commit his reserves', he later wrote in his memoirs, 'so that the American forces would meet less opposition in their advances to gain the territory which was vital to the west.' Although Montgomery understood what was meant to happen (it was his plan after all) and remained supremely confident throughout, there was mounting unease at the slow progress and high casualties which this 'hard fighting' caused among the British and Canadian troops. However, his plan was certainly succeeding and von Rundstedt had already urgently requested – and been granted – reinforcements. He did not, though, get a free hand on how they were to be employed. Hitler taking a personal interest in every detail and decreeing that they would 'fight and die where they stood', rather than being able to withdraw to other positions when the tactical situation required.

The Battle for Normandy
'Again and again the same thing, Hitler grasps an operational idea without giving any consideration whatsoever to the necessary means, the necessary time and space, troops and supplies. Those are the fundamental elements of strategy which are necessary for success, but Hitler rarely took them into consideration.' That damning indictment of the Führer came from Gen Walter Warlimont, Jodl's deputy, during an interview just after the war, when he was trying to explain why the Allies were able to break out of Normandy, an area in which the defender should have held all the aces. Certainly Gen Geyr von Schweppenburg felt that it would have been perfectly possible to carry out mass counter-attacks with two or three panzer divisions, even in the close bocage country – 'we would have used the one to two hours of dawn and dusk and attacked with limited objectives during these hours', he said during a post-war interview, on 11th December 1947: 'I suggested these "tiger tactics" to Hitler. If the attack had been successful, effecting a breakthrough, we

would have gotten in among the Allied forces, forcing your air power to quit its attacks, which were a constant menace to panzer forces. Our supply routes would then have suffered from air attacks, but the success would have been worth it.'[1] The interviewer, Lt Robert W. Fye, commented that von Geyr was a very impressive figure who 'did not as yet appear in the grasp of old age, although he has 43 years of active service in the German Army behind him. He is quite tall and well built, with greyish-white hair and a very kindly face; he gives the appearance more of a scholarly college professor than a retired army officer. Since he speaks good English, the interview was held in that language. Gen Pz von Geyr is very expressive, and his conversation was animated by the use of his hands, which were constantly in motion.'

A number of other senior German panzer officers were interviewed about the fighting in Normandy and all blamed Hitler for interfering. They also blamed each other for using the wrong tactics. Guderian, for example, who was at the time Inspector General of Panzer Troops and thus not in an operational command, readily agreed with his interviewer (in August 1945) that not bringing armoured units against the Normandy beach-head had been a mistake, which he put down to a difference of opinion between Rommel and himself:

I was in France in April 44 to ask Rommel for his ideas on the employment of tanks, and I proposed withdrawing the panzer divisions (as did von Rundstedt and von Geyr) to form a panzer army north of Orleans. Rommel was of the opinion that he must retain the panzer divisions on the expected invasion front, which he thought would come at the mouth of the Somme, near Dieppe . . . There were therefore few panzer divisions behind the actual invasion front . . . I proposed to Hitler in May '44 withdrawing the panzer divisions and placing them in the neighbourhood of le Mans, but he refused. This was the real reason that no panzer divisions were in the neighbourhood of the invasion front line. . . . I could make proposals to Hitler, but I had no right as Inspector General to give orders. My proposals, prior to and during the invasion, were rejected by Hitler in favour of the opinions of Rommel and von Kluge. Hitler said that the generals in command at the front were right and my advisers were wrong.

After a further interview three years later, Lt Robert W. Fye commented that, physically, Guderian was not the impressive military figure one might have expected to see. He was a rather short, slight person who looked all of his 60 years. 'He appeared to be a very kindly man, cheerful despite his present circumstances. Throughout the interview, he evidenced an excellent sense of humour and gave the impression of being a very quick thinker, despite his disadvantage of speaking a language other his own.'[2]

'EPSOM' AND 'GOODWOOD' There followed two extremely hard-fought operations, known as 'Epsom' (26th June–1st July) and 'Goodwood' (18th July–20 th July), during which both sides suffered many casualties and lost large numbers of tanks. Certainly the operations drew most of the German armour, so that only two panzer divisions (Panzer Lehr and 2 SS Pz Div) remained opposite the Americans. But British and Canadian progress was continually thwarted, by such dazzling minor operations as the action by Michael Wittmann's small force of Tigers,[3] which held up the progress of the entire

British Seventh Armoured Division at Villers Bocage, almost wiping out their advanced guard of tanks and infantry, their total casualties being 25 tanks, 14 carriers and 14 half-tracks. Wittmann was awarded the Swords to his Knight's Cross for this action, and was offered a safe job in a training establishment, which he refused. He was killed a few weeks later, on 8th August, just south of Caen, during a tank battle with a troop of British-manned Shermans. Villers Bocage was undoubtedly the most remarkable small tank action of the war and Wittmann has gone down in history, characterized, in the words of 'Panzer' Meyer, as '. . . dying as he had lived – brave, dashing and a living example to his Grenadiers'.

Operation 'Epsom' had as its objective the encirclement of Caen, the main attack being made by Gen Sir Richard's O'Connor's VIII Corps, with Gen 'Pip' Roberts 11th Armoured Division playing a leading role. The result was a stalemate, with heavy casualties on both sides – 15th Scottish Division, for example, lost a quarter of their *total* wartime casualties in five days). Monty was delighted with O'Connor's efforts: 'My dear Dick,' he wrote, 'I would like to congratulate you personally and the whole of 8 Corps, on the very fine performance put up in your attack down to and over the Odon valley. The whole corps fought splendidly and displayed a grand offensive spirit; your contribution to the general plan of battle has been immense.'

Gen 'Pip' Roberts had a lucky escape at the start of the battle, when he was blown up on a mine in an unmarked minefield, thus becoming the first tank casualty of 11th Armoured Division in the war! During that first day, Brig John Currie, commander of 4th Armoured Brigade, was killed and his place taken by Brig Michael Carver, who continued to command the brigade for the rest of the war, and would of course reach the rank of field marshal after the war – the very first officer of those initially commissioned into the Royal Tank Regiment to gain such promotion. He was then (in 1944) aged 29 and was the youngest brigadier in the army (like his GOC, who was the youngest divisional commander).

'Epsom' was followed by two further operations ('Windsor' and 'Jupiter') and then 'Goodwood', Montgomery's directive to Second Army being to retain the ability to operate with a strong armoured force east of the River Orne, in the general area between Caen and Falaise. It was decided that O'Connor would command a corps of three armoured divisions (11th, Guards and 7th), although he made strong representations that Crocker (Comd 1 Corps), as the commander on the spot, should take his place, while he also pointed out the difficulties divisions would have operating under unknown corps HQs. He received a sharp rebuff from Monty, who wrote later: 'You must understand that there is no such thing in my set-up as a permanent composition for a corps; Divisions are grouped in Corps as the battle situation demands, and this is a great battle winning factor.'4

CASUALTIES AND COMMANDERS Undoubtedly the continuing heavy attacks were having the desired effect upon the German armour, causing many casualties – by mid-July Rommel estimated that he had lost 225 tanks, and he had received only a handful of replacements. When von Rundstedt was asked by Keitel what should be done he replied, 'Make peace, you fools!' and was promptly rewarded for his honesty by being replaced by FM Hans Guenther von Kluge, who was at that time still 'Hitler's man', the Führer having not only promoted him twice and decorated him highly, but also given him a large sum of money on his 60th birthday. Despite this, von Kluge was not a convinced Nazi, indeed, he was described as an 'eternal fence-sitter'! After the attempt on Hitler's life on 20th July 1944, von Kluge committed suicide, but no concrete evidence has ever been produced that he was one of the plotters. It seems that he was scared of what Hitler would do to him after his mishandling of the campaign in Normandy, in which he allowed the encirclement of a major portion of the German forces at Falaise. He was replaced by another of Hitler's favourites, FM Walther Model. Known by his troops as 'the lion of defence', Model was an energetic and hard-driving commander, one of the few senior German officers to stand up to his Führer on military matters and to be respected by Hitler for doing so. Model, who later became commander of Army Group B, was responsible for much of the planning and execution of the Ardennes offensive and finally shot himself on 21st April 1945, rather than surrender when Army Group B was surrounded in the Ruhr pocket – 'A field marshal does not become a prisoner,' he had once remarked, when he was told about von Paulus's surrender in February 1943.

Even more serious was the loss of Rommel, who was shot up by an RAF aircraft, while driving in his staff car near Livarot, on 17th July. His skull was fractured in three places, his cheekbone shattered and his left eye badly damaged; it was the end of his military career. His last days in France had been unhappy ones. Von Kluge had arrived with preconceived ideas about Rommel, announcing in the presence of Rommel's staff that he would ensure Rommel became accustomed to obeying orders. Rommel was understandably furious and demanded a written explanation. Later, once von Kluge had completed a proper tour of inspection, he changed his tune and fully supported Rommel's reading of the situation. In fact he wrote to Hitler that he entirely agreed with Rommel's forecast that 'the unequal struggle was nearing its end.' Because of his increasing disillusionment with the Führer, Rommel had given tacit support to the bomb plotters, although he had originally merely opted for Hitler's removal from power rather than his assassination. When his part in the plot was uncovered,[5] he was given the choice of committing suicide or facing trial, which would have undoubtedly ended in public disgrace, execution and, worse still, reprisals against his family. He chose suicide and took poison on 14th October, the official story being that he had died of his wounds. Four days later he was given a state funeral and Hitler ordered a day of national mourning. Von Rundstedt read the funeral oration, ending with the words, 'his heart belonged to the Führer', so the pretence was maintained to the last.

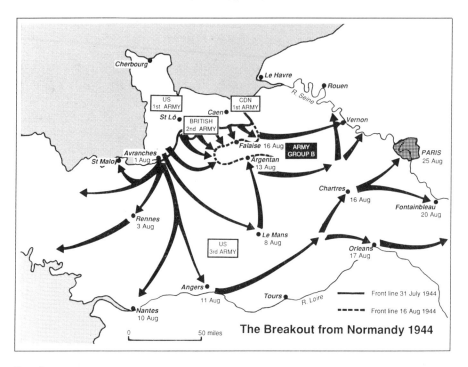

The Breakout from Normandy 1944

Breakout

While Operation 'Goodwood' was threatening Falaise and drawing more and more of the enemy away from the western flank, Patton's Third Army was concentrating around Nehou north of Coutances, while Bradley was putting the finishing touches to his plans for Operation 'Cobra', which was to begin with an infantry/armoured attack by VII US Corps, following a massive air-strike. Once a gap had been punched in the German lines, Patton's Third Army would be released to exploit it. 'Cobra' was timed to start on 24th July, but bad weather caused the aerial attack to be cancelled at the last moment, although not in time to prevent some bombs being dropped on American front-line troops. The same happened again on the 25th when the actual attack began, with more casualties to Allied troops,[6] but this time Gen 'Light-ning Joe' Collins' VII Corps, which had landed at Utah beach, was following as planned right behind the bombing. Bradley had chosen, as he put it, the 'nervy and ambitious Collins as corps commander for Cobra', yet his earlier assessment of Collins speaks of him as having 'unerring tactical judgement with just enough bravado to make every advance a triumph . . . boundless self-confidence . . . tolerable only when right, and Collins, happily, almost always was.' His enthusiasm and frankness had earned for him the nickname of 'The GIs General', but his progress on this occasion was slow, thanks to the deter-mined German resistance – which was small when compared with what was being faced by the British and Canadians on the other front. Nevertheless,

138

some progress was made and 3rd Army, who would lead the breakout, became operational on 1st August.

PATTON AND HIS COMMANDERS   While waiting to go into action that July, Patton had written a poem (he wrote many during his lifetime) entitled 'Absolute War'. The last verse epitomizes just what he intended to do when he got his chance:

> 'So let us do real fighting, boring in and gouging, biting.
> Let's take a chance now that we have the ball.
> Let's forget those fine firm bases in the dreary shell raked spaces,
> Let's shoot the works and win! yes win it all.[7]

With Bradley now in a senior position to Patton, it is interesting to note his evaluation of Patton. Initially he had been hesitant about Eisenhower's decision to give Patton a second chance after the notorious slapping incident. 'Ike assured me that George would submit without rancour,' wrote Bradley later, 'All he wants is the chance to get back into the war. For a time he thought he was through.' And Bradley soon saw that Eisenhower was correct: 'To this day I am chagrined to recall how hesitatingly I first responded to Patton's assignment. For when George joined my command in August 1944, he came eagerly and as a friend without pique, rancor or grievance. My year's association with him in Europe remains one of the brightest remembrances of my military career.' He also comments: 'Few generals could surpass Patton as a field commander. But he had one enemy he could not vanquish and that was his own quick tongue.'[8]

Patton had four corps under command with commanders as follows:

VIII Corps, Gen Troy H. Middleton – 'the most methodical, probably the best tactician, very firm in his relations with other corps commanders' (the words are those of Gen Hobart 'Hap' Gay, Patton's Chief of Staff).

XV Corps, Gen Wade Haislip – Patton had great confidence in Haislip and was 'very depressed' to lose his Corps in the Moselle some months later.

XX Corps, Gen Walton H. Walker – 'always the most willing and cooperative. He apparently will fight any time, any place, with anything that the Army commander desires to give him' ('Hap' Gay's words again).

XII Corps, Gen Gilbert Cook – 'A fine man' whom Patton was very sorry to lose only a few days after the breakout began, with bad arteries (Patton visited him in hospital and remarked in his diary that Cook's circulation was so bad that his toes were turning black. After a long conversation, he told him that, in justice to himself and his men, he could not retain him in command. 'It was a great blow to us both.') Cook's place was taken by Gen Manton S. Eddy, whom Gay described as '. . . always worrying that some other corps commander is getting a better deal than he is, but when the decision is made, he always does as he is told.'

He also had some superlative armoured division commanders, who were to blossom as the breakout developed – men like Maj Gen 'Tiger Jack' Wood, CG

139

of 4th Armored, and Maj Gen Robert W. Grow, CG of 6th Armored, whose armoured columns were soon spearheading the Third Army advance through France. 'Wood's division set the pattern for armor operations in Europe, his division, operating like cavalry, slashed and sidestepped with speed and surprise. It was confident and cocky, and demonstrated a daring, audacious, hard-riding, fast-shooting style'.9 Gen 'Tiger Jack' once declared that his division did not need a nickname like the 1st's 'Old Ironsides' or the 'Super Sixth' – 'They shall be known by their deeds alone', he said. Brig Gen Iryzk had this to say about his commander: 'He was a unique, unusual, and truly great leader – undoubtedly the greatest division commander of World War II.' Liddell Hart, the eminent British historian, military writer and critic, referred to him as 'The Rommel of the American armored forces . . . one of the most dynamic commanders of armour in WW II and the first in the Allied Armies to demonstrate in Europe the essence of the art and tempo of handling a mobile force. . . . His was leadership at its absolute best. He was not only loved and admired, but today is idolized. As Gen Jacob L. Devers simply stated, "They would follow him to hell today".'

Gen 'Bob' Grow was also a much admired commander, although unlike his flamboyant and theatrical army commander, he was methodical and businesslike. Patton nevertheless called him 'one of the best armored-force commanders the war produced.' In his history of 6th Armored, George F. Hofmann explains that only on rare occasions did the division engage in tank versus tank combat. Because the German tanks had better guns and armour, Grow always preferred his armour to break through the enemy lines.

PUNCHING THE HOLE Before Patton's thrusting armoured division commanders were able to take up the race through France, 'Lightning Joe' Collins' VII Corps had first to 'punch the hole' with three infantry divisions concentrated on a front of just over four miles, to be followed by one infantry and two armoured divisions for the immediate exploitation. These were the 2nd and 3rd Armored Divisions. The 2nd, nicknamed 'Hell on Wheels', had pre-war been commanded by Patton and then in North Africa by Harmon, and was now under the able leadership of Maj Gen Edward H. Brooks, while 3rd's CG was Maj Gen Maurice B. Rose. Born on 26th November 1899, son of a rabbi, Rose had tried to join the army as a buck private in 1915, in order to volunteer for Pershing's expedition into Mexico. Rose was discharged after a few weeks, when they discovered he was only 15! Once the USA entered WW1 in 1917 there was no stopping him and he was commissioned, aged only 17, into the infantry. By the end of the war he was a captain, but then left the service for a short time and returned, rising to the rank of major by 1941. Volunteering for the armoured branch, his first important wartime appointment was as chief of staff 2nd Armored for the 'Torch' operations in North Africa. He took over 'Spearhead', as the 3rd were called, from Maj Gen Leroy Watson during the breakout from Normandy, after commanding CCA in 2nd Armored. As Col Haynes W. Dugan told me:

Maurice Rose had as much tactical experience in tank fighting as any American general in the second World War . . . He was the only one killed in action. Our 3rd Armored Division, along with 2nd Armored, were the only 'heavy' armored divisions in WW2, each having six battalions of tanks to three of infantry. As a consequence we frequently had attached infantry from another division in the corps. Initially in Normandy the 3d was commanded by Maj Gen Leroy H. Watson, a West Point classmate of Gen Eisenhower. He was a very nice fellow but in the middle of the Normandy breakout he was relieved of command. . . . Brig Gen Maurice Rose, who commanded Combat Command A of the 2d Armored, was named to relieve Watson, but did not actually take command until after the Mortain action and before the Falaise Gap action. From then on there was no question as to who was in command and if we were on the move and the Germans dislodged we did not stop when the sun went down and if there was any holdup one could expect General Rose on the spot shortly.

Over six feet tall, erect, with finely chiselled features, always immaculate, he was described by one war correspondent as looking like Hollywood's idea of a soldier. Rose was definitely no 'armchair strategist' – he directed operations from a jeep at the point of the cutting edge. He invariably travelled with the forward elements of his command, leading from the front in the tradition of all great tank commanders. That is where he was on a dark evening in late March 1945, near Paderborn, when he was killed in action when his small command group bumped into a Panther tank. War correspondent Hal Boyle wrote at the time: 'Rose lived and died as a professional, in a career he loved and had followed since he was a boy of 17. He would be the last to regret that he had a soldier's ending.'[10] His bullet-pierced helmet is now displayed in the Patton Museum at Fort Knox.

The key to 'Cobra', a massive aerial bombardment which would immediately precede the ground movement, was designed to destroy enemy communications and generally create havoc. The other 'ace in the hole' was a simple solution to the problem of getting through the thick bocage hedgerows – a steel-pronged hedgecutter, nicknamed the 'Rhino', which was the brainchild of Sgt Curtis Culin of 2nd Armored's Cavalry Reconnaissance Squadron. It was mass-produced from steel girders that had been part of the German beach defences and three out of five of the US tanks taking part in the breakout were fitted with them. In addition, the problems with the weather and the delay in the aerial bombardment made the Germans think that they had thwarted the major attack, so they were even more surprised when the second bombardment started a day later. Gen Fritz Bayerlin's Panzer Lehr Division took the brunt of the initial assault and was annihilated, its remnants being absorbed into 2nd SS Panzer Division. After the war Bayerlin explained during an interview: 'The next day, your attack was launched and the fighter-bombers destroyed about 1100–1200 men. . . . The Americans advanced southward in the best American attack I have ever seen. Very little artillery was used, but there was excellent tank-airplane co-operation. Fifty to sixty tanks liquidated my position.' Earlier, asked which American generals in his opinion were especially capable, he answered: 'In the beginning, I thought Patton was the best because of his quick and fearless exploitation of opportunities and his breakthroughs with armored forces. From our reports, we later learned to respect Bradley even more as a cool, clear, and determined commander with more directional genius. Hodges also was considered good.' He also readily admitted that one of the main German errors in the battle of Normandy was underestimating the fighting ability and the tactical and strategical leadership of the American forces.

THE FALAISE POCKET At the same time as Third Army began their momentous sweep, Hitler ordered the remaining panzer divisions to assemble in the Mortain area with the object of attacking the Americans in the flank and then cutting off their forward troops. Although the panzers reached Mortain, they were unable to make any further progress. At the same time, the British, Canadians and Poles had been pushing slowly and steadily on south of Caen and were now advancing towards Falaise. The Allied armies were thus in a position to cut off the bulk of the German forces in Normandy, provided they moved swiftly. Montgomery, though, had already lost too many men and preferred to move with caution. Patton was furious with Montgomery's slowness: 'Let me go on to Falaise', he stormed to Bradley when he was ordered to hold at Argentan, 'and we'll drive the British back into the sea for another Dunkirk!' 'Nothing doing,' replied Bradley firmly and kept Patton halted, because he was seriously worried about the two armies colliding. As a result, although over 40,000 of the enemy were taken prisoner and many tanks were destroyed, some 60,000 Germans managed to escape. Rightly or wrongly the blame for this failure was placed upon Maj Gen George Kitching, GOC 4th Canadian Armoured Division, who was sacked by his Corps Commander, Gen Guy Simonds, on orders from Montgomery. However, it could be argued that the Canadians had been set too difficult a task to achieve. 'Harry felt that either Monty's mind wasn't on the job or he hadn't studied a map of the area. Instead of an eight-mile advance into Falaise the Corps was now being asked to cover 20 miles and take Argentan as well. We were already having a hard enough time to reach Falaise.' In that quote from *Meeting of Generals* by Tony Foster, 'Harry' is his father, Maj Gen Harry Foster, who was to take over 4th Armoured from Kitching. In his memoirs, *Mud and Green Fields*, Kitching explains why he thinks he was relieved of command: 'Had I been an experienced armoured divisional commander with six or eight months of tank battles to my credit, I believe that matters might have developed quite differently in Normandy. With that kind of experience to back me up Guy Simonds would have listened more seriously to changes I recommended at times to his plans. But both Maczek and I were commanding armoured divisions in action for the first time and Simonds preferred to rely on his own experience and judgement.' Foster would himself not remain in command of 4th Armoured for long, being switched in mid-November with Chris Vokes, then GOC 1st Infantry Division in Italy. Vokes, Montgomery's 'plain cook' would command 4th Armoured for the rest of the war.

Maczek's Poles too had a difficult time at Falaise, being nearly overwhelmed by waves of Germans attacking in a suicidal frenzy as they tried to escape. The Poles lost some 20% of their strength and 40% of their tanks. However, among the mass of Germans who were captured at Falaise were several thousand Polish conscripts, who happily changed sides, thus making up for 1st Polish Armoured Division's casualties at a stroke!

The panzer divisions were now down to a handful of tanks – Army Group B consisting of only 100, so they were outnumbered by at least 20 to 1, and despite the individual superiority of the German tanks, those odds were just too great. Von Kluge, who had had to shelter from a heavy air attack after being caught away from his headquarters, committed suicide. His epitaph is pronounced by Richard Brett-Smith in *Hitler's Generals*: 'It is not by Avranches that Kluge will best be remembered. It is as a high commander, promoted above his ceiling but still in authority, who by his own decision at a critical moment in history let down both his soldiers and himself, and, having nothing to offer, in the end found nothing.' German resistance in Normandy was virtually at an end and the race for Paris and the Seine had begun.

Operation 'Dragoon'

The Germans also had another threat to face, namely the Allied landing on the south coast of France, known as Operation 'Dragoon' (earlier called 'Anvil') on 15th August 1944. The Germans had only one panzer division in their Nineteenth Army, which controlled the troops in Mediterranean France. This was 11 Panzer Division, commanded by Maj Gen Wend von Wietersheim. Its tactical value was limited because it could not be moved without the Führer's personal approval. However, it covered the withdrawal of the Nineteenth Army up the Rhône valley expertly, but was unable to prevent the steady advance of the landing forces, which included the French 1st Armoured Division (1st Division Blindée) as part of Gen de Lattre de Tassigny's French II Corps. 1st DB had been formed on 28th January 1943, under Gen Touzet du Vigier, at Mascara in Tunisia and took part in the landings, going on to take Toulon and Marseilles. 5th DB, which had been formed at Oran on 1st June 1943, under Gen de Vernejoul, did not leave Oran until 16th September and then also landed in the south of France, fighting as part of the French First Army. Their fighting spirit was praised by Gen von Mellenthin, Chief of Staff of Army Group B: 'The French tanks, reflecting the temperament of their Army Commander, Gen de Lattre de Tassigny, attacked with extraordinary spirit and élan.'

Command Rivalries

Only 10 days after the 'Dragoon' landings, another French armoured division, Maj Gen Jacques Philippe Leclerc's 2nd DB, was liberating the French capital. Patton had noted in his diary: 'Leclerc of the 2d French Armored Division came in, very much excited . . . he said, among other things, that if he were not allowed to advance on Paris, he would resign. I told him in my best French that he was a baby, and I would not have division commanders tell me where they would fight, and that anyway I had left him in the most dangerous place. We parted friends.' However, Eisenhower ruled that Leclerc must be allowed to liberate Paris, supported by the US 4th Division and working under the orders of Gen Leonard T. Gerow's V Corps in Gen Hodge's First US Army. 'Go and liberate Paris', they were told, which is exactly what they did, so Patton was prevented from making a triumphal entrance into the French capital ('I wish I could see you going down by the Arc de Triumph in your tank', his sister Nita had written, 'You are a modern knight in shining armour'). However, Third Army was first across the Seine (a combat team of the 79th on 20th August) and continued their spectacular advance – 'I wish I were Supreme Commander', Patton wrote in his diary, 'His [Bradley's] motto seems to be, "In case of doubt halt".' It must have also been particularly galling for him to hear Gen Eisenhower on the radio a few days later (1st September) describing Monty as 'the greatest living soldier' and to learn that his rival had been promoted to field marshal, especially after his Third Army had, in a single month, over-run 500 miles of French territory, from Brest to Verdun: 'The Field Marshal thing made us sick, that is Bradley and me', he wrote in a letter to his wife that day.

The new field marshal, however, felt rather differently, having just been relieved of his role as commander of all the ground forces (both American and British); he was now in charge only of 21st Army Group, while Eisenhower assumed command of all ground forces. As there were now five American armies operating and only two British, this seemed only fair to the American public. There was, though, a difference of opinion between the two Allies as to how best to continue the ground war. Montgomery favoured a single thrust towards the Ruhr, with his own troops in the lead, while the Americans favoured an advance on a much broader front. As Lord Chalfont says in his biography of Montgomery, Eisenhower disliked Montgomery's proposal on both political and military grounds, but he realized that 'Montgomery could never be *persuaded* to adopt a particular course of action; he had to be *ordered*. So Montgomery had to be demoted.' It was a blow not only to his pride but also to his confidence, and was partly due to his inability to explain his strategy to others. It is only now, with hindsight, that it is possible to appreciate how vital to the success of Patton's breakout and subsequent 'belly to the ground gallop' across France was Montgomery's 'hard pounding' on the other flank. Unfortunately the bitterness and distrust between them continued to worsen as the war progressed towards its conclusion.

Into Belgium

Maj Gen 'Ernie' Harmon had returned to the USA from 1st Armored in Italy, expecting to receive his third star and the command of XXIII Corps, then at Camp Bowie in Texas. Instead he was asked by Army Chief, Gen George C. Marshall, to forego his promotion and take over 2nd Armored in France.

'Once again that third star of a lieutenant general, which had seemed almost on my shoulder, was flitting out of reach. But down deeper I knew that the job of getting the war won was more important to me than personal promotion. "When do you want me to go?" I asked. Marshall's face crinkled into a grin. "Since the day before yesterday," he said.'[11] Harmon took over the 'Hell on Wheels' Division from Maj Gen Edward Brooks in September, as it was nearing the Belgian border. He soon discovered that some of the men in his new command remembered him from North Africa, overhearing one soldier say to another as he drove his jeep through a small Belgian village: 'Don't you know who that man is? That's the son of a bitch who gave us the eggs at Mazagan!' He stopped the jeep, walked over and shook hands with the soldier, asking him if he had been with the division in Morocco. 'Yes sir', he replied. 'We are all mighty proud to have you back commanding the division again.' Harmon comments wryly in his autobiography that the Americans tend to link the drive across France with just the name of George Patton and his Third Army. 'But the Second Armored and the Third Armored, both components of the First Army, paced off nearly as many miles and fought with the same gallantry, even if the Third Army collected more headlines.'

On the other flank, the British and Canadians were also now making good progress. Entering Belgium, the 11th Armoured Div reached the vital port of Antwerp on 4th September, while the Guards Armoured Div liberated Brussels on the 3rd. However, by the end of September, the American 'gallop' had come to a halt along the German border, delayed by autumnal rains and supply problems, which brought Patton's armoured spearheads to a complete standstill. In 21st Army Group, the Canadians were clearing the Scheldt estuary so that Antwerp could be properly used, while Second Army was endeavouring to deal with a large pocket of enemy in the difficult, marshy area west of the Maas. 7th US Armored Division, under Maj Gen Lindsay Silvester, was attached to O'Connor's VIII Corps for this operation and appeared to perform perfectly well, although as one history puts it, 'Their morale was rather higher than their skill'. However, after meeting Silvester, Montgomery formed the opinion that he was too old for his job and arranged with Eisenhower to have him removed, without saying anything to O'Connor, who was understandably most upset when he found out. He thought that this was a matter of honour and that he should on account of it ask to be relieved. 'Can't you imagine what he [Silvester] will think of me?' he wrote to his wife, 'Complete underhand treachery, as I treated him all the time most cordially. He is like a big dog and just won't understand. But his family [his division] having trusted me completely will never do so again. So that is that. . . . in all probability I shall ask to be relieved of my command, which will undoubtedly be accepted, if I do, as I mean it.'[12] And so it turned out. O'Connor, who had performed so brilliantly in the early days in the desert, but who was perhaps, as he said himself, 'getting too old for the job' in what was now a 'young man's war', left the European battlefield for good.

Battle of the Bulge

This slowing down of Allied progress led to an ambitious British plan being approved for 21st Army Group to shorten the war by bypassing the Siegfried line – going around it to the north, across the canals and rivers of northern Belgium and Holland. A vital part of this plan was to capture a series of bridges – over the Maas north of Eindhoven, the Waal at Nijmegen and lastly, at Arnhem, across the lower Rhine. Operation 'Market Garden' was initially partly successful, but unfortunately II SS Panzer Corps was refitting nearby and was able to deal with the isolated and lightly armed paratroops. The Germans were also to halt Horrocks' XXX Corps and prevent them from achieving a link-up with the paras, so the hopes of an early victory were frustrated.

Nevertheless, the Allies had made a remarkable advance – 'Tiger Jack' Wood's 4th Armoured for example, which had been leading on the right flank, had clocked over 700 miles since the breakout, with individual tanks showing as much as 1,500 miles on their speedometers since then. British armour had also covered an astonishing mileage and all were still confident of eventual victory, being convinced that the Germans were beaten. They were therefore taken completely by surprise when three German armies – Sixth SS Panzer, Fifth Panzer and Seventh Army – containing over a quarter of a million men, launched an all-out offensive through the snows of the Ardennes on 16th December 1944. The Battle of the Bulge that followed was the worst crisis to confront the Allied command in North West Europe. It came as a complete surprise due to the most appalling battlefield intelligence failure of the war – equalled only by a similar discounting of all the obvious signs which

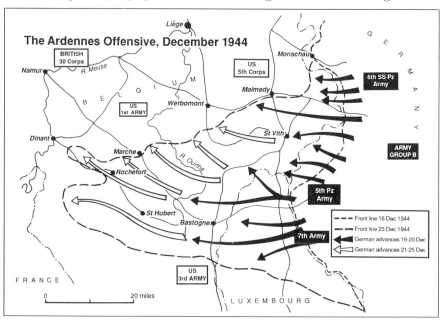

The Ardennes Offensive, December 1944

- - - Front line 16 Dec 1944
━━━ Front line 25 Dec 1944
German advances 16-20 Dec
German advances 21-25 Dec

BRITISH 30 Corps
US 5th Corps
US 1st ARMY
US 3rd ARMY
6th SS Pz Army
5th Pz Army
7th Army
ARMY GROUP B

Liége
Namur
Monschau
Malmedy
Werbomont
Dinant
St Vith
Marche
R. Ourthe
Rochefort
St Hubert
Bastogne
R. Meuse

BELGIUM
GERMANY
FRANCE
LUXEMBOURG

0   20 miles

had preceded that other fateful attack through the same area in 1940. More than a million men would become involved in this last desperate gamble by Hitler to end the war in the west so that he could concentrate on Russia.

'Soldiers of the West Front!' wrote FM Gerd von Rundstedt, once again appointed as German CinC in the West, in a pre-battle message, 'Your great hour has arrived. Large attacking armies have started to advance against the Anglo-Americans. I do not have to tell you anything more than that. You feel it yourselves. *We gamble everything!* You carry with you the holy obligation to give everything to achieve things beyond human possibilities for our Fatherland and our Führer!' The plan, known as *Wacht am Rhein* ('Watch on the Rhein') was Hitler's brainchild, and he sent copies to von Rundstedt and Model, marking the cover: 'Not to be altered.' The High Command were secretly appalled by the plan, but, in the aftermath of the unsuccessful attempt on the life of the Führer, no one dared argue.

Hitler chose Sepp Dietrich to command the Sixth SS Panzer Army, which was to play the leading role, with Gen Baron Hasso von Manteuffel's Fifth Panzer Army on its left and Gen der Panzertruppen Erich Brandenberger's Seventh Army protecting the left flank of the entire operation. FM Model (Army Group B) would be in overall operational control. Von Rundstedt was so staggered by the plan when he first heard it, considering it far too am-bitious for the number of troops and tanks available, that he proposed a much more limited attack, to take out the Allied salient around Aachen. After the war he commented 'It was only up to me to obey. It was a nonsensical oper-ation and the most stupid part was the setting of Antwerp as the target. If we reached the Meuse we should have got down on our knees and thanked God – let alone try to reach Antwerp.'[13] Surprisingly, there was also opposition to the plan from Sepp Dietrich, who took his protests to Generaloberst Alfred Jodl, but got nowhere. (During an interview after the war, Jodl commented that he thought Dietrich was '. . . a good soldier, who never ran down the Army like some SS generals.') Dietrich was to make the main effort of the attack with his four SS panzer divisions, while Manteuffell's army panzer divi-sions would play only a supporting role – a deliberate slap in the eye for the Army, whose officers had tried to kill the Führer.

Gen von Manteuffel was a tough and loyal commander, who had dis-tinguished himself in Russia, when GOC 7th Panzer Division. He then com-manded the Grossdeutschland Panzer Division before being promoted directly to command 5th Panzer Army, thus missing out the corps level of command. A Prussian, he won the Knight's Cross with Oak Leaves, Swords and Diamonds (the Brilliants being awarded on 18th February 1945) and went on to command 3rd Panzer Army – the 'last hope of the Third Reich' – in the East, when he was only 48 years old. Like von Rundstedt and Dietrich, he did not hold out much hope of getting beyond the Meuse and he was clearly worried as to what his divisions would encounter, if they were lucky enough to get thus far relatively unscathed. Manteuffel showed his bravery even before the battle began, going to the front disguised as an intelligence colonel and personally directing the intensive patrolling prior to the attack. Brandenberger was also worried about his role, having only a handful of AFVs to support the four infantry divisions with which he must defend the southern flank against Patton's Third US Army – and Patton was a commander for whom the German generals had a healthy respect!

The German armour of eight panzer divisions (opposite) were supported by 17 Volksgrenadier divisions, a panzergrenadier division and two parachute divisions, plus numerous other brigades and special units, making the assembly for 'Wacht am Rhein' the most formidable force ever to be pitted against the British and Americans in one operation. They were also to be supported by II Fighter Corps and III Flak Corps from the Luftwaffe.

Opposite this formidable force, as it moved silently into its attack positions along roads and tracks spread with straw to muffle the noise, was probably the worst-held area of the Allied line, both in numbers and in quality of troops. There were just six American divisions from V and VIII Corps, whose units were either green with little or no battlefield experience, or under-strength and battle-weary. H hour was first light on 16th December. Helped by bad weather, which grounded the Allied air forces and the panic which their unexpected attack brought, the Germans initially succeeded in making good progress and causing some inexperienced commanders to surrender. In other places, however, reactions were different. One such location was the small Belgian town of St Vith, where one of America's greatest tank commanders would write his name into history. This was Gen (then Brig Gen) Bruce C. Clarke. Clarke had enlisted in 1918, aged 17, served in the ranks and been commissioned into the Corps of Engineers in 1925. In 1940, when the Armored Force was born, he became CO 24th Engineer Battalion and acting engineer officer for the force. Later he was Chief of Staff 4th Armored and went overseas in December 1943 as CO of CCA 4th Armored. After some of the heaviest fighting, in August 1944, he was awarded the DSC and the Silver Star, then in November 1944, he became CG of CCB 7th Armored Division. Thanks to his leadership, the hodgepodge of units in St Vith was welded into a cohesive fighting force and was able to hold off all the enemy thrusts, using mobile 'hit and retire' tactics that after the war Manteuffel described as 'one of the best models of this method of fighting.' Clarke commented:

As the commander of CCB, I analysed the situation and decided that the probable objective of the German attack was not just St Vith or a bridgehead over the Salm River, but rather a decisive objective far to my rear, probably toward the English Channel. I could well afford to be forced back slowly, surrendering a few kilometres of terrain at a time to the German forces while preventing the destruction of my command and giving other units to my rear the time to prepare a defence and a counterattack. Therefore by retiring a kilometre or so a day, I was winning, and the Germans, by being prevented from advancing many kilometres a day, were losing; thus proving my concept that an armored force can be as effectively employed in a defence and delay situation as in the offensive.[14]

148

5th Panzer Army

47th Panzer Corps (under Gen der Panzertrüppen Heinrich von Luttwitz), containing 2nd Pz Div (reorganized after heavy losses in Normandy; 9th Pz Div (another veteran division, which had fought in Normandy, moved to Holland and now to the Ardennes, with over 100 tanks, including some attached heavy Tigers); Pz Lehr Div (rebuilt after being virtually annihilated in Normandy. In addition was the special Führer Begleit Brigade, organized around Hitler's HQ guard, plus a tank battalion from the Gross Deutschland Pz Div.

5th Panzer Corps (under Gen der Panzertrüppen Eugen Walter Krueger), containing 116th Pz Div (known as the 'Greyhounds', the division had also suffered in Normandy but been rebuilt with good reinforcements and now had over 100 tanks).

29th Panzer Corps (under Lt Gen Karl Decker), containing no panzer divisions, brought forward at the end of December.

Baron von Luttwitz had previously commanded first the 20th, then the 2nd Pz Div and would direct the seige of Bastogne in the battle; Walter Krueger had been acting commander of two Panzer corps and commanded 1st Pz Div in 1942–43; Karl Decker had previously commanded 3rd Pz Div. All were thus experienced, able commanders, who had already seen plenty of armoured action.

6th Panzer Army

1st SS Pz Corps (under SS Gruppenfuehrer Hermann Priess), containing 1st SS Pz Div ('Leiberstandarte Adolf Hitler') (one of the most powerful German divisions, with 501 SS Heavy Tank Battalion attached); 12th SS Pz Div ('Hitler Jugend') (rebuilt after Normandy but lacking experienced commanders). In addition there was 150th Panzer Brigade, a makeshift formation assembled under the dashing Otto Skorzeny, who had rescued Mussolini in September 1943.

2nd SS Pz Corps (under SS Obergruppenfuehrer Willi Bittrich), containing 2nd SS Pz Div ('Das Reich') (which had fought in Russia and Normandy and had a reputation for brutality); 9th SS Pz Div ('Hohenstaufen') (also rebuilt after Normandy and Holland).

Hermann Priess held the Knight's Cross with both Oak Leaves and Swords and had previously commanded both 1st and 3rd SS Pz divs; Wilhelm Bittrich, who had been a fighter pilot in WW1, was a courageous and able soldier; initially he had been an ardent Nazi but was now 'sick and tired of Berlin's orders and the sycophants around Hitler'.

'Clarke of St Vith' as he came to be called, undoubtedly prevented a link-up between 5th and 6th Panzer Armies and upset the German timetable. He went on to command both 4th and 1st Armored Divisions after the war, I and

VIII Corps during the Korean War, 7th US Army and later Central Army Group of NATO during the Berlin crisis.

Of course, small isolated actions such as Clarke's at St Vith or the equally famous defence of Bastogne by Gen McAuliffe's 101st Airborne Division (his contemptuous reply of 'Nuts!', when the Germans demanded that he surrender, has also gone down in history), would not on their own have stopped the German assault. That required far more organized operations. Eisenhower decided on 19th December that Montgomery should take over command of both the First and Ninth US Armies, north of the penetration, while Patton was ordered to break off his operations in the Saar, turn his Third US Army through ninety degrees and strike northwards into the flank of the German penetration. In addition, Eisenhower's only reserve – the 82nd and 101st Airborne Divisions – was sent immediately into the Ardennes. Montgomery deployed XXX Corps in a blocking position on the Meuse, while making Hodge's First Army contain the enemy on the northern shoulder of their attack. It was thus far more an American battle than a British one, indeed probably the greatest they fought in the war, and one in which they suffered some 78,000 casualties. Patton's part, his most spectacular of the war, was undoubtedly made easier by the fact that he had some days earlier ordered his staff to study just such a problem, namely counter-attacking through First Army sector. The speed with which Third Army moved was quite remarkable, resulting in the epic relief of the beleaguered 101st Airborne in Bastogne by Wood's 4th Armored. The confidence in what Patton could do was shared by soldiers at all levels: 'If Georgie's coming we have got it made!' was one soldier's reaction in St Vith, when told of the intended advance.

The Germans nevertheless pushed on hard, endeavouring to side-step obstacles, but gradually running out of steam as the American resistance stiffened. By Christmas the offensive had been sealed off within the general line Elsenhorn-Malmedy-Hotton-Marche-St Hubert-Bastogne and all routes to the Meuse were blocked. The weather had also cleared and the full weight of Allied air power came into operation. By mid-January, First and Third US Armies had linked up and the Army Groups readied for the final assault on Germany. Although some of the attackers were able to withdraw in good order, they had lost over 100,000 casualties and some 800 irreplaceable tanks. Montgomery later wrote: 'The battle of the Ardennes was won primarily by the staunch fighting qualities of the American soldier . . . Had the quality of the German formations been of the same high standard as in the early war years, with junior leaders of great dash and initiative, the temporary effects of the counter stroke might well have been more grave; the enemy failed to exploit his success in the first vital days, and the fighting showed he was no match for the splendidly steady American troops.'15 Unfortunately Montgomery said some other things about his taking control, which upset both Bradley and Patton so much that both swore that they would resign rather than serve under him. 'After what has happened I cannot serve under Montgomery',

Bradley said to Eisenhower, 'if he is to be put in command of all ground forces, you must send me home, for if Montgomery goes in over me, I will have lost the confidence of my command.'[16]

By the end of January it was all over and American troops were back in the positions they had held on 16th December. It had been a hard battle, with over 75,000 Allied and 120,000 Germans killed, wounded or captured. Undoubtedly this had a devastating effect upon the Third Reich and seriously weakened its ability to defend itself against assaults from both east and west. Although 'Wacht am Rhein' had delayed the Allied advance for some six weeks it had also undoubtedly hastened the final defeat of Germany.

To the Oder

On the morning of 12th January 1945, the Russians launched their largest offensive of the war, aimed at the very heart of Germany, to take Berlin. It had been brought forward by eight days in order to relieve the pressure in the west caused by the Nazi's Ardennes offensive. Along the entire front, from the Baltic to the Carpathians, no fewer than five armies moved relentlessly against the enemy. In the south, Koniev's 1st Ukrainian Front, his tanks outnumbering the German panzers by at least seven to one, pushed back Fourth Panzer Army 12 miles on the first day. To their north, other Fronts were also attacking – Zhukov's 1st Belorussian, Rokossovky's 2nd Belorussian, Chernyakovsky's 3rd Belorussian, Bagramyan's 1st Baltic and Yeremenko's 2nd Baltic. The Germans were forced to give ground everywhere, individual divisions and units scoring limited successes, but as Bryan Perrett explains in *Knights of the Black Cross*: 'No coherent strategy was ever evolved . . . the enemy possessed too many tanks, too many anti-tank guns and too many aircraft for it to be otherwise. . . . However, the final days of the Panzerwaffe were not marked by a series of fatal conflicts on a stricken field; rather, the demise of the arm came about as a result of the severing of the arteries of mechanised war.' As the German supply system disintegrated, the fuel, ammunition, spare parts, rations and all the rest dried up, forcing the German forces to discard or destroy their equipment and join the ever increasing flood of survivors rushing westwards to surrender to the Western Allies before the Red Army could catch up with them.

Zhukov reached the Oder on 31st January after a 300 mile advance, with Koniev a couple of weeks or so later. They were undoubtedly helped by Hitler's extraordinary decision to counter-attack through Hungary. Guderian, now acting Army Chief of Staff, begged his Führer to concentrate his forces on the defence of the Oder, but to no avail. On hearing of Hitler's decision to transfer Sixth Panzer Army to Hungary, Guderian 'lost my self-control and expressed my disgust to Jodl in very plain terms, but could get no reaction from him whatever beyond a shrug of the shoulders. . . . Hitler could not accept my opinions and reaffirmed his intention to attack in Hungary, to throw the Russians back across the Danube and relieve Budapest.' Needless to say, 'Heinz Hothead' did not last much longer in Hitler's service, being sacked again on 21st March. He then decided to go to the Tyrol, where he 'sat down and waited for the end of the war.' After the surrender he accompanied this staff into American captivity.

This last offensive, known as *Frühlingserwachen* ('Spring Awakening') was doomed to failure from the very beginning. The Nazis were facing overwhelming odds. They had also assumed that the ground would be frozen, which it was not and Sepp Dietrich was soon forced to withdraw, abandoning most of his heavy equipment, including some 500 tanks and assault guns. As Bryan Perrett comments in *Knights of the Black Cross*: 'The Panzerwaffe had fought its last major battle . . . Disillusioned, they now fought only to survive and to avoid capture by the Russians . . . desertion was now rife and . . . the troops had lost confidence in their leaders.' Hitler's reaction on hearing the news was to fly into a rage, order Himmler to tell them that they had disgraced him and that they should remove their special cuff titles, bearing such once-proud names as 'Leiberstandarte SS Adolf Hitler'. It is reputed that when the 1st SS Panzer Division received the order, its soldiers removed all their cuff titles *and* decorations and sent them to their Führer in a latrine bucket!

Into the Fatherland

In the west the situation was very similar, as three massive army groups – Montgomery's 21st in the north, Bradley's 12th in the centre and Dever's 6th in the south – pressed forward, with armour well to the fore in all areas. Patton's Third Army, for example, was, by early April 1945, some 60 miles east of the Rhine, its armoured spearheads rolling steadily forward against only scattered resistance. On 21st April their direction of attack was changed and they began to cross the Danube, entering Czechoslovakia and Austria, Panzer divisions surrendering to them en masse. The first eight days of May saw the end of the German war machine, as the Third Army split the Reich in half and gave the defeated enemy no chance to make the last 'glorious' stand Hitler wanted. In a total of 281 days of campaigning Patton's men had liberated an estimated 12,000 cities, towns and communities of more than 50,000 people. They had killed 144,500 enemy, wounded 386,200 and captured a staggering 1,280,688. They had travelled further and faster than any other Army had ever done in the entire history of war. Undoubtedly much of their greatness they owed to one man, their hard-driving commander, Gen George Smith Patton. He would not live long enough properly to savour his victories, dying on 21st December 1945 from the injuries he sustained when his staff car was in collision with a big truck on the Frankfurt-Mannheim road on 9th December. Patton, who had always said that he would like to die from the last bullet of the last battle, confided to his brother-in-law that 'this was a hell of a way for a soldier to die'. *The New York Times* said later:

History has reached out and embraced Gen George Patton. His place is secure. He will be ranked in the forefront of America's great military leaders. . . . Long before the war ended, Patton was a legend. Spectacular, swaggering, pistol-packing, deeply religious and violently profane, easily moved to anger because he was first of all a fighting man, easily moved to tears because underneath all his ill-mannered irascibility he had a kind heart. . . . Hot in battle and ruthless too, he was icy in his inflexibility of purpose. He was no more a hell-for-leather tank commander but a profound and thoughtful military student. He was not a man of peace. Perhaps he would have preferred to die at the height of his fame, when his men, whom he loved, were following him with devotion. His nation will accord his memory a full measure of that devotion.

The Decisive Arm

When WW2 ended, the tank had undoubtedly earned the title 'Queen of the Battlefield' that had originally been given to the Matilda Mk 2 in 1940. As the US Army Lineage series *Armor-Cavalry* puts it: 'Armor as the ground arm of mobility, emerged from World War II with a lion's share of the credit for the Allied victory. Indeed armor enthusiasts at that time regarded the tank as being the main weapon of the land army.' Tank commanders at all levels had once again proved themselves to be the battle-winners, although, to be fair, it was the mobile armoured force of all arms that tank formations had eventually become in all armies that was the battle-winner, and not the tank on its own. However, the tank was probably the most important and indispensable part of this force, bringing to it those three essential, basic characteristics of firepower, protection and mobility, which Guderian, Rommel, Zhukov, Rokossovsky, Patton and all the rest had used so brilliantly. Now, new, even more powerful weapons were making their appearance. Would the atom bomb, which had so dramatically heralded in the nuclear age, lead to the demise of the tank and the eclipse of the tank commander?

NOTES TO CHAPTER 9

1 *World War II German Military Studies* Vol. 2, Report No 13

2 *World War II German Military Studies* Vol. 2, Report No 39

3 Wittmann was then an SS Oberstürmführer commanding a company of six Tiger tanks, of which only four were roadworthy when the action started.

4 As quoted in John Baynes, *The Forgotten Victor*

5 When von Stauffenberg attempted to blow up Hitler on 20th July 1944, Rommel was still in a French hospital and he did not recover sufficiently to be moved home to Herrlingen until 8th August. He might never have been implicated had not another plotter, Gen von Stulpnagel, the military governor of France, jumped the gun and had all Nazi officials in Paris arrested, after being wrongly told that Hitler was dead. Gen von Stulpnagel tried to commit suicide on the journey back to Berlin, where he had been ordered to report by Keitel, but only succeeded in blinding himself.

He was rushed into hospital for an emergency operation and as he came round uttered just one word: 'Rommel'.

6 These casualties included Gen Lesley McNair, who had been visiting the front at the time. McNair was Chief of Staff at GHQ US Army and had been responsible for establishing the vast training machine all over America.

7 Martin Blumenson, *The Patton Papers*, Vol. 2

8 Omar N. Bradley, *A Soldier's Story*

9 Brig Gen Albin F. Irzyk, 'The "Name Enough" Division', in *Armor*, July–August 1987

10 *Spearhead in the West, the history of 3d Armored Division 1944–45.*

11 *Combat Commander* by Maj Gen E.N. Harmon.

12 *The Forgotten Victor.*

13 As quoted in *Hitler's Generals*

14 Gen Bruce C. Clarke, 'The Battle for St Vith', in *Armor*, Nov–Dec 1974.

15 FM Montgomery, *Memoirs.*

16 *A Soldier's Story.*

10 THE FAR EAST 1942–1973

During WW2 tanks had little impact on the battlefields of the Far East. The Americans, both the US Army and the US Marine Corps, used them in limited numbers during their island-hopping operations in the South Pacific. Tank units in the Pacific theatre were also equipped with the Landing Vehicle Tracked (LVT), which came into existence in early 1941, and owed much of its basic design to the pre-war work of Donald Roebling Jr, grandson of the builder of the Brooklyn Bridge, who in the mid-1930s had designed a tracked amphibian for rescue work in the Florida Everglades. By the end of the war some 18,000 LVT had been built, including over 3,000 LVT (Armored), which were tanks in all but name and used in very similar ways.

WW2: the Pacific Theatre
In battles such as the retaking of Tarawa in 1943, Peleliu in 1944 and Leyte in 1944, tanks and LVTs got the job done, but suffered heavy casualties from the fanatical Japanese defenders. As Gen Donn A. Starry commented in the introduction to his book *Mounted Combat in Vietnam*: 'In the war in the Pacific there was slow, difficult fighting in island rain forests. No armored division moved toward Japan across the Pacific islands. Neither blitzkrieg tactics nor dashing armored leaders achieved literary fame in jungle fighting. It was an infantry war; armored units were employed, but what they learned was neither widely publicised nor often studied.'

Although the Japanese had set up a tank-building industry between the wars, they did not see the tank as a battle-winner – building priority and finance being lavished on aircraft and naval vessels instead. Between 1931 and 1945, only about 3,500 tanks of all types were built and most were not up to Western standards. When used, they were to be found in small numbers and invariably in a supporting role. Japanese tanks were designated by a type number, which indicated the year in which they were first produced. The year was taken from the Japanese calendar, which began on the legendary date of the foundation of the Japanese empire – 660BC in Western terms. Thus the Type 92 was built in the year 2592 or 1932 in Western parlance. Later, from 2601, they used just the last digit, together with a short name describing the tank's function. Despite the fact that there were three Japanese armies in Burma, there was only one tank unit there – the 4th Tank Regiment – which was committed piecemeal and suffered accordingly.

BURMA CAMPAIGN   It was left to the British and Indians to make the fullest use of armour in a jungle setting, namely in Burma, where they gave the Imperial Japanese Army a taste of mechanized war from which it never recovered. The fighting in Burma and on its borders lasted for three years, but not continuously. Tanks were involved in the spring of 1942, briefly again in the spring of 1943 and then on an increasingly large scale through 1944 and up to the end of the war in the following year. In conditions where the arrival of a single tank could have an effect out of all proportion, tank commanders at all levels intervened decisively on a number of occasions. Perhaps the most important was the timely arrival in February 1942 of the 7th Armoured Brigade, fresh from their victories in the Western Desert as part of the 7th Armoured Division. 7th Armoured Brigade, who wore a green desert rat instead of a red one, acted as rearguard during the epic retreat to India, effectively dealing with the Japanese sadly at the cost of the majority of their light Stuart tanks, which could not get across the final barrier of the Chindwin and had to be left behind after being made unbattleworthy. This 'magnificent formation' as the great Gen (later FM) 'Bill' Slim called it, comprised just two armoured regiments – 7th Queen's Own Hussars and 2nd Royal Tank Regiment. It was commanded by Brigadier J.H. Anstice DSO. Gen Alexander later wrote of it: 'I must also mention here the excellent work done by the 7th Armoured Brigade, whose high morale and great fighting capacity I have frequently stressed. . . . No praise is too high for this formation. . . . Without the 7th Armoured Brigade we should not have got the army out of Burma.'[1]

Unfortunately, the next time tanks were used they were a dismal failure. This was during the ill-fated advance down the Mayu Peninsula in the Arakan, in January 1943, when a small detachment of Valentines was sent in at short notice to support an attack which had already failed twice. The attack failed for a third time and all the Valentines were knocked out and their crews killed. This led so-called 'armour experts' in India to say that armour would be of little use in the recapture of Burma. Fortunately, however, there were still those who had faith in tanks, especially Slim himself, so when XIV Army was formed it did contain three armoured brigades – the 50th, 254th and 255th. They rapidly showed their worth both as 'bunker busters' and by providing immediate, accurate and easily controllable direct firepower. By the end of the battles on the Imphal plain they had effectively silenced their critics in this the static phase of the campaign. From then on they went from strength to strength and, once the winter monsoon was over and the advancing columns had reached the better going beyond the Irrawaddy, then armour really came into its own. Both corps' advances were led by armoured formations – 255 Bde with 4 Corps and 254 Bde with 33 Corps, the tanks doing much to hasten the disintegration of Japanese resistance. The last phase of these operations has been described as one of the greatest pursuits in the history of British arms, with the armoured brigades going hell for leather, trying to reach Rangoon before the weather yet again clamped down. There were few tank v tank engagements, no major pitched battles on the scale of the Western Desert, Russia or North West Europe, nevertheless the tanks and armoured cars of XIV Army can be justly proud of their achievements in the most difficult theatre of operations. Certainly Slim thought so, writing: 'The Royal Armoured Corps and Indian Armoured Corps silenced all their critics and had no greater admirers than the infantry who they had supported so staunchly, and with whom they had co-operated so closely and so skilfully.'[2]

It would perhaps be invidious to try to choose a great tank commander from this theatre as there just were not enough armoured actions to make a proper choice. However, typical of the commanders who fought so well in such difficult conditions was Maj Gen Ralph Younger CB, CBE, DSO, MC, DL, who was probably the only senior RAC officer to serve throughout the entire campaign in Burma. He was second-in-command of the 7th Hussars when they landed in 1942 and took part in the long retreat to India. When 7th Armoured Brigade left to go to Italy, he was selected to command the 3rd Carabiniers during the vital Imphal battle. Later he became deputy commander of 255 Tank Brigade, which carried out the decisive thrust at Meiktila and then led the famous dash for Rangoon in 1945.

The Korean War

'Scattered showers were falling along the 38th Parallel on the morning of 25 June 1950, when to the sound of sporadic thunder was added the deafening roar of artillery and mortar fire. As much as an hour separated the periods of opening fire, but everywhere they signalled the commencement of a series of co-ordinated attacks across the entire width of the Peninsula. . . . Stunning successes in the western (1 NK Corps) sector paved the way for the assault on Seoul. The main thrust, spearheaded by more than fifty tanks, with 8,000 to 10,000 infantry troops was directed down the historical Pochon-Uijongbu Corridor. A second column, tipped with some forty tanks, drove on Seoul from Kaesong.'

That is how Daniel S. Stelmach described the opening moments of the Korean War (1950–1953), in a paper he wrote for his PhD at St Louis University in 1973, entitled 'The influence of Russian armored tactics on the North Korean Invasion of 1950.' He goes on to explain that the basic tactical pattern for the whole of the North Korean offensive was a strong artillery-supported frontal attack to fix the enemy in place and break up his defensive positions, then a double envelopment to encircle and annihilate him. The frontal assault, whenever the country allowed, was spearheaded by tanks, which preceded the infantry by anything from fifteen to forty-five minutes. In typical Soviet tactical style, once the line had been penetrated, the artillery and mortars would lift to engage pre-arranged targets in depth, while the tanks continued to press on, destroying enemy command posts, seeking out their close-support weapons and cutting off all avenues of escape. Stelmach, after explaining in some detail how the teachings of the great Russian tank expert

Tukhachevsky became the basis of the North Korean armoured doctrine, comments that nowhere was the North Korean superiority in training and equipment more clearly visible than in '. . . the aggressor's skilful employment of armored vehicles along the main line of advance in the opening weeks of the war.' He goes on to say: 'The use of tanks during this period proved to be one of the most tactically efficacious ploys of the entire Korean war, causing considerable concern among American military leaders, who feared that the NKPA [North Korean Peoples Army], spearheaded by armored formations, would crush all resistance before substantial aid could be rushed to the Peninsula.'

In fact, the NKPA possessed a mere handful of tanks by WW2 standards – just one weak division – the 105th Armoured Division, which was the only identified tank unit in the invading army. It never fought as a unified force, but rather had its individual regiments allocated in support of designated infantry divisions. After capturing Seoul it was awarded the honorary title of 'Division', but in fact was never really more than a brigade of three tank regiments (107th, 109th and 203rd) plus supporting arms and services, such as the 206th Mechanized Infantry Regiment and the 603rd Motorcycle Regiment. It did not contain a heavy-tank regiment, mortar regiment, AA regiment or rocket-launcher battalion, as found in its Soviet counterparts. It was also very much weaker in tank strength, the NKPA tank company containing only the equivalent of a Soviet tank platoon. Each regiment was equipped with just 40 medium T34 tanks, mounting the 85mm gun, which were divided into three battalions of 13 tanks each, plus one more for the regimental commander. Tank companies comprised three platoons, each of just a single T34. The 105th Tank Division was commanded by Lt Gen Yu Kyong Su, who had, like so many other North Koreans, served in the Red Army during the Great Patriotic War. After graduating from a Red Army tank school in 1938, he served as a tank platoon and company commander with a Russian tank unit and saw a fair amount of action. One of his regimental commanders, Maj Gen Pir U Chang, fought with the Russians all the way to Berlin.

They and the other North Korean tank commanders initially had spectacular successes, because the South Koreans had no armour and the Americans could only muster some M24 Chaffee light tanks which were easily dealt with. Later, when the Americans got their act together and produced M26 Pershings and M4 Shermans, then the story was very different; as Stelmach explained, by September, after the Inchon landing and the resultant buildup in US tank power, the Red Armored Forces lost their bravado, becoming cautious to the point of inactivity. During August 1950, six US medium-tank battalions were landed in Korea, containing Pershings, Shermans (M4A3 version) and including one battalion of the more modern M46 Pattons. Tank battalions averaged 69 tanks. By the third week in August there were more than 500 US medium tanks within the Pusan perimeter. At the beginning of September American tanks outnumbered the enemy's by at least five to one. A month earlier, on 13 July, one of the late Gen George Patton's former corps commanders, Lt Gen Walton H. Walker, took over command of the United Nations forces in Korea, which were by then known as the US Eighth Army. A tough, pugnacious Texan, nicknamed 'Johnny' after a famous brand of Scotch whisky, Walker was very much in the same mould as Patton. He believed in letting his soldiers see who was commanding them and left the day-to-day administration of his HQ to his staff. Above all he was a fighter, and swiftly informed his men that there would be no more 'bugging out' or 'Dunkirk-type' rescue and equally, no surrender. They would hold the tiny Pusan perimeter into which they had been forced to the last man and the last bullet. Fortunately this did not prove necessary and their spirited defence held.

Walker continued to command the UN forces during their breakout from Pusan, but he never had large quantities of armour, although tanks certainly played their part in the advance up to the Yalu River. By now the force was truly representative of the United Nations, and included a small number of British and French tanks – the British Centurion proving to be undoubtedly the best tank of the campaign. The war looked to be drawing to a close, but on the night of 25th November, 180,000 Chinese troops launched a massive offensive against the right flank of the Eighth Army and forced it into headlong retreat. The lightly equipped Chinese troops had no armour whatsoever, but were ideally suited to the rugged terrain and bitter winter weather, quickly nullifying the superior firepower of their road-bound opponents. Gen Walker managed briefly to stabilize the situation on the 38th Parallel, but on 1st January 1951 the enemy launched another all-out attack and captured Seoul for a second time. A few days later, 'Johnny' Walker was killed in a jeep accident[3] and his place taken by another famous WW2 soldier, Gen Matthew Bunker Ridgway – known affectionately as 'Old Iron Tits', because of his penchant for carrying two primed hand-grenades on his chest! Fortunately, the Chinese attack began to run out of steam and Ridgway was able to go onto the offensive. By early April the front had been stabilized along the 38th Parallel. From then on neither side made a great deal of use of tanks, except as mobile pillboxes, firing from semi-static positions, in support of the infantry in an equally static WW1-type trench-warfare situation. Armour, denied its basic mobility and flexibility, ceased to play a dominant role. So, once again, as in the Far East operations of WW2, tanks in the Korean War cannot be said to have had a major effect upon the battlefield, except during the opening phase. It is true to say that, before 25th June 1950, no-one apart from a few generals in the NKPA had ever thought that it was possible for tanks to operate in such rugged terrain and so the use of armour in both attack and defence was written off. The ability of the North Koreans to utilize the striking power of the tank undoubtedly took the Americans and South Koreans completely by surprise and provided a good example of the blitzkrieg tactics of Guderian and the Panzerwaffe as adopted by the Red Army and then the

North Koreans, being used to perfection. So Lt Gen Yu Kyong Su earns his place in this book, although his career was seemingly short.

Indo-China and Vietnam

The terrain of the Indo-China peninsula presented similar problems to those found in Burma, ranging from mountains to deep valleys, from close jungle to open rice paddies, the type of country in which tanks were not supposed to be of much use. Certainly the French, in their early battles against the Viet Minh, made only limited use of armoured vehicles in their unsuccessful attempts to retain Indo-China. Even the sending of one of their most distinguished WW2 soldiers, Gen Jean de Lattre de Tassigny, to become CinC, had no effect. He returned to France, dying of cancer, in 1951 and his successor, Henri Navarre, planned to lure the Viet Minh into a set-piece battle around the isolated fortress of Dien Bien Phu. In doing so he seriously underestimated his enemy and France suffered a humiliating defeat at the hands of the peasant armies of Ho Chi Minh in the summer of 1954. In the Armistice talks that followed, the country was divided at the 17th Parallel, the north being controlled by the Communists, the south by the nationalists, with whom the West would find themselves allied – a situation similar in many ways to Korea.

The armoured vehicles that had been used by the French in their four years of campaigning were American WW2 equipment, totalling some 452 tanks and tank destroyers, plus 1,985 scout cars, half-tracks and amphibious armoured vehicles. However, these were spread over an area of 228,627 square miles. By comparison, when it came to be the Americans turn to fight in the area, they would have some 600 tanks and 2,000 armoured vehicles of other types deployed over an area less than one-third that size. The French found the wide deployment of their armoured forces a perpetual headache; armoured units were fragmented and many small posts had as few as two or three armoured vehicles. The only viable French striking force, Groupement Mobile 100, was destroyed after a series of ambushes, and the story of this disaster led to the unfortunate conviction in high places that armoured combat in Vietnam was impossible.[4] In actual fact the striking force was mainly composed of truck-mounted infantry and artillery with just 10 light tanks – hardly an armoured column by any standards.

A study of the terrain in Vietnam carried out by a team of US armour officers in 1967, showed that nearly half the country could be traversed by armoured vehicles all the year round, the most difficult areas being the Mekong Delta and the Central Highlands. Like the Viet Minh, the lightly equipped, fast-moving Viet Cong moved on foot and were superb jungle fighters, capable of carrying out full-scale mobile war, not simply the uncoordinated guerrilla war that the Americans imagined. They even had some armoured forces, supplied by both the People's Republic of China and the Soviet Union, but did not use them particularly well in their early encounters.

However, they learned their lessons well and in early 1975, actually spearheaded their final assaults into South Vietnam with armour.

The South Vietnamese also initially had some light AFVs – armoured cars, half-tracks and scout cars – but had inherited the totally negative French concept of the use of armour which denied its use for offensive action. The first US advisers, who arrived in the mid-1950s, included a small number of armour officers, but it was not until the 1960s that they were available in sufficient quantity to be attached to units in the field. US armoured units followed, initially the main vehicle being the M113, which was used almost like a light tank, with the crew remaining mounted. They earned the local nickname of 'Green Dragons', partly from their green camouflage and partly from the fire and smoke belching from their machine-guns and engines! It was probably the best land vehicle for the terrain and its use meant that armoured units could abandon the French tactic of sticking to the roads and move at will across most of the country. The first light tanks, some M41 Walker Bulldogs, arrived in January 1965, to replace the older M24 Chaffees left behind by the French. Later, M48 and M60 tanks were sent to Vietnam as the war escalated. However, as Gen Westmorland, the American CinC saw no use for tanks, these early armoured units had a frustrating time, their heavier AFVs often being withdrawn to squadron bases on orders from higher authority. Starry comments that armoured units arriving early in Vietnam literally had to invent their own tactics and techniques and then convince the Army that they worked. On occasions the results were spectacular, such as the last major armoured action in Junction City, in March 1967. Fire Base Gold was in imminent danger of being overwhelmed, the Viet Cong being within half-a-dozen yards of the battalion aid station and within hand-grenade range of the command post. Into this chaos came the tanks and APCs of 2nd Battalion, 34th Armor, commanded by Lt Col Raymond Stailey, firing with their 90mm guns and machine-guns:

The ground shook as tracked vehicles moved around the perimeter throwing up a wall of fire to their outside flank. They cut through the advancing Viet Cong, crushing many under their tracks. The VC, realizing that they could not outrun the encircling vehicles, charged them and attempted to climb aboard but were quickly cut down. Even the tank recovery vehicle of Co A, 2nd Battalion 34th Armor, smashed through the trees with its machine guns chattering. . . . It was just like the late show on TV, the US Cavalry came riding to the rescue. . . . When the smoke cleared, it was apparent that the enemy had not only been defeated but had lost more than 600 men.[5]

As early as 1965, there had been discussions about the employment of armour from other nations, which began with the proposed use of a tank company from New Zealand. This did not materialize, but when the Australian task force arrived an APC troop was included and was attached to the US 173rd Airborne Brigade. Small armoured elements of the Republic of the Philippines and the Royal Thai Army also arrived, while a request from the South Koreans for permission to deploy a tank battalion were refused, on the grounds that the area was 'inappropriate for tanks'! Finally, in 1967–8, the

Australians sent 'C' Squadron,[6] 1st Armoured Regiment (medium tanks) and 'A' Squadron 3rd Cavalry Regiment (APCs). The tanks were the British Centurion, in its day one of the finest tanks in the world. They fought a number of highly successful actions, including sweeps and ambushes, before their withdrawal in 1971–2. One of the most important actions was in June 1969 at Binh Ba, a village only three miles from the Australian task-force base at Nui Dat. The North Vietnamese – a regular infantry battalion – let it be known that they had come to stay and would never be evicted. But 'it turned out to be armour's greatest day. The enemy was cleared out of Binh Ba lock, stock and barrel.' The main action was undertaken by four Centurion tanks, supported by a company of 5th Battalion, Royal Australian Regiment. In four hours of hard and savage fighting, two MCs and one MM were awarded to RAAC personnel for their bravery.[7]

NEW COMMANDER, NEW TACTICS   In the summer of 1968, there was a change of leadership, Gen Creighton W. Abrams taking over from Gen Westmorland as Commander of the US Military Assistance Command, Vietnam. Abrams had shown himself to be one of the great commanders of small armoured units in WW2 and later commanded an armoured division and a corps, before becoming Vice Chief of Staff of the US Army. He had also been Westmorland's deputy for a year before taking over and had concentrated on the Vitenam Army, gaining a tremendous rapport with them. Like other famous American cavalry and armour generals, his name would later be used to 'christen' an American AFV, the highly effective current main battle tank, the M1 Abrams, which first came into service in the early 1980s. Under his guidance all armoured units, in particular armoured cavalry, found themselves being used more and more frequently. 'The ability to move men and vehicles rapidly into battle was ideal for small, widely separated, independent engagements. Cavalry could move quickly and bring heavy firepower to bear at critical points. . . . Rapid reinforcement of a unit in combat was nicknamed 'pile-on'. . . . In this period of widespread small actions, some form of pile-on became the usual mode of operation.'[8] The tactic became highly successful; one armour officer, writing later about a particular action at Binh An, said: 'We had once more stumbled into a situation and had been able to turn it to our advantage. But it was more than stumbling and it was not luck that brought success. It was soldiers in hot steel vehicles out in the glaring sun looking and poking until the enemy, North Vietnamese and Viet Cong, never knew when or where an armored column would crop up next.'[9]

New equipment to arrive in the late 1960s included the Sheridan light tank, which did not prove to be a great success, especially because its main weapon system, the 152mm anti-tank missile, was never used, while conventional ammunition fired from the same tube gave constant problems. Mine ploughs and other methods of clearing anti-tank mines were also brought in, as the enemy use of mines became more widespread. Tank *v* tank combat took place only once, at Ben Het in March 1969, between two tanks of 1st Battalion 69th

Armour and some PT76s from 16th Company, 4th Battalion, 202nd Armored Regiment of the North Vietnamese Army. Specialist 4 Frank Hembree was the first American tank gunner to fire at the enemy armour; 'I only had his muzzle flashes to sight on,' he wrote later, 'but I couldn't wait for a better target because his shells were landing real close to us.' However, this was enough, his second round turning the enemy tank into a fireball. Two PT76s and an enemy troop carrier were knocked out, the Americans also suffering casualties, although none of their tanks was knocked out. Tanks did not clash again until South Vietnamese M41s clashed with North Vietnamese tanks in Laos in March, 1971.

Gen Abrams began using large armoured formations to attack enemy base areas, once safe havens, in order to disrupt their logistical system. Next they were used to seal the borders, armoured and airmobile units rapidly becoming the mainstay of such operations, especially in III Corps area north of Saigon. Based at Phuoc Vinh, the 1st Cavalry Division, with three brigades of airmobile infantry and operational control over 11th Armored Cavalry, carried out border operations, the helicopter gunships, tactical air and artillery all co-operating with ground armour to prevent the enemy crossing the border in strength. At the same time, South Vietnamese armoured units began to play a larger part in operations, their 1st Armoured Brigade being awarded a US Presidential Citation for the success of its first large-scale operation.

Meanwhile, plans for turning the war over to the Vietnamese and the withdrawal of US forces were under secret consideration, with 'armor units (which had been specifically excluded from the build up until late 1966) anchoring the withdrawal of American combat units from Vietnam.'[11] This must have been a relatively novel use of armour, quite the opposite to its blitzkrieg role at the start of the Korean war. Armoured units in Vietnam provided a maximum of firepower and mobility for the minimum number of US troops left on the ground. For example, when, by the end of 1970, the withdrawal of American units was in full swing, 14 armoured battalions or squadrons remained in Vietnam. In December 1971, armoured units represented a staggering 54% of the US manoeuvre battalions still in Vietnam. The last US ground cavalry unit to carry out operations was F Troop, 17th Cavalry, which left Da Nang on 6th April. The last ground cavalry unit to leave Vietnam was the 1st Squadron, 1st Cavalry, which began its return on 10th April. Air Cavalry units, with the primary mission of supporting South Vietnamese army forces, were the only active Army combat units left in Vietnam in 1972.

VIET CONG ARMOUR   Until the end of 1973, Viet Cong armour made only brief appearances on the battlefield, on just four occasions, but each time the amount of armour employed increased. The first instance was at Lang Vei special forces camp near Khe Sanh on 6th/7th February 1968. Here a combined-arms attack was supported by more than a dozen PT76 light tanks and in a single night's action stormed and over-ran the entire camp. The sudden appearance of enemy armour had a tremendous shock effect, which spread throughout the US forces: 'Jesus, they had tanks! Tanks! . . . After

Lang Vei, how could you look out of your perimeter at night without hearing the treads coming?'[12] In 1969 the North Vietnamese again used armour, this time at Ben Het. Then, two years later, when South Vietnamese forces attacked into Laos, the enemy committed an entire tank regiment and staged, as Gen Starry puts it, 'well-coordinated tank-infantry attacks'. In their spring offensive of 1972 in South Vietnam, the North Vietnamese used the largest tank forces of the war, complete tank companies storming objectives with the infantry following up close behind. Russian-built T54s and their Chinese equivalent, the T59, fought it out with the M48A3 tanks of the South Vietnamese 20th Tank Regiment (later reconstituted into the 1st Armor Brigade). Unfortunately, the South Vietnamese had not only let the initiative pass to the enemy, but also used their armour mainly in static defensive positions where, as Gen Starry puts it, 'the inherent advantages of firepower, mobility and shock effect could not be exploited, inviting piecemeal destruction.' He goes on to comment that the tactical situation that existed immediately before and for some time after the cease fire 'was ideal for the employment of armored forces as mobile reserves.'

Thus, once again, a seemingly unsophisticated, 'peasant' Communist army had showed its better-equipped and more armour-conscious opponent how armour should be handled. It is easy to draw wrong conclusions from such unhappy conflicts as the two wars in Indo-China/Vietnam and the UN action in Korea, but the evidence is clear that, given the will, armour could be used effectively in such extreme conditions of terrain and climate, and could produce the same spectacular successes that had already been achieved by the 'Queen of the Battlefield' in other wars and in other theatres of operations. Despite the heroism of individual tank commanders (there were no fewer than nineteen armour recipients of America's highest battlefield award for bravery, the Congressional Medal of Honor, during the period 1966 to 1971 in Vietnam) the great tank commanders were mainly to be found on the 'other side of the hill'.

India and Pakistan at War

On 14th August 1947, India and Pakistan became separate countries within the British Commonwealth, this momentous event being accompanied by widespread communal violence which led to the deaths of over one million people. Ever since their independence the two countries have been uneasy neighbours, with violence flaring up again and again in various disputed areas. Three of these have so far been large enough to be classified as 'wars', with armour being used to good effect in all of them.

CONFLICT OVER KASHMIR   The first took place in November 1947, when Pakistani troops went to the assistance of a Moslem revolt against the Hindu ruler of Kashmir. Armour was used, but only in limited numbers and only by India. The first occasion was on 5th November in the Battle of Shalateng, when an armoured car troop, under Lt N.G. David, created havoc by attacking the enemy rear and inflicting over 500 casualties. Lt David was awarded the Vir Chakra, India's third highest award for bravery. Later, Stuart tanks of 7th Cavalry, under Lt Col Rajindar Singh (affectionately known as 'Sparrow') took part in highly successful operations in the Himalayan mountain pass of Zoji La, some 11,300 feet above sea level. 'The decision of the Indian commanders to take tanks to Zoji La was a historic one,' wrote Lt Col (Retd) Dr Bhupinder Singh in the introduction to his book on the 1965 war. For his part, 'Sparrow' went on to command a division in the 1965 war and a corps in 1971.

THE RANN OF KUTCH   Kashmir was formally annexed by India on 26th January 1957, despite protests from Pakistan. Fighting soon began between the two countries in the disputed border area of the Rann of Kutch, and, despite Britain managing to arrange a cease-fire on 1st July, further violence was inevitable, especially after large numbers of Pakistani irregulars had crossed the cease-fire line into Kashmir. By 5th August the Indians were claiming that a full-scale invasion had taken place and so retaliated. Pakistan's reaction was to launch an offensive themselves in brigade strength, supported by over 70 tanks, in the Chamb area on 1st September. Five days later, the Indians retaliated by launching their own attacks against Lahore, Sialkot and Hyderabad. Once again the UN mediated and a cease-fire was effected on 23rd September, but not before a number of major battles had taken place, including many tank engagements. This fighting saw the more sophisticated American-built M48 Patton tanks of the Pakistanis being taken on and beaten by the less sophisticated Indian-manned British-built Centurions. 'The sheer modernity of the Patton was its undoing,' wrote one reporter, 'Indian tanks would fire off three shots while the Pakistanis were twiddling with their computers.'[13] As Lt Col Singh comments acidly: 'The Pakistanis themselves admit that their overreliance on sophisticated weaponry (particularly the armour and their air arm) had also generated the risky habit of over-rating one's own chances of success and taking victory for granted. Sophistication of the equipment should, therefore, be commensurate with the mental capability of those who are to handle it.' This is, of course, the Indian view. Other reports from Pakistan claimed that they were well satisfied with their more complicated tanks, saying that the large number of hits on the turrets of enemy Centurions was entirely due to having better equipment. Nevertheless, there was clear evidence that the Patton was vulnerable to the Centurion's 20-pdr and, for that matter, to the 75mm of the AMX13.

As far as numbers were concerned, Pakistan had some 900 main battle tanks at the start of the war, mainly M47s and M48s, with some older Sherman M4s. They were faced by about 800 Indian tanks, mainly Shermans, but with some 300 Centurions. Both armies were organized along British lines and used the tactics and battle procedures they had learnt from the British. The armed forces of India were far larger than those of her neighbour (869,000 as compared with at best 208,000), while in fully fledged divisions within the two armies the balance was 20 Indian to six Pakistan, but the latter were certainly better equipped. The Indians could not of course deploy all their forces, requiring to leave a fair number defending their long border with China. The two armies were basically 'infantry-orientated', with a proportion of their armoured regiments within infantry divisions. Pakistan had two armoured divisions (1st and 6th) each (on paper at the start of hostilities) containing four armoured regiments, one armoured recce regiment and three armoured infantry battalions (motorized). 1st Armd Div was the pride of the Pakistani Army, but 6th had only recently been formed and was still incomplete. India had one armoured division (1st) containing four armoured regiments, a motor battalion and three lorried infantry battalions and one strong armoured brigade (2 Independent), plus some light tank regiments. The 22-day War of 1965 was the largest ever fought on the Indian sub-continent and the largest tank war ever fought in Asia. Over 1,500 tanks were involved and many were knocked out. The main tank battles occurred in two areas – the Sialkot and Labore sectors. In the former, the fighting was between 1st (Indian) Armoured Division and 6th (Pakistani) Armoured Division, in the latter between 1st (Pakistani) Armoured Division and 2 (Indian) Independent Armoured Brigade. An independent report, written shortly after the war had ended, summarized the tank fighting thus: 'The picture that emerges is that on both sides the armour was committed without proper reconnaissance in an area unsuited to the use of tanks on the scale employed and that they allowed themselves to be drawn into a tank melee in which the tactical handling of armour was conspicuous by its absence.' Nevertheless, great bravery was shown on both sides. A Pakistani history of the campaign speaks of many of its armoured corps officers winning one of their highest awards for gallantry, the *Sitara-i-Jurat* (Star of Bravery). On the Indian side, they awarded the *Param Vir Chakra*, their equivalent of the VC, to Lt Col Ardeshir Burzorji Tarapore, CO of 17 Horse (The Poona Horse), then part of 1st (Indian) Armoured Division. His citation tells how, on 11th September 1965, he was given the task of delivering the main armoured thrust to capture the Phillora sector in Pakistan. While they were moving between Phillora and Chawinda they were suddenly counter-attacked by heavy Pakistani armour. Lt Col Tarapore, who was at the head of his regiment. '. . . defied the enemy's charge, held his ground and gallantly attacked Phillora with one of his squadrons supported by an infantry battalion. Though under continuous enemy tank and artillery fire, Lt Col Tarapore remained unperturbed throughout this action and, when wounded, refused to be evacuated.' Three days later, despite his wounds, he led his regiment in an attack, this time to capture Wazirawali. Two days afterwards he was back in action again, when

unmindful of his injury, he again gallantly led his Regiment and captured Jasoran and Butur-Dograndi on 16th September. His own tank was hit several times, but despite the odds, he maintained his pivots in both these places and thereby allowed the supporting infantry to attack Chawida from the rear. Inspired by his leadership, the Regiment fiercely attacked the enemy's heavy armour destroying approximately sixty enemy tanks at the cost of only nine tank casualties, and when Lt Col Tarapore was mortally wounded, the Regiment continued to defy the enemy.

It was in this action that the Poona Horse earned for themselves the nickname *Fakr-i-Hind* ('Pride of India').

Operating in the same attack on Phillora on 11th September was Hodson's Horse (4 Horse), under Lt Col (now Brig) Madan Mohan Singh Bakshi, who had the dual task of protecting the left flank and of intercepting the enemy's armour as it withdrew astride the Gadgor-Phillora road. The citation to his *Mahar Vir Chakra* (India's second highest gallantry award) explains how, while the squadrons were moving up and RHQ 4 Horse was engaged in reconnaissance, Bakshi suddenly saw a squadron of enemy tanks in hull-down positions astride the Libbe-Phillora road.

Without the slightest hesitation, he engaged and knocked out two enemy tanks. Soon after, the other tanks of the enemy squadron directed their guns on Lt Col Bakshi's tank. Undeterred, Lt Col Bakshi advanced again to charge through the enemy tanks, though he had by now received two direct hits on his tank. Despite these odds, he gallantly charged with his single tank, crossed the road and knocked out another enemy tank. By now his tank had been hit for a fourth time and had caught fire, whereupon he ordered the crew to bale out. While doing so Lt Col Bakshi and his crew came under intense machine gun fire and were also surrounded by the crew of enemy tanks who had bailed out earlier from their burning tanks. Bakshi and his crew defied capture and took cover in an adjacent sugarcane field, from where they were retrieved by the advancing tanks of 17 Horse. Meanwhile one sqn of 4 Horse had advanced and engaged the enemy armour, thereby diverting the enemy's attention from their CO. Thereafter Lt Col Bakshi resumed command of the Regiment. His inspiring leadership made a material contribution to the capture of Phillora.

The day before the Phillora action, over in the Lahore sector, Maj Gen Nasir, commander of Pakistan's 1st Armd Div, was killed with his entire recce group, after being ambushed. His three tanks were knocked out in a hail of artillery, anti-tank and small-arms fire. This clearly shows that Pakistani armoured commanders were operating well forward and it was also the same among the Indian tankers. Gen Singh, 'Sparrow', then GOC 1st (Indian) Armoured Division, was awarded a bar to his *Mahar Vir Chakra*, his citation reading: 'By his presence in the thick of the battle in utter disregard to his personal safety, Maj Gen Rajinder Singh [Sparrow] inspired our tank crews to engage the enemy forces closely'. In commenting upon the use of armour in the 1965 war, Lt Gen O.P. Dunn, commander of the 1st (Indian) Corps, agrees that the tanks used by both sides were probably too complicated for simple peasant soldiers. However he adds that 'This proves the old dictum that it is not the machine, but the man behind the machine, who always has the last say.'[14]

THE LIGHTNING WAR   On 10th January 1966, India and Pakistan signed an agreement to renounce the use of force, but the uneasy peace did not last for long, there being increased unrest within East Pakistan for autonomy. Eventually, in 1971, the Awami League declared East Pakistan to be the independent

166

republic of Bangladesh, so Pakistan sent in troops to deal with the rebels. Their harsh and repressive measures caused thousands to flee over the border into India, who deliberately began fostering the unrest by arming and training the rebels. Pakistan eventually decided that the only way to deal with the situation was to attack India from West Pakistan, whilst India retaliated by sending a massive force of some eight divisions into East Pakistan. The 'Lightning War' that followed ended in a complete disaster for the Pakistanis, who were forced into a humiliating surrender, in order to prevent a full-blooded Indian invasion of West Pakistan. Armour was used in strength, but this time the Indians had vastly increased their tank strength with some 450 T55 Soviet tanks and 300 home-produced Vickers Vijayanta, to bolster up their faithful Centurions, plus AMX13s and amphibious PT76s, which were invaluable for reconnaissance, especially in riverine terrain. Singh Sparrow was now a lieutenant general commanding a corps, while the late Lt Col Tarapore's Poona Horse was once again in the thick of things. During the battle of the Basantar River on 16th December 1971, 2nd Lt Arun Khetarpel of Poona Horse was posthumously awarded the *Param Vir Chakra* for his courage that day, showing, in the words of the citation, 'qualities of leadership, tenacity of purpose, a will to close with the enemy and courage of the highest order. His daring exploits reached a grand climax in the fast and furious tank *versus* tank action . . . and this young officer sacrificed his young life for the greater glory of his Regiment and his country.'

NOTES TO CHAPTER 10

1 As quoted in Brig George Davy, *The Seventh and Three Enemies*

2 As quoted in Bryan Perrett, *Tank Tracks to Rangoon*

3 After his death Gen Walker joined that very special group of American generals who have had tanks named after them, the light tank M41 'Little Bulldog', which came into service in 1951, being renamed the 'Walker Bulldog'.

4 The destruction of Groupement Mobile 100 was described vividly by Bernard B. Falls in his book *Street Without Joy*. Gen William C. Westmorland, the US commander in Vietnam from 1964 to 1968, kept a copy of Fall's book on the table by his bed. He later said that the defeat of Groupement Mobile 100 was always on his mind. Westmorland was no armoured soldier and was clearly far too influenced by this book and also by a staff briefing held at the Pentagon in July 1965, when a general officer stated that tanks were not needed in Vietnam.

5 *Mounted Combat in Vietnam.*

6 Sub-units were rotated thereafter, so other squadrons also served in Vietnam.

7 See Maj Gen R.N.L. Hopkins, *Australian Armour*, for a full description of this and other RAAC actions in Vietnam.

8 *Mounted Combat in Vietnam*

9 *ibid.*

10 Now General (Ret)

11 *Mounted Combat in Vietnam*

12 Michael Herr, *Dispatches*

13 The Pentagon was so worried that, immediately the war ended, they initiated some serious discussions about the poor performance of the Patton, as a loss of export orders was feared.

14 As quoted in Col Robert J. Icks, *Famous Tank Battles*

11   ISRAELIS VERSUS ARABS

It is somewhat ironic that after WW2 the dashing image of the Panzerwaffe of a decade earlier should have been taken over by the tank commanders of the Nazi's most hated peoples, the Jews. The Israeli Armoured Corps was born in battle from very small beginnings in the early days of Israel's nationhood, yet quickly became one of the most formidable armoured forces the world has ever seen. Its early commanders at all levels had to gain most of their expertise the hard way – on the field of battle – swiftly putting the lessons they learnt into practice and instituting a rigorous system of discipline while not allowing individual initiative or flair to be stifled. The resulting potent mixture has enabled them to overcome the far larger, better equipped forces of their Arab neighbours on every occasion that they have fought.

We have to look back to the days before the establishment of the State of Israel in 1948, to learn about the build-up of their first ramshackle collection of AFVs, most of which they acquired by very devious means to protect their burgeoning state from the onslaught of their Arab neighbours, whose armies were far better trained and equipped. The tank commanders of those days were a mixture of Jewish settlers and soldiers of other nationalities, including some British 'deserters' who had decided to support the Jewish cause. Their very first AFVs were two armoured cars – a GMC and a Daimler – which were driven out of British camps by sympathetic soldiers and then handed over to waiting Haganah[1] crews. The British authorities were furious and demanded their return, but as Col David Eshel explains in his stirring history of the Israeli Armoured Corps, *Chariots of the Desert*, the Jewish authorities were unable to comply even if they had wanted to because '. . . only a handful of Haganah members had been part of the plot. Within a few days, both cars were brought out of hiding and used to help the Haganah rout a massive Arab force from the Kastel redoubt on the main road to Jerusalem.'

Next they acquired a tank – a derelict Sherman, one of a number scheduled to be scrapped before the end of the British Mandate, by the simple expedient of being taken up Mount Carmel and pushed over a sheer cliff. 'Finding a sympathetic ear among the British troops whose job it was to carry out the destruction of the AFVs, the Jews were able to arrange for the clandestine abduction of one of the Shermans, while it was on its way up the mountain by night. It was transferred to a waiting Jewish transporter and spirited away to Tel Aviv, while the obliging British soldiers signed the necessary forms to confirm its

168

destruction.'² Sadly their 'prize' was not immediately battleworthy, being minus its guns and sighting equipment, with an unserviceable engine and missing various track plates and bogies! A great deal of ferreting in junkheaps at the recently evacuated REME dumps and other similar places was then necessary.

While such clandestine operations were taking place, the Jewish convoys running between their settlements were being protected by lightly armoured trucks known as 'Sandwiches' (because their 'armour-plate' consisted of a sandwich of plywood, 5in thick, between two thin 5mm sheets of steel). Better armoured cars were, however, soon available from Europe, based upon the Dodge and White 4 × 4 and fitted with an LMG turret. A new organization was also introduced, known as the Armoured Service, which comprised 100 of the new armoured cars. It was led by Yizhak Sadeh, 'an already legendary figure, who had served alongside Capt Orde Wingate in the Special Night Squads (SNS) in the thirties and had led the Palmach since its inception in the forties.'³ Sadeh organized the first operational armoured formation, known somewhat optimistically as 8th Armoured Brigade. He was thus the founder of the Israeli Armoured Corps. A Pole by birth, he emigrated to Palestine in 1920 and joined the Haganah. He was the first to appreciate the importance of mobility and had put his ideas to Wingate while they were both serving in the SNS. He reached the rank of major general and died in 1952.

The War of Independence

1948 saw the Israelis endeavouring to organize their existing armour into effective fighting units, while at the same time trying to obtain tanks from all over the world. These efforts produced extraordinary results – Col Sadeh's 8th Armoured Brigade for example, contained just one tank battalion, comprising one company of French Hotchkiss tanks (smuggled into Israel under the guise of farm machinery) manned by Russians who spoke only Russian and a little Yiddish, and one company of the two Cromwells and the Sherman, manned by British and South African volunteers who spoke only English. Sadeh spoke all these languages, but his orders still had to be passed on using a series of interpreters, so it is easy to see how mistakes could occur. The second battalion in the brigade was 89th Commando, commanded by another legendary figure, the one-eyed Moshe Dayan, who had lost his eye fighting the Vichy French in the Middle East in WW2.

The first major operation carried out by Sadeh's brigade was Operation 'Danny', a two-pronged attack on Lydda airport. It started well; the English-speaking tank company took the ex-RAF camp within half an hour of reaching the airport. However, the Russian-speaking company lacked updated maps and could not understand their orders anyway, so they quickly got lost! It took time to sort things out, concentrate the battalion again and get it moving. In the meantime Dayan's commandos had captured all their objectives and were waiting for the tanks to arrive. Dayan realized that the road to the town of Lydda further to the south was wide open, so he decided to disobey his brigade commander's orders and to mount a surprise attack on the town, which was a great success despite heavy fighting. Dayan received an imperial rocket from his boss, but nevertheless had achieved a remarkable victory. As David Eshel says: 'The blooding of Operation Danny was the first of many Israeli Armoured Corps "success stories" later to establish the foundation of the IDF concept for mobility.'[4]

Sadeh and his makeshift armoured brigade continued to perform miracles, such as the capture of a heavily reinforced concrete fort nicknamed 'the Monster', which was the lynchpin of the main Egyptian position at Iraq Suweidan, a hill controlling the whole of the Faluga intersection. But there were failures, too, and casualties, from mechanical breakdowns, mines and enemy fire. The Israeli Defence Minister, David Ben Gurion, decided to try to form another armoured unit, but as there were no tanks available, the new brigade – 7th Brigade – was equipped with M3 half-tracks and armoured cars. Recruits came mainly from those illegal immigrants whom the British had originally sent to detention camps in Cyprus, so they were unfamiliar with the topography of their new country. Their first major engagement took place at Latrun, halfway along the road between Jerusalem and Tel Aviv, a fierce fight in which they suffered many casualties. Ben Gurion then chose a Canadian war veteran, Lt Col Ben Dunkelman, to reorganize the shattered brigade, a job which he had only just started when he was ordered to take his unit north to assist in the liberation of Galilee. Force-marching his brigade into position, he brilliantly utilized an unguarded access route and captured Nazareth, at the same time dealing with Arab amoured cars that were blocking the town's approaches. Later he freed the road from Safed to Kibbutz Sassa on the Lebanese border, bringing the Israelis to the banks of the Latani River. As Eshel comments, '. . . he set a precedent of excellence in the 7th Brigade – which was to become the IDF's foremost armoured formation in later wars.' Although this first Arab-Israeli war was mainly an infantry battle, the armour did show that they were capable of exploiting the principle of mobility to the full and were thus able to overcome much larger and better equipped enemy forces.

BUILDING AN ARMOURED CORPS   The 1949 Armistice was followed by a major reorganization and reduction within the IDF, which initially led to 7th Brigade becoming the only armoured brigade, inheriting 82nd Tank Battalion from the disbanded 8th Brigade. Now reorganized into four tank companies, the brigade was completely equipped with Shermans, the Hotchkiss having been 'retired'. However, they still boasted an amazing variety of Marks of Sherman which would have done any tank museum proud! 'A' Company had M4s acquired in Italy from ex-US Army surplus dumps, 'B' Company was not quite so lucky. They had a mixture of Shermans of various types, mainly with 75mm guns for which ammunition supplies were very limited, plus one Sherman 'Firefly' for which there was no ammunition whatsoever. The other two companies had no tanks at all, just half-tracks, while the imposingly titled 'Armour School' boasted only three Shermans, all of different Marks, with virtually no training ammunition to go with them. Commanding the Armour School was Desmond Ruthledge, a British ex-regular warrant officer from the RTR, quickly promoted to chief instructor with the rank of major. His students learnt the hard way – driving, repairing, maintaining and manoeuvring their tanks as best they could – creating original ideas, concepts and tactics, which would later develop into one of the most successful armoured techniques in the world. The school's first students included Abraham 'Bren' Adan and Shmuel Gorodish (Gonen), both of whom would rise to senior command in the Israeli Armoured Corps.

In addition to this do-it-yourself training, the IDF High Command decided to send a group of hand-picked officers to attend a tank officers' course at the French Armour School at Saumur. David Eshel tells how, on the same course, there were a group of Syrian officers with whom the Israelis became quite friendly, swopping their wartime experiences of being on opposing sides. He also tells how, on the command-level manoeuvres in 1952, Lt Col Uri Ben Ari, then 21C of 7th Armoured Brigade, drove his force of tanks and half-tracks 80 miles into the Negev, to emerge on the flank of the Central Command defensive line and then attacked, routing an entire infantry brigade in panic and thus upsetting a carefully prepared exercise plan. The high brass was not amused, but Prime Minister Ben Gurion, who fortunately happened to be present, was greatly impressed and saw to it that the much-depleted armoured corps received funds for new tanks and ammunition. Uri Ben Ari, who went on to become the Commander of the Israeli Armoured Corps (1956–7) was one of the IDF's most brilliant young officers in the 1950s. Born in Berlin in 1925, he survived the Holocaust only because his parents sent him to Palestine, where he was educated in a kibbutz. He joined the Palmach, commanded a company at the age of 21, then in 1948 commanded a battalion in the fighting around Jerusalem and in the Negev. There he became convinced that fast-moving armoured columns were the ideal forces to operate in Israel – which he ably proved in the 1952 exercise and again in 1956, when he commanded 7th Armoured Brigade in the lightning Sinai campaign. Shortly before this campaign the IDF managed to obtain from France several hundred SuperShermans and AMX13s, which were secretly landed at Haifa. With French help, the IDF managed to fit into their Shermans the new French 75-mm gun, considered to be the best in the world, and to design suitable *ad hoc* gun-control equipment. Col 'Bren' Adan – commanding 82nd Tank Battalion – and Col Bar Lev were both intimately involved in the trials of the new gun and equipment, fitted, trialled and modified in secret on the French tank ranges at Bourges. The result was the Sherman M50, which came into service in mid-1956 and was 'blooded' a few months later in the Sinai.

Suez and Sinai

The year 1956 saw an upsurge of violence in the Middle East, following the nationalization of the Suez Canal Company by the Egyptian government on

26th July. Both Britain and France were worried that major trade routes to Australasia and the Far East would be threatened and that oil supplies from the Persian Gulf would have to go all the way around the Cape. This led to them adopting a joint resolution which provided for free open transit through the canal, with Egypt's sovereignty being respected. Secretly, however, they had agreed with Israel to attack Egypt if Nasser, the Egyptian President, did not agree to their proposals. Naturally he did not respond to their demands and the joint plan went into effect, Israeli paratroopers being dropped on the Mitla Pass on 29th October. A combined British and French force landed at Port Said and Port Fuad and 6th Royal Tank Regiment, equipped with Centurions, rapidly took Port Said. However, the major armoured effort was in the Sinai, where the Israeli 7th Armoured Brigade, commanded by Col Uri Ben Ari, and 27th Armoured Brigade, under Col Haim Bar Lev, were both part of the two divisional task groups that made up the invasion force. Bar Lev, like Ben Ari, had been born outside Palestine, in Austria in 1924, emigrating to a kibbutz in 1939. He served as a platoon commander in the Palmach in 1942, commanded a battalion in the Negev brigade and took part in the first tank *v* tank action in 1949 near Rafa. He would command the Armoured Corps in 1958 and become Chief of Staff of the IDF in 1968.

The lightning campaign was a triumph for Israeli armour, 7th Armoured Brigade, for example, reaching the Suez Canal in under 100 hours, having travelled 150 miles and fought several fierce battles. 27th Armoured Brigade did equally well, but, as David Eshel says: 'In assessing the campaign from an armoured viewpoint, the performance of 7th Armoured Brigade and its brilliant commander stands out clearly as the outstanding feat of the war. . . . In those few days the IDF Armoured Corps had earned its coveted spurs and the Israeli combat doctrine would change completely – the armour thereafter becoming "king" of the battlefield.' In typical blitzkrieg style armoured commanders up to and including brigade commander led from the front by personal example, dealing with each battle on the spot – neglecting their rear links, which cannot have endeared them to senior commanders! Nevertheless, their success would have a profound effect on IDF doctrine, with Moshe Dayan, now Chief of Staff, being the foremost advocate of a strong armoured force. Up-and-coming officers, including some of the best infantry officers, were assigned to senior armoured posts. These included Col David Elazar, who later became Chief of Staff, and Col Israel Tal, perhaps the most famous of all Israeli tank commanders. 'Talik', as he is known, was born in Israel in 1924, joined the Haganah and later served in the British Army, as a member of the Jewish Brigade in Italy, where he was sergeant in a Vickers machine-gun platoon. During the Sinai campaign he had commanded an infantry brigade, now, after a thorough conversion course, he took over as commander of 7th Armoured Brigade. Elazar attended the same course and became deputy to Maj Gen Bar-Lev, then commanding the Armoured Corps.

Re-organization

A major period of re-organization followed, in which the IDF became highly mechanized, a number of new armoured brigades being formed, with medium tanks and mechanized infantry. Various organizations were tried out, but eventually the strength of each tank company was set at three platoons of three tanks, with two more in Coy HQ, making the 'lean eleven tank company', as David Eshel calls it, which was the ideal size for young company commanders to control in battle. It also meant that there were more officers leading tanks, which helped when units had to be re-grouped due to breakdown or battle casualties. It was about this time (1960), that the IDF took delivery of the British Centurion, undoubtedly the finest tank in the world in its day, although more complicated than the existing Shermans, which did not initially endear it to Israeli tankers. Even when the newly acquired British 105mm L7 guns were fitted, it was difficult to raise much enthusiasm for the new tanks. Fortunately for the IDF this situation was to change dramatically with the assumption of command of the Armoured Corps by 'Talik', who appreciated the full potential of the Centurion, realizing that it was outdated gunnery procedures that were at fault and not the equipment. Gen Tal also matched words with action, swiftly becoming the best tank gunner in the entire Israeli Armoured Corps! He proved his prowess during an engagement with the Syrians near Alkmagor north of Lake Galilee. A Jewish tractor, working in the fields, had been fired on by Syrian tanks and a rescue squad had also been pinned down. A platoon of Centurions (with Tal as one of the tank gunners) engaged the Syrian tanks, knocking them all out, then engaging and destroying various other enemy vehicles, which fondly imagined they were well out of range. The Centurion was vindicated in the short battle, which had the direct result of stopping the Syrians from their activities in the area.

Expansion and modernization continued, newer tanks, such as the M48A2 Patton, were obtained, while the armoured commanders were given more status within the IDF, the Commander Armoured Corps being promoted to major general and becoming a member of the General Staff, where his views on mobile warfare could be properly aired. First to hold this post was Maj Gen Haim Bar-Lev, followed in 1964 by 'Talik'. His period of command was to be the longest to date (1964–9), during which great strides were made in all aspects of the corps' work. However, they were not allowed to make this progress unhindered, because in 1967 they faced their greatest test ever – the 'Six Day War'.

A Lightning Campaign

'By 1967 the Armoured Corps was ready for action. It was a highly trained, motivated force containing top professionals in their various trades. The Corps could face the growing Arab armour with full confidence and the test was soon to come.'[5] For the very first time in its short history, Israel considered itself strong enough to take on its Arab opponents, and so, instead of waiting to be attacked by the enormous forces that were being built up all around their tiny State, they decided to pre-empt the inevitable and to attack first. The armour played a vital role in the plan, especially in Sinai, where large Egyptian forces were massing – more than five infantry and two armoured divisions – ready to mount a two-pronged attack through the Gaza Strip and Abu Agheila towards the heart of Israel. The IDF carried out successfully a major deception plan, aimed at getting the Egyptians to redeploy their main armour well south, away from the border area. Gen Tal's armour carried out the first ground action of the Six Day War on 5th June, immediately following the Jewish airstrikes on enemy airfields which gave them virtual control of the skies. 'We shall be the first formation to open the assault,' Gen Tal told his tank commanders,

the outcome of the war will depend upon our performance. Our division has the best brigades in the Army and we are expected to succeed. If we fail, the outcome will be disastrous for the whole campaign. . . . There will be heavy fire and the Egyptians will fight well, so keep moving. If you stall the attack, you will be subjected to tons of steel coming on top of you; therefore keep moving under all circumstances and fire from as far as possible, knocking out the enemy tanks and anti-tank guns at long range.

As David Eshel explains, Tal had trained his crews to become top gunnery performers, always striving to achieve kills at maximum range, going for a first round knockout, which, considering the state of the gun-control equipment of the period, was no mean achievement

The resulting battle was every bit as fierce as Gen Tal had predicted, but despite the Israelis being outnumbered by at least three to one in tanks alone, and their Arab opponents showing great bravery, the superior skills of the IDF commanders won the day. Typical of their young commanders was Lt Avigdor Kahalani, who was in the lead tank of 7th Armoured Brigade, who would later become the most decorated officer in the IDF. Close behind him was his battalion commander, Maj Ehud Elad, already severely wounded, but, as David Eshel describes 'still erect in his turret hatch', while beside him was his ops officer, Lt Amram Mitzna, also wounded but refusing to leave his post. Kahalani's company led the southern attack, but his Patton was soon hit and ablaze. Maj Elad took over the lead to maintain the momentum of the attack and was killed in the thick of the battle. Mitzna then took over and continued to fight until he could contact the deputy commander, who was some way behind. At this point the brigade commander intervened and personally directed the attack, smashing through the strong Egyptian defences, the audacity and speed of the Israeli armour taking the enemy completely by surprise. This was typical of the Jewish tank commanders, who, like all great tank commanders in history, commanded from the front and carried the day as much by their personal example and bravery as by their tactical skill and professional competence. Israeli tank crews fought for over sixty hours without rest, outfighting their more numerous opponents all the way to the Suez Canal, which they reached on the early morning of 9th June, having destroyed or captured most of the enemy's 960-strong tank force. Despite their individual bravery, the Egyptians had handled their armour badly and with little imagination, keeping their tanks static and mainly locating them far behind their forward defended localities. Individual tank-gunnery skills were far more in evidence on the Jewish side, 90mm Patton tank gunners completely dominating for example, the 122mm JS IIIs, which they knocked out without losing a single tank themselves. Even the lightly armed AMX13s showed that they could outmanoeuvre and outshoot enemy 100mm T 55s by night, knocking them out from a flank with their 75mm guns.

On the other fronts around Jerusalem, in Samaria and on the Golan Heights, the action was just as fierce, Col Uri Ben Ari's Shermans dealing swiftly with Jordanian thrusts on Jerusalem, while Col Moshe Bril dealt with other Jordanian armour in Samaria. On the Golan, Maj Gen David Elazar had only been allotted three brigades, of which only one was armour, but nevertheless he managed to capture the heights after some extremely fierce fighting. The Syrian forces retreated from Kuneitra and the war was won. It had been a triumph for the Israeli mobile armoured forces over a far larger enemy who employed semi-fixed defences. In the notes he wrote in *Chariots of the Desert*, Brigadier Bryan Watkins makes the point that it is impossible to overstate the importance of the very high standard of tank gunnery that Gen Tal had ensured was the norm among his men. Watkins explains how successful engagements at over 4,000 yards were quite usual and that there was even one recorded at a staggering 12,000 yards, albeit against a soft target. 'When speaking about the Six Day War, General Tal will often describe how a battalion of his tanks completely destroyed a much larger Egyptian force by standing off and knocking out the opposition at long range – a tactic to which the enemy had no response, except to flee.'[6]

Uneasy Peace

The Six Day War was followed once again by a period of relative calm, while the beaten Arabs licked their wounds and tried to repair their shattered forces. The IDF armoured forces were in the ascendancy and Israel now controlled an area four times as large as they had before 1967! Unfortunately, instead of signing a peace treaty and recognizing the State of Israel, the Arabs decided, at a summit meeting in September 1967, not to recognize Israel and not to make peace. There followed what the Jews now call 'the War of Attrition', when, for a period of some three years, there was continual activity on all fronts, the Jordanians supporting the PLO (Palestine Liberation Organization) against the West Bank, the Syrians stirring things up on the Golan Heights and the Egyptians making constant raids on the Sinai and Suez Canal fronts. However, in 1970, the United Nations managed to persuade President Nasser to agree to a cease-fire.

The IDF had apparently fully subscribed to the theory and practice of mobile warfare enshrined in the 'Ugdah Concept of Command' originally developed by Moshe Dayan during the 1956 campaign, but now enlarged to take in a more all-arms approach, including the US Army 'Constant Flow' echelon support system which kept supplies moving forward without waiting for specific demands from the front-line. However, although this flexibility was the very cornerstone of IDF thinking, they had also allowed themselves to adopt the costly (over £30 million) and controversial building of the 'Bar-Lev' Line along the Suez Canal, in other words to adopt an element of static defence. This was justified as being necessary in order to maintain observation along the canal, provide bases for armoured operations and, first and foremost, to give the troops employed on these onerous and boring tasks some protection against the constant heavy Egyptian shelling. Although this line did perhaps give Israel a sense of security, it also gave the Arabs something to aim for which they could have a sporting chance of achieving – the breaching of these defences by a surprise amphibious assault across the Canal. President Nasser died in November 1970 and was succeeded by Anwar el Sadat, who was determined to recover all the territories Egypt had lost. He appreciated however that, initially anyway, it would be playing into Israel's hands to attempt a major breakout into the open wastes of Sinai, where the Israeli armour had already twice shown its superiority. Therefore the Egyptians planned to cross the canal, take the Bar-Lev Line and then consolidate. Planning was the responsibility of the Egyptian Chief of Staff, Gen Saad el Din Shazli, an extremely able officer who had fought in the Six Day War.

I visited the IDF in the early summer of 1973 and remember being very impressed with the high standard of their armoured forces and the general competence of their individual soldiers, yet somewhat surprised by the false sense of security that seemed to colour all our discussions. They had licked the Arabs on every previous occasion and were well placed to do so again. The Bar-Lev Line was virtually impenetrable, and besides, their armoured forces were more than a match for those of any potential enemy force that was lucky enough to break through. Such new developments as man-portable anti-tank guided missiles were laughed off – good tank gunnery was the thing that mattered, it would overcome whatever new weapons appeared on the battlefield. The supreme arrogance came when they chose to ignore all the signs from their early warning system (and that of the Americans) that an attack was imminent. 'Yom Kippur' would indeed prove not to be a day for reconciliation and atonement, but rather one for blood and fire.

Yom Kippur

At 1350 hours on 6th October 1973, while most of Israel celebrated the Day of Atonement with prayers in their homes and neither public transport nor broadcasting were operating, Egypt launched its massive surprise attack across the canal. It was an operation they had rehearsed minutely and it went very much according to plan. Over 2,000 guns opened fire on the Bar-Lev Line and, although the fortifications were able to withstand the 10½ thousand shells which rained down on them at the rate of 175 a minute, the defenders were rendered incapable of preventing the initial assault waves from crossing the Canal virtually unscathed. The Egyptians had deployed over 280,000 troops and 2,000 tanks for the assault, which was protected not only by the artillery barrage but also by direct tank gunfire from a series of high ramps on the west bank, where their T55 and T62 tanks were able to engage Israeli armour on the east bank, as it arrived from the armoured reserve positions to defend the Bar-Lev Line. The high sand ramps the IDF had built on their side of the Canal were blasted apart at the crossing places, not by explosives but by high-pressure water hoses! There were heavy tank casualties on both sides and it is certain that many Israeli tanks were knocked out by the hordes of man-portable Soviet made 'Sagger' guided missiles that the Egyptian soldiers had carried across in their 'suitcases'.[7]

By the morning of the 8th October the Egyptian Army had, to quote David Eshel, '. . . achieved a tremendous feat of arms. Having crossed the 200 metres wide Suez Canal water obstacle with five divisions two days ago, they now had two major army corps bridgeheads on the east bank with eight heavy duty bridges operating.' The one aspect of the Egyptian plan that had not been successful was the attempted capture by heli-borne commandos of the Mitla and Gidi Passes. Most of their helicopters were shot down en route and those that did manage to land were swiftly wiped out. The lightly equipped Egyptian 130th Marine Brigade, which had crossed the Great Bitter Lake to link up with these commandos, was also destroyed. Nevertheless, the Israelis were by now extremely worried. Yom Kippur forgotten, their reserve soldiers were rushing to join their units, while their hard-pressed and outnumbered front-line forces strove to hold back the enemy. There is no doubt that they had underestimated the Egyptians. Most of the Bar-Lev Line fortified positions were captured or destroyed, while heavy casualties were suffered trying to rescue the remaining garrisons. The two Israeli reserve armoured divisions (143rd under Sharon and 162nd under 'Bren' Adan) reached Sinai during the night of the 7th and the Israeli commander of their Southern Command, Gen Shmuel Gonen, decided to employ Adan's division in a north-to-south counterstroke against the expected Egyptian breakout, while Sharon's force covered the southern sector. However, as Bryan Perrett points out in *Desert Warfare*, the Israelis '. . . made the fundamental error of assuming that the Egyptians would break out of their bridgeheads into Sinai, as the Israelis would have done. . . . In fact, beyond making local improvements to their positions, neither Egyptian army had any intention of breaking out, and had not Adan's reconnaissance unit been detached in pursuit of enemy commandos he would have learned the true situation.' Adan's 'ill-fated counterattack' (Eshel's words) was launched on the morning of 8th October. There followed a disastrous period for the Israelis in which Adan lost some 70 tanks without achieving anything. The Egyptians fought well and withstood all the Israeli attacks, while IDF senior officers had an embarrassing argument with everyone trying to blame someone else for the débâcle!

It was clear that the Israelis must do something unexpected if they were to seize the initiative and unbalance the now-jubilant Egyptians. Therefore, instead of letting the battle develop into a bitter slogging match which they could ill afford, or allowing the Egyptians to build up any further so as to be in a strong enough position to achieve a proper breakout from their bridgeheads, the Israelis decided they must themselves mount a reverse crossing of the canal, in order to take control of the battle and get their armour operating behind Egyptian lines, where it could do the most damage. The Egyptians had by now decided that they must launch a major offensive to capture the Tassa, Mitla and Gidi Passes, then to take the Israelis' main Sinai base at Bir Gifgafa, which would effectively destroy the Jewish hold on Sinai and force them to withdraw. Gen Bar-Lev, who knew of the Egyptian preparations for this offensive, decided to postpone his attack across the canal and instead to launch one against the Egyptian bridgeheads, to deal with the enemy build-up. This assault was launched at 0630 hours on 14th October and a massive tank battle ensued, probably the largest since WW2, with some 1,500 Egyptian and 500 Israeli tanks involved. The superior Israeli gunnery in their battle-tested Centurions, Pattons and M6os, won the day and they knocked out many of the enemy Russian-built T62s and T55s – the Egyptians losing over 250 tanks in the first day. Amazingly, despite being well outnumbered, the IDF lost a mere handful of their tanks – some reports put the figure as low as 10 – so Bar-Lev decided to reactivate 'Gazelle' – the Canal crossing plan – and at dawn on the 15th, the assault began again, while the advance guard of Gen Sharon's armoured division smashed into the flank of the Egyptian Second Army near the shores of the Great Bitter Lake. 'Completely surprised by the unexpected direction of the Israeli move, the anti-tank barrier across the road had not opened fire on the vanguard, which was now in the midst of the Egyptian compound firing at anything which moved, and there was plenty! A savage battle now raged, with firing in all directions turning the whole area into a turmoil.'[8] Sharon was by now at the canal and had decided to press on with the crossing, despite the chaos raging to the north. Supported by tanks, Israeli paratroops recrossed the canal on the night of the 15th and, by first light on the following morning, achieved a bridgehead some three miles wide on the west bank. The first tanks crossed by raft, broke out of the bridgehead and started to destroy Egyptian missile sites. More tanks were soon across and the Israeli build-up continued, with heavy bridging equipment moving slowly through to the canal, while the Egyptians tried desperately to prevent it. By the 19th, the Israelis had the best part of three tank divisions across – Sharon's, Adan's and Magen's. The latter was a veteran tank officer who had served as Tal's operations officer in the Six Day War and commanded the 7th Armoured Brigade in the War of Attrition, when he was severely wounded while leading a patrol along the canal road. The Israeli forces were now across in two places. North of the Great Bitter Lake Sharon had not only turned south to link up with the lower bridgehead, but was also poised to strike westwards towards Cairo itself. Below the Little Bitter Lake, Adan and Megen now threatened Suez, Port Tewfik and the Gulf of Suez, encircling the 3rd Egyptian Army Corps and forcing them to accept a cease-fire. Gen Shazli, who had, by any standards, fought a magnificent campaign, collapsed with nervous exhaustion and was replaced by Gen Abdel Ghani Gamasy. The cease-fire came into operation on the evening of the 22nd, but this did not hold and it was not until the 24th that the three weeks of costly fighting came to an end.

ON THE GOLAN 'The Golan Heights, scene of such gallant and bitter fighting in the Six Day War, was about to witness a defensive action, fought chiefly by the Israeli Armoured Corps and the Israeli Air Force, which must go down in history as one of the truly great defensive battles of all time – ranking with Cassino and Kohima. The time was 1400hrs on 6th October 1973.' That is how Col David Eshel begins his account of this epic battle, in which the Syrians fielded some 1,400 tanks, including 400 modern T62s, plus nearly 1,000 artillery pieces deployed along a 20-mile front. The Syrian offensive was an integral part of the overall Arab concept for the October war, which envisaged a simultaneous, co-ordinated, surprise offensive on both the Canal and Golan fronts, in the hope that the IDF would be off-balance and looking in two directions from the very outset. Thus, the battle for the Golan was in no way a minor front, even though the Israelis could normally only spare just one two-battalion armoured brigade of Centurions (188th Barak Brigade) and one reserve infantry battalion, manning 12 fortified OPs, with two armoured Ugdah formations as back-up. Just before war began, the IDF had moved two further Centurion battalions of the 7th Armoured Brigade to the north of Kuneitra, in order to beef-up the 188th positions.

The Syrian plan envisaged a swift attack by three mechanized divisions that would completely overwhelm the tiny defending force. Once the initial assault was under way, then joint armoured-airborne operations would be mounted to capture the Jordan bridges – heli-borne commandos, supported by two complete armoured divisions. It was a well-planned operation, which, on paper at least, had every chance of success as the attackers had such over-whelming odds. But the Syrians had underestimated the ability of the Israeli tanks and their crews, men like Lt Col Avigdor Kahalani, now CO of the senior of the two Centurion battalions from 7th Armoured Brigade, and Col 'Yanosh' Ben-Gal, the lanky, 38-year-old brigade commander, who had told his commanders that morning: 'We shall go to war today. . . . I don't know the exact time, probably between early afternoon and dusk, but the Syrians are going to attack in an all-out effort, simultaneously with the Egyptians at Suez – it's going to be tough!'9 His commanders were all seasoned tank soldiers, who had come up the hard way, gaining their promotion from the ranks by their proven prowess in battle. Just as 'Yanosh' was finishing his briefing a 'thunder in the sky' announced the arrival of enemy jets and the first bombs and rockets landed all around them. 'Then came the shout, unmistakably clear, as "Yanosh" briskly ordered "everyone to his tanks – move!" and the officers, gathering their maps, raced, ducking among the searching bullets from strafing MIGs on their second pass.'[10] The war had begun!

The Syrians attacked *en masse*. 188 Barak Brigade, outnumbered by at least ten to one, fought back bravely but were forced to give ground. They did so slowly, because they knew that they had to buy as much time as possible, but as the fighting went on one after another of the Israeli tanks was knocked out. Individual crews continued to fight even when their tank was immobilized, the brigadier fighting to the last just like everyone else. The Syrians pushed steadily forward, their attack seemingly going according to plan. They reached the main tank obstacle, which was over-watched by the Israeli tanks on high ramps. Here their mine-clearing tanks and engineer equipment came forward and was shot to pieces, but they pressed on, sacrificing tanks in order to get across the obstacle. The Syrians displayed great bravery and David Eshel mentions in particular, Brig Omar Abrash, commander of the Syrian 7th Infantry Division, a graduate of both the American and Soviet Staff Colleges, who was 'clearly one of the best educated field officers in the Syrian Army.' He had advanced in a three-brigade attack in typical Soviet style, reaching the anti-tank obstacle and using his supporting tanks to engage the Israeli Centurions on the ridge, which were busy knocking out his engineering equipment. There were Syrian tanks everywhere and the pressure upon the outnumbered Israelis to give ground was enormous. Then, just at the critical moment, Lt Col Kahalani's tanks arrived and the line held.

The battle continued as night fell, when the advantage passed to the Syrians, who had better night-viewing equipment on their T55s. However, by making use of their antiquated IR binoculars, the Israeli tankers could just make out the enemy IR lights and Kahalani ordered his crews to hold their fire until the Syrian tanks had closed to an effective night-fighting range. The Syrian tanks came boldly up the hill, but as they reached the top all hell broke loose, the Israelis firing as fast as possible from ranges of under 300 yards even down to point-blank engagements at 50 yards or less. Soon there were burning tanks everywhere, with those crews who had survived desperately seeking shelter on foot. The Syrian attack stalled, then went into reverse, as the Israeli Centurions rallied and regained their ramp positions. But the Syrians attacked again at first light. Some 500 tanks of their 46th, 51st and 43rd Armoured Brigades pushed forward, past the still-burning hulks from the night battle. The Barak brigade was now down to a handful of individual tanks, but they fought on. Their commander, Col Ben-Shoham, held a vital blocking position with his tiny command group, he and most of his staff officers dying in their tanks as they fought to the last man.

The Syrians had now reached positions overlooking the Sea of Galilee, but were held up there by the leading tanks of the Israeli reserve brigade and forced back, but it was touch and go. There were many examples of heroism on both sides, such as the manning of two trackless Centurions, which had been undergoing repairs, by brigade staff officers, who fought to the last man, knocking out several Syrian tanks on the very wire. Up on the Golan Heights, 7th Armoured Brigade clung doggedly to its positions, but they were by now in a very parlous state. In the nick of time, a small force of Centurions, which had been hastily assembled in the valley below by Jossi Ben Hannan (who had just arrived from leave abroad), made its way to the front and enabled the brigadier to rally his forces. Some 300 Syrian tanks and countless other vehicles were knocked out by 7th Armoured, who had been outnumbered by almost fifteen to one but had saved the day with their superior gunnery. The immediate crisis was over.

More Israeli reserves now started to arrive and the Syrians were pushed steadily backwards, out of Israel. From 11th October the threat was now towards Damascus and not Jerusalem, as the Israelis mounted their own offensive, with 7th Armoured Brigade still playing a major role, despite the fact that they and the Barak brigade could muster only 60 fit Centurions between them. With Kahalani's tank battalion once again in the lead, 7th Armoured spearheaded the northern arm of a three-pronged advance, the other two prongs being Gen Dan Laner's armoured division of about 100 tanks and Gen Moshe Peled's of about the same strength. Soon they had to face a new threat. The Iraqis, having decided to come to Syria's aid, sent an armoured brigade to help defend Damascus. To give some idea of the odds against the Israelis at this time, according to David Eshel the 900 tanks the Syrians had lost in the Golan battles had already been made up from their reserves, while Laner's division alone now faced a total Arab force of nearly 1,300 tanks. Nevertheless the Israelis pressed forward and were soon able to bring long-range artillery fire to bear onto Damascus. The Arabs had had enough and the war on the Golan was virtually over.

THE PRICE AND THE LESSONS   The three week-long Yom Kippur War had cost both sides dear. David Eshel gives the following figures:

	Arabs (total all armies)	Israelis
Tanks	2,150	440
APCs	1,000	not known
Guns	550	not known
Casualties		
killed	15,000 plus	2,222
wounded	40,600	5,596
captured	8,811	294 (mostly in the Bar-Lev Line positions)

The IDF was well pleased with the way in which their tanks had operated, despite the high attrition rate which had quickly reduced brigades to battalions, battalions to companies. Their system of command allowed for junior leaders immediately to replace commanders who became casualties, thus maintaining the momentum. However, they particularly worried about the heavy tank-crew casualties, a fact which was to influence strongly the design of Gen Tal's new main battle tank, the Merkeva. In addition, it had quickly become apparent – as it had done to both sides in WW2 – that tanks were not always effective operating on their own. The all-arms team was introduced and tried out for the first time in June 1982, when Israel invaded Lebanon, in an operation called 'Peace for Galilee', which was brought about by the continual harassment of Israel by PLO rocket batteries and artillery located within Lebanese territory. A cease-fire eventually came into being, after the armour had once again proved a major battle-winning factor, the new tank fully proving its worth. Since then, no major conflict has broken out between Israel and her neighbours. Egypt has genuinely tried to make peace, the Iraqis were concerned with their own war against another enemy, the Israelis have been in continual conflict with the PLO, the various factions in Lebanon have gone on fighting each other, with Syria playing a major role – in other words it has been 'business as usual' in the troubled Middle East. The Israeli Armoured Corps has seen great changes since its early days of ramshackle tanks, its tankmen now rating among the finest in the world, their tank commanders all seasoned by many years of fighting.

NOTES TO CHAPTER 11

1. The Haganah was an illegal Jewish citizens defence group, formed in 1920. Until 1938, it tried to co-operate with the British Mandate and to avoid politics. However, the Arab revolt in 1936 made all the Jewish communities unite in their common defence, so that by 1937, virtually all members of Jewish settlements were members of the Haganah.

2 George Forty, *M4 Sherman*

3 The Special Night Squads (SNS) were formed from a mixture of British soldiers and Jewish auxiliary police, with the aim of 'out-terrorizing' Arab terrorists. The Palmach was a Haganah unit of assault companies. It was a full-time professional military force which has been described as being the academy for the future Israeli Army, containing as it did some of their most expert early commanders.

4 *Chariots of the Desert*

5 *ibid*

6 *Chariots of the Desert*, note to Chapter 6

7 David Eshel says that contrary to popular belief there were just as many tank casualties from the tanks firing off their elevated ramps as from the Sagger missiles. However, of the 279 tanks in Sinai on 6th October – he is able to quote the exact figure from records – only 110 were left fit for battle at first light on the 7th. By midday the total number of Israeli tanks destroyed or damaged was 153, but some were later restored to combat status.

8 *Chariots of the Desert*

9 *ibid*

10 *ibid*

12 THE GULF WARS

Until the recent hostilities in the Balkans, there has been no major military conflict in Europe since the end of WW2. Nevertheless, the tank played a major part in preserving peace in the long and bitter Cold War between West and East. After WW2, all the victorious Allies stationed troops and a large proportion of their armour in Germany. For half a century war was prevented by the certain knowledge of the terrible consequences that would follow any attack by either side, in the shape of the subsequent nuclear exchange. However, the 'Shield and Sword' of NATO and the Warsaw Pact have both contained an increasingly large number of main battle tanks. Deciding how they should be employed has involved the best tank brains on both sides. In the same way as the period between WW1 and WW2 was given over to the formulation of theories on how the tank should be used, some of which were then tried out in peace-time manoeuvres, so war games became the norm in Europe on both sides of the now defunct Iron Curtain. The fact that the East never attacked is perhaps due in no small measure to the success of the plans made by great tank commanders in waiting, while the awesome power of the Russian steamroller attack was fortunately never released against the NATO defences. Now it appears that many of the thousands and thousands of tanks currently in existence all over Europe are rapidly becoming just so much scrap iron. If disarmament talks between East and West continue to go well, then there will be a great turning of swords into ploughshares once both sides agree to drastic arms limitations.

During the same period we have seen the AFV become even more sophistic-ated. The modern main battle tank may look much like its predecessor and its three basic characteristics of firepower, protection and mobility still remain pre-eminent, but what changes have taken place! The vast improvements to tank guns and gun-control equipment, in particular to their night-fighting capabilities, the power and reliability of improved engines and transmissions, and above all, the significantly higher level of protection now offered by new types of armour, have all changed the tank greatly, refining and honing its battlefield capabilities. Nevertheless, such improvements remained unproven in battle, they were merely claims in the glossy brochures of the tank builders. Most sensible people, despite the enormous cost of maintaining such hi-tech equipment, were prepared to see it as the price they had to pay for world peace and stability while their politicians strove to find a better solution. But they had reckoned without the ambitions of Saddam Hussein. Proof positive of the power of the modern main battle tank was on its way and, after what now seems like a rehearsal, would be given on a desert battlefield – not only to the combatants but to millions of viewers on TV screens all over the world. However, first comes that 'rehearsal'.

Iran versus Iraq

The Iran-Iraq conflict must rank as the longest-running war of this century. It started when President Saddam Hussein of Iraq attacked Iran on 22nd September 1980. He expected victory in three weeks – a blitzkrieg campaign in which his 3,000 mainly Soviet-built tanks would play a major part. Instead, on 20th October, when he had hoped to be announcing complete victory, he was having to make excuses as to why victory had eluded Iraq, because of 'geographical injustice' and the superiority of Iran's arms and military training. 'Their tanks are among the most sophisticated Western tanks,' he claimed. In fact Iran had only 2,000 British and American AFVs, which had been in the deposed Shah's army. Many of them were unusable as they were miles away on the Soviet and Afghan borders, while without Western back-up – spares and advisers – many of the 900 tanks immediately available were in a parlous state. And the situation did not improve as the war continued. Neither side used its armour particularly well – it was a question of 'brute force and bloody ignorance' rather than the skilled manoeuvering and competent gunnery displayed by the Israeli Armoured Corps. No great tank commanders emerged on either side, as the war dragged to its unsatisfactory conclusion eight years and more than a million casualties later. It had achieved nothing. America and the West had been determined that Ayatollah Khomeni and his Islamic Revolution would not win, especially after the humiliations the US had suffered when the Shah was deposed. Of course, the arms dealers in the West were only too happy to supply both sides with weapons, even though the traffic to Iran had to be kept under wraps. Saddam Hussein seemed to be the lesser of two evils, despite the unspeakable horrors he perpetrated upon his own people – such as using poison gas on the Kurds.

Unfortunately, politics in the Middle East are never straightforward, as subsequent events showed only too clearly. However, following the ceasefire, which took effect on 20th August 1988, the area returned, albeit briefly, to its normal mixture of continual minor unrest: the smaller, but still just as bloody, street battles within the Lebanon, trouble between Jew and Arab on the West Bank, raids on Israel by the PLO and the IDF's subsequent retaliations. It seemed, in other words, like 'business as usual' in the Middle East.

The Gulf War

The invasion of tiny oil-rich Kuwait in early August 1990 by its powerful neighbour Iraq sent shockwaves around the world, as the fourth largest army in the world marched across the border on 2nd August, using large numbers of its thousands of mainly Russian-built tanks to spearhead an attack in typical blitzkrieg style. The similarities with the Nazis' unprovoked aggression in the 1930s were uncanny. First, the Iraqi dictator had manufactured a crisis by accusing Kuwait and the United Arab Emirates (UAE) of exceeding OPEC oil quotas, then he had moved large numbers of his troops to his neighbour's border. When Kuwait responded by putting its forces on full alert, Saddam pretended to be ready to defuse the situation by agreeing to discuss the matter, but almost immediately invaded his then off-guard neighbour. At the same time he threatened Saudi Arabia, apparently supremely confident that the world would react in the same way as it had done to Adolf Hitler's initial territorial claims. He refused to listen to calls from the UN to withdraw, formally annexing Kuwait and threatening that the 'Mother of all Battles' would be visited upon anyone who dared to interfere with him.

'DESERT SHIELD' The strength of the Iraqi forces lay mainly in their field army and in particular in their much-vaunted Republican Guard, whose armoured formations had apparently done so well in the long drawn-out Iran-Iraq war. These crack troops, with their Russian-built T72s and T62s, would be far too strong for anything the rest of the world could produce, or so the dictator boasted. They were backed by masses of modern artillery, well-equipped infantry and terror weapons, like the poison gas Hussein had already used on his own people. He was confident that he held the upper hand. But he could not have read world opinion more wrongly. Apart from a small number of prophets of doom and those who always advocate appeasement whenever conflict threatens, Saddam found few friends willing to support him, while the US and most of her allies quickly showed that they were prepared to take positive action in support of the UN resolutions ordering Iraq to withdraw. A sea blockade was swiftly imposed, followed by one of the fastest and most impressive build-ups of sea, land and air forces the world has ever witnessed. Operation 'Desert Shield' saw large quantities of the most modern and sophisticated hardware pouring into Saudi Arabia, and, more importantly, the men to man them came not just from the West but also from Iraq's Arab neighbours, such as Syria, Egypt, Saudi-Arabia and the UAE. By early in 1991, the Coalition Forces, as the alliance was called, were ready. In the meantime, of course, Iraq had not been idle. As well as finding every pretext to play for time, they had been building massive ground defences inside Kuwait, while systematically looting the country and committing atrocities in Kuwait City.

'DESERT STORM' Vengeance was on its way and while a seemingly confident President Saddam Hussein continued to spout his rhetoric and to find pretext after pretext supposedly to search for peace – although not for one minute actually being prepared to give up any of his conquests – time ran out for Iraq and its dictator. The UN ultimatum to Iraq to withdraw from Kuwait was not complied with and, on 16th January 1991, the air onslaught of Operation 'Desert Storm' began. Spearheaded by the US Air Force, the Coalition air forces unleashed their tremendous power upon not just the Iraqi forces in

Kuwait but on the entire Iraqi nation. Baghdad soon heard the wail of sirens
and the crack of anti-aircraft guns, as London had done in the Blitz. However,
there was little comparison between the weaponry of the 1940s and that of the
1990s. Laser-guided missiles launched both from the air and from naval
vessels off the coast, terminally guided bombs, special runway-cratering devices and all the rest of this amazing gamut of new technology rained down
upon the Iraqi nation, as the Coalition air forces dealt coldly and clinically
with their chosen targets, showing a degree of accuracy that was amazing. The
Iraqi air force hardly flew a mission. Those aircraft that were not destroyed on
the ground wisely stayed in their specially reinforced bunkers, or legged it
over the border to Iran, who promptly impounded them. Air retaliation was
limited to the launching of a number of the wildly inaccurate Soviet-made
Scud missiles, at targets in both Saudi Arabia and Israel – the latter being in
the hope that the Israelis would be drawn into the conflict, thus causing
problems for the Arab partners of the Coalition. Fortunately this did not
happen; Israel suffered its civilian casualties and forebore to make its usual
swift riposte. They were assisted in their steadfastness, and many casualties
were prevented in both Israel and Saudi, by the great success of the Patriot
anti-missile missile, which shot down many Scuds before they could reach
their targets. Air superiority over the entire battle area was quickly gained, to
such an extent that virtually no Iraqi troop formations could leave their
boltholes without inviting total destruction.

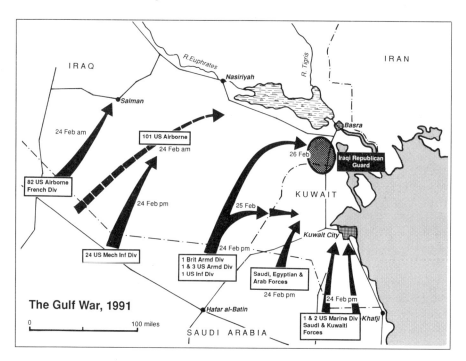

At sea, it was a similar story. The Coalition naval forces, having sunk most of the Iraqi navy, bottled the rest up in port and then joined in the bombardment of enemy positions, the massive 16-inch guns of the USS *Missouri* and *Wisconsin* for example, firing just as effectively as they had done in WW2.

'DESERT SABRE' On 23rd February, the Coalition launched its ground offensive, known as 'Desert Sabre'. The attack had been meticulously planned by Gen H. Norman Schwarzkopf and his staff many months before. It was a bold and imaginative plan which largely depended for its success upon being able to convince the enemy that the main attack would be a frontal assault into Kuwait, supported by a seaborne landing. Instead, it was basically a fast-driving left hook, with armour to the fore and the main battle tank in particular playing a major role. It was also another example of an all-arms team attack, ably supported from the air and with complete air superiority. It was, too, a night war, the vastly superior night-fighting capability of the British Challenger and the American Abrams being proved from the very first engagement. The 'Apache' anti-tank helicopter and the A10 tank buster also more than proved their worth, while modern artillery, like the MLRS (Multi-Launch Rocket System), which is known with good reason as the 'Grid-Square Remover', quickly showed that the gunners had lost none of their expertise.

The main assault, which began at 0400 hours on 24th February, was made by VII (US) Corps and XVIII (US) Airborne Corps, the former containing the British 1st Armoured Division. In the four-day battle that followed, they encircled almost the entire Iraqi Army in the Kuwait theatre of operations. Far over to the west, the French 6th Light Armoured Division, reinforced by a brigade from the US 82nd Airborne, moved rapidly deep into Iraq to secure the left flank, destroying an entire Iraqi infantry division and capturing Salam airfield, before deploying a screen to protect XVIII Airborne's left flank. Just to the east of the French the helicopter-borne 101st Airborne (Air Assault) Division established a forward operating base known as 'Cobra', also deep inside Iraqi territory. Meanwhile Gen Schwarzkopf had directed the Arab Joint Force Command North (containing Saudi-Syrian-Egyptian-Kuwaiti-Pakistani troops) to breach the centre of the Iraqi lines on the Kuwaiti border in order to convince the Iraqis that his plan was for a head-on assault. To their west, the Joint Force Command East (Saudi-Kuwaiti-Omani-UAE troops) made directly for Kuwait City astride the coastal road, while the US 1st and 2nd Marine Divisions breached the Iraqi defences further inland.

The battle went so quickly and so well that many observers could scarcely believe what they saw on their TV screens all around the world. Thousands and thousands of the enemy were killed, wounded or captured, the amounts being out of all proportion to the tiny number of casualties suffered by the allies. The shocked and demoralized Iraqi soldiers could not wait to surrender. Many had been deserted by their officers and left to fend for themselves, so, although a few isolated pockets fought bravely, most gave themselves up without even firing a shot. The much-vaunted Soviet-built tanks had been dug in so deeply that they could not traverse their turrets, while their vehicle batteries were being used to light their underground shelters rather than to work the vehicle electrical circuits, so they were unable to function properly. The fourth largest army in the world turned out to be a paper tiger, their tanks being overwhelmed by the sheer professionalism of the Allied tank crews. Senior Pentagon officials estimated that some 4,000 Iraqi tanks were destroyed in the 100-hour battle that brought the 43-day campaign to a close. When the cease-fire came into effect, on 28th February, the VII and XVIII Corps had cut the road from Kuwait to Basra, thus preventing the bulk of the battered, defeated Iraqi Army from escaping.

Postscript to the Gulf War

Many books will now be written about this remarkable war, one in which the much-vaunted Iraqi Army was found to be totally out of its depth in the context of a modern land-air battle. Here, however, this short description forms but a postscript to our study of great tank commanders. No doubt, when the full details are known, the abilities of the commanders of the American, British, French, Kuwaiti, Saudi and all the other Coalition tank forces will be studied minutely and names will emerge – I think I can state confidently, however, that there will be no Iraqi names among them! Gen H. Norman Schwarzkopf, Commander of US Central Command, the overall ground commander has undoubtedly shown himself to be in the same classic mould as the great hard-driving commander of the US Third Army of WW2, Gen George S. Patton Jr. However, with such a wide-ranging, multi-national command, all carrying out very different tasks, it was not a time for him to lead from the front, but rather to remain at the 'hub' of his highly effective communications network, with his finger firmly on the pulse of operations. The senior British commander, Lt Gen Sir Peter de la Billiere, rightly named 'Stormin' Norman' as 'man of the match', but no doubt some field tank commanders will emerge. Listening to Brig Christopher Hammerbeck, the commander of the British 4th Armoured Brigade, telling how he had personally engaged and knocked out enemy tanks with the 120mm gun on his Challenger during the battle, certainly proves that both he and Brig Patrick Cordingly, commander of 7th Armoured Brigade, were right up at the sharp end, in the best traditions of 'Strafer' Gott and 'Jock' Campbell of the original Desert Rats.

For now suffice it to say that, without a shadow of a doubt, the tank had once again proved itself still to be a potent force on the battlefield, provided it is used by professional, properly motivated, well-disciplined and well-trained tank crews, and above all, in conjunction with the other arms and air support. It is still the all-arms team that wins battles, and it is the human element, in the shape of the man who commands, the 'great tank commander', who is still the most important ingredient.

BIBLIOGRAPHY

Blumenson, Martin *The Patton Papers* Houghton Mifflin, 1972

Brett-Smith, Richard *Hitler's Generals* Osprey, 1976.

Browne, Capt D.G. *The Tank in Action* William Blackwood & Sons, 1920.

Carell, Paul *Hitler's War with Russia* Harrap, 1964.

Chalfont, Alun *Montgomery of Alamein* Weidenfeld & Nicholson, 1976.

Essame, Maj Gen H. *Patton, the Commander* Batsford, 1974.

Eshel, Col David *Chariots of the Desert* Brassey's, 1989.

Forty, George *Afrika Korps at War*, Vol. 1, Ian Allan, 1978.

Forty, George *M4 Sherman*, Blandford 1987.

Forty, George *A Photo History of Tanks in Two World Wars* Blandford, 1984.

Forty, George *The Royal Tank Regiment: A Pictorial History 1916–1987* Spellmount Ltd, 1988.

Forty, George *United States Tanks of World War II* Blandford, 1983.

Fuller, Col J.F.C. *Tanks in the Great War 1914–1918* John Murray, 1920.

Garthoff, Raymond L. *How Russia Makes War* Allen & Unwin, 1954.

Grow, Maj Gen Robert W. *The Ten Lean Years* privately published, 1969.

Guderian, Gen Heinz *Panzer Leader* Michael Joseph, 1952.

de Guingand, Francis *Operation Victory* Hodder & Stoughton, 1947.

Harmon, Maj Gen E.N. *Combat Commander* Prentice-Hall, 1970.

Herr, Michael *Dispatches* Alfred A. Knopf Inc. 1977.

Hiro, Dilip *The Longest War* Grafton Books, 1989.

Horne, Alistair *To Lose a Battle* Macmillan, 1969.

Jones, Maj Ralph E., Rarey, Capt George H. and Icks, Robert J. *The Fighting Tanks from 1916 to 1933* We Inc., 1933.

Kurcz, F.S. *The Black Brigade* (trans Peter Jordan), Atlantis Publishing, 1943.

Lewin, Ronald *Man of Armour* Leo Cooper, 1976.

Liddell Hart, Capt Sir Basil *The Rommel Papers* Collins, 1953.

Liddell Hart, Capt Sir Basil *The Tanks* (two vols) Cassell, 1959.

Macksey, Maj K.J. *Guderian, Panzer General* Macdonald & Co Ltd, 1975.

Macksey, Maj K.J. *The Tank Pioneers* Jane's, 1981.

Manstein, FM Erich von *Lost Victories* Greenhill Books, 1987.

Milsom, John *Russian Tanks 1900–1970* Arms & Armour Press, 1970.

Montgomery, FM the Viscount *Memoirs*, Collins, 1958.

Ogorkiewicz, Richard M. *Armour: the Development of Mechanised Forces and their Equipment* Atlantic Books, 1960.

Perrett, Bryan *Desert Warfare* Patrick Stephens, 1988.

Perrett, Bryan *A History of Blitzkrieg* Robert Hale, 1983.

Perret, Bryan *Knights of the Black Cross* Robert Hale, 1986

Ramspacher, Col E.G. *Le Général Estienne, 'Père des Chars'* Charles Lavauzelle, 1983.

Schmidt, H.W., *With Rommel in the Desert* Harrap, 1951.

Shirer, William L. *The Rise and Fall of the Third Reich* Secker & Warburg, 1960.

Simpkin, Brig Richard *Deep Battle* Brasseys, 1987.

Singh, Lt Col Dr Bhupinder *1965 War: Role of Tanks in India-Pakistan War* BC Publishers, 1982.

Starry, Gen Donn A. *Mounted Combat in Vietnam* US Department of the Army, 1981.

Stern, Lt Col Sir Albert G. *Tanks 1914–1918: the Log Book of a Pioneer* Hodder & Stoughton, 1919.

Swinton, Maj Gen Sir Ernest *Eyewitness* Hodder & Stoughton, 1932.

Swinton, Maj Gen Sir Ernest, *Over My Shoulder* George Ronald, 1951.

Wilson, Dale E. *Treat 'em Rough!* Presidio, 1989.

Zaloga, Steven J. *The Polish Army 1939–45* Osprey, 1982.

INDEX

Abrams, Gen Creighton W.   126, 161, 162

Abrams, M1 tank   161, 187

Abrash, Brig Omar   180

Adair, Maj Gen Allan   125

Adan, Gen 'Bren'   171, 177, 178

AEF (American Expeditionary Force)   30 *et seq*

Agedabia   76

Airmobile units   162

Alam Halfa   80

Aldinger, Lt Hermann   77

Algiers   87

Alexandria Recommendation   59

Alexander, Field Marshal   80, 82, 90, 91, 114, 115, 116, 118 *et seq*, 155

AMX 13 light tank   164, 167, 175

Anstice, Brig J.H.   155

Antwerp   145, 147

Ardennes   63, 146 *et seq*

Arakan   155

Argentan   142

Ari, Gen Uri Ben   171, 172, 175

Armoured Car Companies (RTC)   39

Armoured divisions; *see under* country of origin

Armored Force (USA)   59 *et seq*

Army Groups, British 21st AG   118, 123, 144, 145, 146, 152
   USA, 1st AG   123; 6th AG   152; 12th AG   152

Armies, British 1st   91; 2nd   123; 3rd   24; 4th   36; 8th   79, 83, 84 *et seq*, 91, 114, 116, 119; 14th   156
   Canadian 1st   123
   French 1st   63; 2nd   63; 3rd   36; 5th   21; 6th   37; 9th   63; 10th   36, 37
   German: *see* Panzer
   Italian   83
   USA 1st   123, 144, 150; 3rd   123, 126, 128, 138, 144, 145, 148, 150, 152; 5th   119; 7th   114

Arnim, Gen Jurgen von   81, 89

Arras counterattack (1940)   66 *et seq*

Artillerie d'assaut   14, 49

A7V heavy tank   16, 37

Ashplants, first use   20

Auchinleck, Gen Sir Claude   74 *et seq*, 79, 81

Australian Tank Corps   43; 6th Australian Div Cavalry   85; in Vietnam   161; Light Car Patrols   43; Volunteer Automobile Force   42

Autocars   16

'Avalanche', Operation   119

Avonmouth   16

Babcock, Lt Col Conrad S.   34

Bach, Hauptmann Wilhelm   79

Bacon, Maj Robert   32

Baade, Gen Ernst   115, 116

Baku oilfields   104

Balbo, Marshal Italo   71, 92

Barak Brigade   179, 180

'Barbarossa', Operation   53, 87, 95, 96 *et seq* 97 (map), 101, 112

Bardia   78

Bakshi, Brig Madan   166

Barmin, Junior Political Officer   101

Bastogne   149, 150

Bagramyan, Marshal   151

'Battleaxe', Operation   78 *et seq*

Bangladesh   167

Bar-Lev, Gen   171, 172, 173, 178

Bar-Lev Line   176, 177

Bayerlin, Gen Fritz   81, 95, 131, 141

'Baytown', Operation   119

Beda Fomm   73 *et seq*

BEF (British Expeditionary Force)   61 *et seq*

Belgium   61 *et seq*, 63, 144

Ben-Gal, Col 'Yanosh'   179 *et seq*

Ben Het   161

Ben-Shoham, Col Yizak   180

Berlin   78, 106

Bermicourt   19, 33

Berry au Bac   21 *et seq*

'Big Wheel'   8

'Big Willie' (also 'Mother' and 'HMLS Centipede')   11 *et seq*; plan of test   23

Bibergan, D.   51

Billiere, Gen Sir Peter de la   188

Bir Hakeim   80, 116

Bisley (Siberia Camp)   12

Black beret, adopted by British RTC   40; by Australians   43; by Panzerwaffe (*Schutzmutze*)   59

'Black' Brigade, Polish   58

Black Sea   97

'Blitzkrieg'   46, 48, 55 *et seq*, 55 (plan) 69, 84, 89, 100, 103, 109, 158, 185

Bock, Field Marshal Fedor von   54, 96, 102, 103

Boer War   9, 18

Bossut, Chef d'Escadrons Louis-Marie-
  Ildefonse   21, 22
Bittrich, SS Obergruppenfuehrer Willi   149
Bovington Camp   20, 34, 39
Bradley, Gen Omar   89, 90, 116, 117, 128,
  138, 139, 142, 144, 150, 151, 152
Bradley, Lt Col R.W.   12 *et seq*, 18
Brandenberger, Gen Erich   147
Brandenbergers   63
Brandt, Capt Alfred   90
Braine, Lt Elgin   32
Brauchitsch, Gen Walther von   75
Brett, Maj Sereno   35 *et seq*, 44
'Brevity', Operation   78 *et seq*
Briggs, Maj Gen Raymond   84
Bril, Col Moshe   175
Birks, Maj Gen Horace   84
British armoured divisions, 1st   67; 2nd   76;
  7th   70 *et seq*, 78
British tanks, first   10 *et seq*; first training
  school   12; first tank action   17 *et seq*
Broad, Lt Gen Sir Charles   41, 62
Brooks, Maj Gen Edward H.   140, 145
Brough, Lt Col   18
Browne, Capt D.G.   19 *et seq*
Bruce, Capt E.M.   40
Brutinel, Brig Gen Raymond   16
Bucknall, Lt Gen G.C.   126
Bulge, Battle of the   146 *et seq*, 146 (map)
Buq-Buq   72, 73
Bug River   98, 112
Burma   118, 155, 159
Burns, Maj Gen E.L.M.   121
Byng, Gen Sir Julian   24

Caen   130, 132, 134, 136, 142
Cairo   78, 179
Call, Cpl Donald M.   35
Cambrai, Battle of   24 *et seq*, 28 (map)
Campbell, Maj Gen 'Jock'   82, 83, 188
Camp Borden   43
Camp Colt   34, 43
Camp Polk   43
Canada, first AFVs (Autocars)   16; 1st
  Canadian MMG Brigade   16, 43; Royal
  Canadian Armoured Corps   43
Capper, Maj Gen Sir John   22
Cardenas, Julio   31
Carver, Field Marshal Lord   136
Casablanca   87, 88, 114
Cassino   116, 119, 121
'Centipede HMLS'; *see* 'Big Willie'

Centurion tank   158, 161, 164 *et seq*, 172,
  173 *et seq*, 178, 179, 180, 181
Chaffee, Gen Adna Romanza   15, 41, 45 *et
  seq*, 59 *et seq*
Chaffee light tank   157
Challenger tank   125, 187
Chang, Maj Gen Pir U.   157
Chernyakhovsky, Gen Ivan Danilovich   111,
  151
Chibisov, Gen   112
Chinese Peoples Republic   158, 159
Christie, Walter J.   41, 53
Chuikov, Gen Vasily Ivanovich   104, 105,
  106
Churchill, Winston   8, 9 *et seq*, 59, 65, 74, 78,
  79, 84, 91, 114, 123
Churchill tank   125
'Citadel', Operation   107 *et seq*
Citroen-Kegresse   42
Clark, Gen Mark   118, 121
Clarke, Gen Bruce C.   126, 148 *et seq*
'Cobra' Operation   138, 141
Cold War   183
Collins, Gen 'Lighting Joe'   138, 140
Colours, for tank corps, Australian   43;
  British   22; USA   33
'Compass', Operation   72 *et seq*
Condor Legion   48
Congressional Medal of Honor   35, 163
Conrath, Gen Paul   115, 116
Cook, Maj Gen Gilbert   139
Cordingly, Brig Patrick   188
Corps, British I   126, 136; III   17; IV   155;
  VIII   123, 126, 145; IX   91; X   82;
  XII   83, 123; XIII   78, 82, 83; XIV   17;
  XV   17; XXX   79, 82, 126, 146, 150;
  XXXIII   155
  Canadian 2nd   126;
  Polish 1st   58; 2nd   12
  French 5th   21; 21st   65; 32nd   21
  German; *see* Panzer Corps
  North Korea, 1NK   156
  USA 1st   59; 2nd   90, 116, 120, 127;
    3rd   127; 4th   30, 127; 5th   127, 144,
    148; 6th   127; 7th   127, 138, 140, 187;
    8th   123, 127, 139, 148; 9th   127;
    12th   139; 15th   139; 18th   187;
    19th   123; 20th   139
Coutances   138
Cramer, Gen Hans   81, 91
Creagh, Maj Gen Michael O'More   71, 73,
  83

Crerar, Gen Henry 121
Creusot, Le (Schneider Works) 14
Crocker, Gen Sir John 41, 62, 67, 91, 126, 136
Cromwell tank 125, 169
Cruewel, Gen Ludwig 80 *et seq*
'Crusader', Operation 79 *et seq*
Culin, Sgt Curtis (hedgerow cutter) 141
Cunningham, Lt Gen Sir Alan 79
Currie, Brig John 136
Cyrenaica 79, 87

D Day 123 *et seq*
Dally-Jones, Lt Col 12
Da Nang 162
'Danny', Operation 169 *et seq*
David, Lt N.G. 163, 164
Davidson, George 43
Davis, Dwight F. 44
DD tanks 131, 132
Dayan, Gen Moshe 169, 170, 172, 176
'Death Zone' 130, 133
Decker, Lt Gen Karl 149
de Gaulle, Gen Charles 42, 49 *et seq*, 66, 69
Deitrich, SS Gen Joseph Sepp 130, 147, 152
Dempsey, Gen Sir Miles 82
Derna 78
Desna, River 112
'Desert Fox'; *see* Rommel
'Desert Rats'; *see* British 7th Armd Div
'Desert Sabre', Operation 187
'Desert Shield', Operation 185
'Desert Storm', Operation 185
Deutsches Afrika Korps (DAK) 74 *et seq*, 80, 86
Devers, Gen Jacob 140, 152
d'Egencourt, Tennyson 10
Diplock caterpillar tracks 8
Divisions, armoured, British 1st 62, 67, 82, 187; 2nd 76; 6th 119; 7th (Mobile Div) 70 *et seq*, 72, 73, 78, 82, 85, 119, 124, 125, 136; 11th 84, 91, 124, 125, 126, 145; 79th 91, 124, 131 *et seq*; Guards 125, 136, 145; general organisation 124
Canadian 4th 126, 142; 5th 119, 121
French 1 DCR 50, 63, 65; 3 DCR 65; 4 DCR 66; 1 DB 143; 2 DB 126, 143; 5 DLM 65; general organisation 69
German; *see* Panzers
Indian 1st 165
North Korean 105th 157

Pakistan 1st 165; 6th 165
Polish 1st 58, 126
South African 6th 119, 121
USA 1st 60, 90, 119, 120, 127; 1st Cav 162; 2nd 60, 119, 127, 140, 149; 3rd 127, 140, 145; 4th 126, 127, 140, 146, 148; 5th 126, 127; 6th 126, 127, 140; 7th 145, 148; 8th 127; 9th 127; general organisation in WW2 127
Dnieper, River 98, 112
Don, River 104
Doumenc, Gen 48, 49
'Dragoon', Operation 118, 143
Duncan, Maj Gen Nigel 124
Dunkleman, Col Ben 170
Durham Light Infantry 66 *et seq*
Dyle Line 61, 63
'Dynamo', Operation (and Dunkirk) 65, 67, 69

Eddy, Gen Manton S. 139
Eisenhower, Gen Dwight D. 34, 44, 87, 89, 114, 117, 118, 139, 141, 144, 145, 150, 151
El Agheila 76, 80
El Alamein 80, 83, 85 *et seq*, 122
Elazar, Maj Gen David 172, 175
Elad, Maj Ehud 174
Elles, Maj Gen Sir Hugh 18 *et seq*, 22 *et seq*, 24 *et seq*, 27 (special order of day), 33, 39, 42, 50, 57
Eltinge, Lt Col LeRoy 30, 31, 32
Elveden 14
'Epsom', Operation 135, 136
Erskine, Gen 'Bobbie' 84, 125
Estienne, Gen Jean Baptiste 7, 14 *et seq*, 23, 48, 49, 50 *et seq*
Evans, Maj Gen Robert 67
Evelegh, Maj Gen V. 119
Experimental Mechanised Force, British 41, 44, 63
   USA 45 *et seq*
   USSR 51

Falaise 126, 136, 138, 141, 142 *et seq*
'Fall Blau' 103
'Fall Gelb' 59, 63 *et seq*, 95
'Fear Naught' motto 22
Fehn, Gen Gustav 81
Feuchtinger, Lt Gen Edgar 131, 132
Fiat 2000 tank 16
Finland 60, 94, 100, 180
First tank versus tank action 37

Flavigny, Gen 65

Flers, Battle of 17 *et seq*

Flesquieres 26, 29

FMAH (*Compagnie des Forges d'Homercourt*) 14

Foch, Gen 38

Fort Capuzzo 72, 85

Fort Knox 46, 141

Foster, Maj Gen Harry 126, 142

Foster, William & Sons 10 *et seq*

France, first tanks 14 *et seq*; first training schools 14; first tank action 21 *et seq*; German invasion (1940) map 62; interwar reorganisation 49 *et seq*; in Indo-China 159

Frendenhall, Gen 87

Fruehlingswind 'Spring Breeze', Operation 89

Fruelingswachen 'Spring Awakening', Operation 152

Freyberg, Gen Sir Bernard 121

Fritsch, Gen Werner von 54, 75

Fronts, Russian Army 90, 103, 108, 110, 151

Frunze, Michail 52

Fuller, Maj Gen J.F.C. 19, 22, 25, 33, 39, 40, 41, 49, 53

Funck, Gen Baron von 75

'Funnies'; *see* Specialised armour

Gambier-Parry, Maj Gen M.D. 76 *et seq*, 78

Gamelin, Gen 49

Gatehouse, Maj Gen Alex 84

Gay, Gen 'Hap' 139

Gaza Strip 174

Gazala 80, 83

George V, King 11 *et seq*

Germany, first tanks 16; rise of panzers 46 *et seq*

Gerow, Gen Leonard T. 144

Gillem, Gen Alvan C. 59

Goering, Reichsmarshal Hermann 106

Golan Heights 175, 179

Gonen-Gorodish, Maj Gen Shmuel 171

'Goodwood', Operation 135, 136, 138

Gordon-Finlayson, Gen Sir Robert 70, 71

Gordov, Gen V.N. 104

Gothic Line 119, 121

Gott, Gen 'Strafer' 82, 83, 188

Graziani, Marshal Rodolfo 71 *et seq*, 75, 119

Great Patriotic War 52, 94 *et seq*

Groupement Mobile 100 159, 167

Grow, Maj Gen Bob 45, 46, 140

Guderian, Gen Heinz 42, 47 *et seq*, 49, 54, 55, 56, 57 *et seq*, 63, 64, 65, 66, 68, 95, 96, 97 *et seq*, 99, 100, 101, 102, 107, 130, 131, 135, 151, 153

Guingand, Maj Gen Sir Francis de 82, 84

Gulf War 184 *et seq*, 186 (map)

Gurion, Ben 170

Haig, Field Marshal Earl 11, 16, 18, 22, 24, 26, 30

Halder, Gen Franz 59, 75, 78, 95, 104, 105

Halfaya Pass 79, 83

'Halt' Order 69

Hannibal 7

Haganah 168, 172, 182

Harding, Field Marshal Lord 83, 118 *et seq*

Hardress-Lloyd, Brig 22

Harmon, Gen Ernest 90, 120, 126, 140, 144 *et seq*

Haislip, Gen Wade 139

Hammerbeck, Brig Christopher 188

Hastie, Lt 17

Heavy Section MGC 14 *et seq*, 18 *et seq*

Heavy tanks, British Mk I 11, 18; Mk IV 15, 16, 20 *et seq*, 33, 37; Mk V 16, 31, 40, 44; Mk V* 31; Mk VI 31; Mk VIII 44, 53

Heeresgruppe Afrika 89

Hetherington, Flt Comd, RNAS 8, 11

Heim, Lt Gen Ferdinand 106

Herr, Maj Gen Traugott 121

Hickey, Capt D.E. 29

'Hilda' 28

Hitler, Adolf 48, 54, 63, 65, 67, 69, 86, 93, 94, 95, 96, 98, 101, 102, 103, 104, 105, 106, 107, 113, 120, 129, 130, 131, 132, 134 *et seq*, 137, 142, 143, 147, 151, 152

Hobart, Maj Gen Sir Percy 41, 62, 67 *et seq*, 70 *et seq*, 73, 83, 91, 124 *et seq*

Ho Chi Minh 159

Hodges, Gen Courtney 142, 144, 150

Hoepner, Gen Erich 63, 68, 96, 99, 102

Hoffmeister, Maj Gen Bert 121

Holland, invasion of 63

Holt farm tractor 8, 14

'Hornet', 'Green' 60

Horrocks, Gen Sir Brian 82, 84, 126, 146

Hotblack, Col F.E. 18

Hoth, Gen Hermann 63, 68, 96, 103, 104, 105, 107, 110

Hube, Gen Hans Valentin 115, 116, 121

Huntbach, Maj Gerald 28

'Husky', Operation   114
Hussites   7

Inchon   157
Indian Armoured Corps   156
Indo-China   159
Indo-Pakistan War   163 *et seq*
Iran-Iraq War   184
Israeli Armoured Corps   168 *et seq*
Italy, first tanks   15 *et seq*; defeat at Beda
   Fomm   73 *et seq*; units in DAK   80; allied
   landings   11, 118 *et seq*; panzer units in
   Italy   120

Japan   113, 154 *et seq*
Joffre, Gen   14
Jodl, Gen Alfred   105, 134, 147, 151
Jordanian armour   175
JS III tank   175
'Jupiter', Operation   136

Kahalani, Lt Col Avigdor   174, 179, 180,
   181
Kalinovsky, Col   52, 93
Kasserine Pass   89, 120
Kashmir   163, 164
Kazan   51
Keitel, Field Marshal Wilhelm   137
Kesselring, Field Marshal Albert   86, 115,
   120
Keyes Gen Geoffery   120
Khetarpel, Lt Arun   167
Khruschev, Nikita   103, 109
Kiev   97, 98, 99, 100
Kirponos, Gen M.P.   97
Kitching, Maj Gen George   126, 142
Kleist, Field Marshal Paul Ludwig Ewald   54,
   57, 63, 64, 65, 68, 96, 99, 103, 104, 113
Kluge, Field Marshal Guenther von   63, 102
   et seq, 137, 143
Koniev, Gen Ivan   100, 103, 109, 151
Korean War   150, 156 *et seq*
KOYLI   17
Kravchenko, Gen Andrei Grigorevich   111,
   112, 113
Krueger Gen Eugen Walter   149
Kuneitra   175
Keuchler Field Marshal Georg von   102
Kursk   94, 107 *et seq*, 108 (map), 111
'Kutuzov', Operation   110
Kuwait   184 *et seq*
KV1 and KV2 heavy tanks   99

Lagus, Gen Ernst Ruben   60
Lampered, Lt E.W.   43
Landships Committee   9 *et seq*, 12
Laner, Gen Dan   181
Lang Vei   163
Le Clerc, Maj Gen Jacques Philippe   129,
   143, 144
Le Mans   135
Leeb, Field Marshal Ritter von   96, 98, 99,
   102
Leese, Gen Sir Oliver   82, 118
Leonardo de Vinci   7
Lelyushenko, Gen Demitry, Danilovich   60 *et
   seq*
Lemelsen, Gen Joachim   98
Leningrad   96, 98, 99
Liddell-Hart, Sir Basil   41, 49, 52, 53, 63, 67,
   93, 124, 140
Lieberstein Gen Kurt Freiherr von   81, 95
'Lightfoot', Operation; *see* El Alamein
Lindsay, Maj Gen George   39, 41, 42, 62
List, Field Marshal Siegmund Wilhelm   65,
   105
'Little Willie'   10 *et seq*
Luftwaffe   55, 63, 64, 69, 77, 106, 107, 115,
   133, 148
Lulworth Gunnery School   39
Lumsden, Lt Gen Herbert   82
Lutz, Gen Oswald   41, 48, 54
Luttwitz, Lt Gen Baron von   149
Luxembourg   63
LVT (Landing Vehicle Tracked)   154 *et seq*
Lyubushkin, Sgt   101

M 60 tank   160, 178
MacArthur, Gen Douglas   46
Maczek, Gen Stanislaw   58 *et seq*, 126 *et seq*,
   142
Magen, Maj Gen Kalman   178
Maginot Line   49, 61
Malmedy   130
Maletti, Gen Pietro   73
Manstein, Gen Fritz Erich von   95, 106, 107,
   113
Manteuffel, Gen Hasso von   147, 148
Maps   28, 62, 76, 97, 108, 138, 146, 186
'Market Garden', Operation   146
Marshall, Gen George C.   60, 144
Martel, Gen le Q.   18, 41, 125
Matilda tank   61 *et seq*, 66 *et seq*, 72 *et seq*, 74,
   79, 153
McCreery, Gen Sir Richard   82 *et seq*

Mellenthin, Maj Gen von 99, 143
Mendeleyev, Vasiliy Dmitriev 15
Merkeva tank 182
Mersa Brega 76
Mersa Matruh 72
Messervy, Gen Sir Frank 83
Meuse, River 63, 64, 147 *et seq*
Meuse-Argonne battles 35
Meyer, Maj Gen Kurt 131, 136
Middleton, Gen Troy H. 139
Mitchell, Lt F. 37
Model, Field Marshal Walther 107, 110, 113, 137, 147
Mole, Lancelot de 8
Montgomery, Field Marshal Bernard Law 62, 78, 80, 82 *et seq*, 91 *et seq*, 109, 114, 115, 118, 122, 125, 126, 132, 133, 134, 136, 142, 144, 145, 150, 152
Morgenluft 'Morning Air', Operation 89
Mortimore, Capt H.W. 17
Moscow 96, 98, 100, 101, 103, 109, 111
'Mother'; *see* 'Big Willie'
Motor gun (*motorgeschutz*) 8
Motor Machine Gun Service 12

NATO 183
Nasser, President Abdul 172, 175
Nasir Maj Gen 166
Neame, Lt Gen 78
Nehring, Gen Walther K. 81, 98
Nibweia 72, 73
Nicholls Cpl Alfie 122
Normandy 129, 131 *et seq*, 134 *et seq*, 138 (map)

O'Connor, Gen Sir Richard 71, 72 *et seq*, 74, 78, 83, 126, 136, 145
Oder, River 106, 151
Odessa 113
Omaha Beach 132
Oran 61, 87
Orel, River 107
Orne, River 132

Pacific theatre WW2 154 *et seq*
Pakistan 163 *et seq*
Panther tank 141
Panzer Army 1st 103, 104; 2nd 100; 3rd 147; 4th 96, 103, 104, 107, 151; 5th 143, 147, 149; 6th 149, 151; 7th 147, 149; 9th 107; 10th 57; 14th 58; 6 SS 146, 147, 151

Panzer Corps 5th 149; 12th 98; 14th 104, 105, 115, 121; 15th 63, 68; 16th 54, 57, 63, 68, 95; 19th 54, 63, 64, 65, 68; 22nd 58; 24th 98, 105; 26th 121; 29th 149; 39th 68; 41st 63, 65, 68; 47th 98, 149; 48th 106; 76th 121; 1st SS 130, 149; 2nd SS 149; in Normandy 130, 131
Panzer Divisions, 1st 63, 64; 2nd 63, 140, 149; 3rd 57, 140; 4th 126, 140, 148; 5th 63, 126; 6th 63, 126, 140; 7th 63, 64, 145, 147, 148; 9th 63; 10th 63; 11th 143; 15th 76; 17th 98; 18th 98; 21st 75, 81, 82, 131; 116th 149; 255th 135, 141; Pz Lehr 135, 141, 149; 1st SS 149, 152; 2nd SS 135, 141, 149; 9th SS 149; 12th SS 149
Panzer tanks, Pzkpfw I 48, 58; Pzkpfw II 48, 58; Pzkpfw III 48, 83; Pzkpfw IV 48, 58, 122; *see also* Panther and Tiger tanks
Panzerwaffe 46 *et seq*, 69, 146 *et seq*, 149, 151; in Italy 120
Paris 143, 144
Pas de Calais 127, 132
Patton, Gen George Smith Jnr 30, 31, 33 *et seq*, 44, 57, 59, 60, 87 *et seq*, 89, 114 *et seq*, 116 *et seq*, 127 *et seq*, 138, 139 *et seq*, 141, 142, 143 *et seq*, 148, 150, 152 *et seq*, 188
Patton tanks 157, 163, 164, 173, 178
Paulus, Field Marshal Friedrich 78, 104, 106, 137
Pavlov, Gen Dmitry 51, 53, 94, 96, 99
'Pedrail' 8
Peled, Gen Moshe 181
Penfold, Capt E. 43
Peover Camp 127
Pershing, Gen John J. 30, 31 *et seq*, 44, 140
Pershing tank 157
Phillora 165
Pile, Gen Sir Frederick 62 *et seq*
Poland, Germans attack 54 *et seq*, 113
Polish armour 57 *et seq*, 121 *et seq*
Petain, Marshal 48
PLO 175, 182, 184
Poole, Maj Gen Evered 121
Pope, Lt Gen Vyvyan 41, 79
Porokovskikov 15
Preiss SS Gruppenfuehrer Hermann 149
Pritchard, Maj Gen Vernon E. 120
PT 76 light tank 162, 167
Pusan 157 *et seq*

Rafa   172
Rangoon   155
Rann of Kutch   164
Ravenstein, Gen von   81 *et seq*
Reconnaissance Corps   124
Reductions to tank corps, British   39;
    American   43
Regimental Day (RTR)   30
Reinhardt, Gen Georg-Hans   63, 68
Renault light tank (FT 17)   15, 16, 30, 32,
    34, 36, 44, 51, 88
Regiments, Cavalry KDG   73; 7H   70, 74,
    155; 8H   70; 11H   70, 73, 85;
    13/18H   131; 9L   122; 12L   82;
    4/7DG   132; Sherwood Rangers   132;
    Poona Horse   165, 166, 167; 7th Cav   164;
    Hodson's Horse   166
RTR 2nd   74, 155; 3rd   67; 4th   61, 66 *et
    seq*; 5th   83; 6th   70, 172; 7th   61, 66 *et
    seq*, 72 *et seq*
Renton, Maj Gen Callum   83
Reichenau Field Marshal Walther von   102
Richards, Brig G.W.   84
Ridgway, Gen Matthew Bunker   158
Rimailho, Col   14
Roberts, Cpl Harold W.   35
Roberts, Maj Gen 'Pip'   84, 125, 136
Robertson, Capt Clement   22 *et seq*
Rockenbach, Brig Gen Samuel Dickerson   33
    et seq, 35, 44, 50
Roebling, Donald   154
Rommel, Field Marshal Erwin Johannes
    Eugen   64 *et seq*, 74 *et seq*, 77, 79 *et seq*, 83,
    86, 89, 90, 91, 98, 105, 120, 129, 130, 132,
    135, 137, 153
Rokossovsky, Marshal Konstantin   108 *et seq*,
    110, 151, 152, 153
Rome   120
Roosevelt, President   114, 123
Rose, Maj Gen Maurice   140 *et seq*
Rostov   102, 107
Rotmistrov, Gen Pavel Alexandrovitch   94,
    99, 110, 111
Royal Air Force   72, 79
Royal Armoured Corps   42, 156
Royal Naval Air Service   8, 10
Royal Tank Corps (RTC)   39
Rundstedt, Field Marshal Gerd von   54, 65,
    96, 102, 129, 130, 134, 137, 147
Russia, first tanks   15
'Russian Stunt' The   40
Ruthledge, Maj Desmond   171

Ryder, Capt D.R.   85

Saddam Hussein   184, 185
Sadeh, Maj Gen Yizhak   169
Salerno   119
Sasse, Maj Ralph I.   36
Schneider tank   14, 16, 21 *et seq*, 36
Schmidt, Gen Rudolf   68
Schoerner, Field Marshal Ferdinand   113
Schwarzkopf, Gen Norman   187
Schweppenburg, Gen Baron Geyr von   130,
    131, 134, 135
'Sea Lion', Operation   98
Sedan   63 *et seq*, 65
Seeckt, Gen Hans von   47
Senger und Etterlin, Gen Frido von   115, 121
Seoul   156
Sharon, Maj Gen Ariel   177, 178, 179
Shazli, Gen Saud el Din   176, 179
Sherman medium tank   125, 157, 164, 168
    et seq
Sialkot   164 *et seq*
Sicily   114 *et seq*
Sidi Barrani   72, 73
Sidi Rezegh   79, 82, 83
Seigfried Line   146
Silvester, Gen Lindsay   145
Simmonds, Gen Guy   142
Sinai   171 *et seq*
Singh, Maj Gen Rajinder   164, 166, 167
Six Day War   173 *et seq*
Slim, Field Marshal Bill   155, 156
Smith, Geoffrey   12 *et seq*
Smolensk   98
Sokolovsky, Gen Vasiley   100
Soissons   36
South African armour   85
Spanish Civil War   48, 49, 53
Specialised armour   123, 131 *et seq*
Speidel, Gen Dr Hans   132
Stalin, Josef   51, 52, 53, 94, 97, 100, 104,
    105, 109
Stalingrad   40, 103–105
St Chamond tank   14, 36
St Vith   148
Stanley, Lt Col Raymond   160
Starry, Gen Donn A.   154, 163
Stern, Albert   10, 18
Stuka Ju 87 dive bomber   48, 56, 77
Stumme, Gen Georg   86
Su, Lt Gen Yu Kyng   157
Sueter, Capt Murray, RNAS   8

Suez Canal   72, 171, 174, 176, 177
Summerall, Gen Charles P.   44 *et seq*
Swinton, Maj Gen Sir Ernest   7, 8 *et seq*, 11 *et seq*, 17 *et seq*, 19 *et seq*, 42, 50, 127
Syria   173, 180 *et seq*, 182

T26, T34, T54, T55, T62 and T72 tanks   53, 94, 99, 100, 103, 105, 107, 110, 112, 157, 163, 167, 175, 177, 178, 185, 187 *et seq*
Tal, Gen Israel 'Talik'   172, 173, 174, 175, 178, 182
Tank Corps, British creation   22
Tank Corps Memorial   17
Tank crews, first   12 *et seq*
Tank Detatchment   12
'Tank', first use of name   12
Tank Tips (Swinton's)   12, 13, 127
Tank versus tank, first engagement   37
Tapper, Capt J.H.   18
Tarapore, Lt Col Ardeshir   165, 167
Tassigny, Gen de Lattre   143, 159
Tel Aviv   168
Thoma, Gen Ritter von   81, 86, 92
Tiger tank   107, 110, 111, 135
Timoshenko, Marshal   103, 104, 109
Tobruk   78, 79
'Torch', Operation   87, 120
'Treat 'em Rough Boys'   36
Trench crossing drill   24, 25 (plan)
Tripoli   75, 77, 80, 87
Tritton, William   10
Tsaritsin; *see* Stalingrad
Tukhachevsky, Marshal Mikhail   52, 53, 93, 157
Tulenev, Gen I.V.   97
Tunisia   89
'Typhoon', Operation   100

Ur of Chaldees   7
Urals   99
'Uranus', Operation   105
USA, first tanks   15; first operations   30 *et seq*, 35; first tank school in France   32; armor organisation for D Day   126 *et seq*
Uzielli, Col T.J.   18

Vaerst, Gen Gustav von   81
Valentine tank   155
Vatutin, Gen Nikolai Feodrovich   106, 112
Verney, Maj Gen G.L.   125
Vernejoul, Gen de   143
Versailles Treaty   47, 51

Victoria Cross   22, 82
Vietinghoff, Gen von   98
Vietcong   159 *et seq*, 162
Vietminh   159
Vietnam   159 *et seq*
Vigier, Gen Touzet du   143
Vijayanta tank   167
Villa, Pancho   31 *et seq*
Villers Bocage   136
Villers Bretonneux   37
Vezdekhod   15
Vokes, Maj Gen Christopher   126, 142
Volga River   51, 104, 105
Vollmer, Joseph   16
Volturno River   119
Voorhis, Gen Van   41, 45, 46
Voroshilov, Marshal Kliment Yefremovich   51, 53, 99

Wacht am Rhein   147, 148, 151
Walsh, Capt   40
Walker, Gen Walton H.   139, 158
Walker Bulldog light tank   160
Ward, Gen Orlando   120
Warlimont, Gen Walter   134
Warsaw   54
Watson, Maj Gen Leroy   140, 141
Wavell, Field Marshal Archibald   71, 74, 76, 78, 79
Wietersheim, Gen von   104, 143
Wilson, Lt Walter Gordon   10
Wilson, Lt Gen 'Jumbo'   71, 118
'Windsor', Operation   136
Wingate, Maj Gen Orde   169
Winter War   60 *et seq*
Witt, Gen Fritz   131
Wittmann, SS Obersturmfuehrer Michael   110, 135 *et seq*
Wood, Maj Gen 'Tiger Jack'   126, 139 *et seq*, 140, 146
Worthington, Gen 'Worthy'   43, 126

Yalu River   158
Ypres   8
Yeremenko, Gen Andrei   100, 151
Yom Kippur War   176 *et seq*
Younger, Maj Gen Ralph   156

Zeigler, Gen Heinz   81
Zhukov, Marshal Greogory Konstantinovich   99 *et seq*, 101, 103, 105, 106, 107, 109, 113, 151, 153

NOTES

NOTES